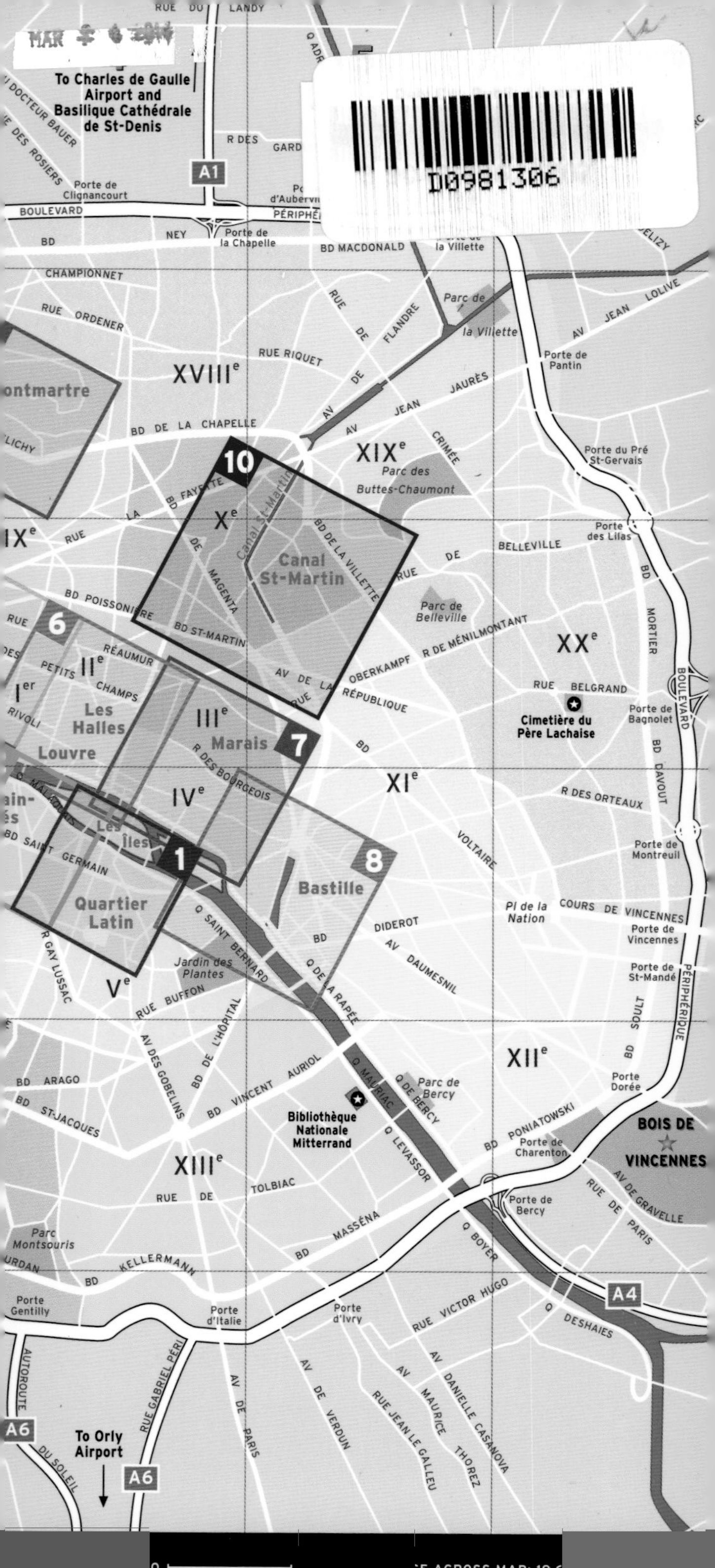
To Charles de Gaulle Airport and Basilique Cathédrale de St-Denis
A1
Porte de Clignancourt
Porte de la Chapelle
BD MACDONALD
la Villette
Parc de la Villette
Porte de Pantin
XVIIIe
Montmartre
XIXe
Parc des Buttes-Chaumont
Porte du Pré St-Gervais
Porte des Lilas
10
X^e
Canal St-Martin
Parc de Belleville
XXe
6
IIe
Ier
Les Halles
Louvre
IIIe
Marais
7
IVe
Les Îles
1
Quartier Latin
V^e
8
Bastille
XIe
Cimetière du Père Lachaise
Porte de Bagnolet
Porte de Montreuil
Pl de la Nation
Porte de Vincennes
Porte de St-Mandé
Jardin des Plantes
XIIe
Porte Dorée
Parc de Bercy
Bibliothèque Nationale Mitterrand
BOIS DE VINCENNES
Porte de Charenton
Porte de Bercy
XIIIe
Parc Montsouris
A4
Porte Gentilly
Porte d'Italie
Porte d'Ivry
A6
To Orly Airport
A6
BD DE LA CHAPELLE
BD DE MAGENTA
BD ST-MARTIN
BD POISSONNIÈRE
BD DE LA VILLETTE
AV DE LA RÉPUBLIQUE
RUE OBERKAMPF
R DE MÉNILMONTANT
RUE DE BELLEVILLE
RUE BELGRAND
R DES ORTEAUX
BD VOLTAIRE
COURS DE VINCENNES
BD DIDEROT
AV DAUMESNIL
BD SAINT GERMAIN
R GAY LUSSAC
RUE BUFFON
BD DE L'HÔPITAL
AV DES GOBELINS
BD ARAGO
BD ST-JACQUES
BD VINCENT AURIOL
RUE DE TOLBIAC
BD MASSÉNA
BD KELLERMANN
RUE VICTOR HUGO
Q DE LA RAPÉE
Q SAINT BERNARD
Q DE BERCY
Q MAURIAC
Q LEVASSOR
Q BOYER
Q DESHAIES
BD PONIATOWSKI
BD SOULT
BD DAVOUT
BD MORTIER
BOULEVARD PÉRIPHÉRIQUE
AV JEAN JAURÈS
AV JEAN LOLIVE
RUE DE FLANDRE
RUE RIQUET
RUE ORDENER
CHAMPIONNET
BD NEY
RUE DES ROSIERS
R DES BOURGEOIS
RÉAUMUR
PETITS CHAMPS
RIVOLI
AV DES GOBELINS
AV DE PARIS
AV DE VERDUN
RUE JEAN LE GALLEU
AV MAURICE THOREZ
AV DANIELLE CASANOVA
RUE GABRIEL PÉRI
AUTOROUTE DU SOLEIL
AV DE GRAVELLE
RUE DE PARIS
D0981306

MOON MapGuide

CONTENTS

PARIS

HOW TO USE THIS BOOK

MAP SECTION

- We've divided Paris into 10 distinct areas. Each area has been assigned a color, used on the map itself and in easy-to-spot map number indicators throughout the listings.
- The maps show the location of every listing in the book, using the icon that indicates what type of listing it is (sight, restaurant, etc.) and the listing's locator number.
- The coordinates (in color) indicate the specific grid that the listing is located in. The black number is the listing's locator number. The page number directs you to the listing's full description.

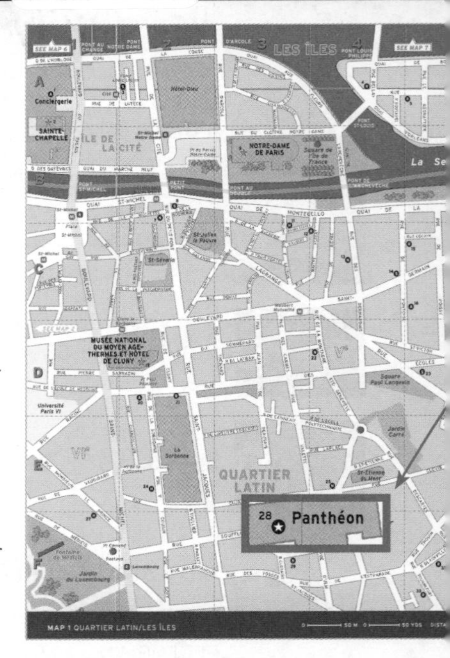

LISTINGS SECTION

- Listings are organized into six sections:
  - SIGHTS
  - RESTAURANTS
  - NIGHTLIFE
  - SHOPS
  - ARTS AND LEISURE
  - HOTELS
- Within each section, listings are organized by which map they are located in, then in alphabetical order.
- Look for ☾ to find recommended sights, restaurants, nightlife, shops, arts and leisure, and hotels.

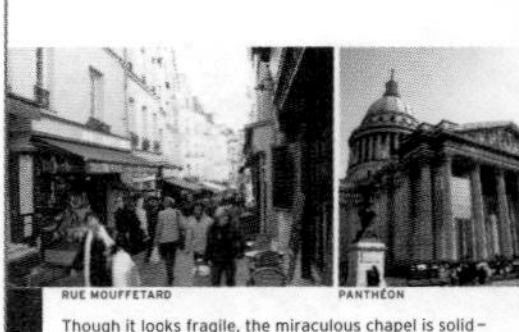

RUE MOUFFETARD   PANTHÉON

SIGHTS

Though it looks fragile, the miraculous chapel is solid–no cracks have appeared in the delicate vaulting in seven centuries. Try to visit on a sunny day and bring binoculars. Take a wall seat and read the windows left to right, from bottom to top. There's also a regular schedule of classical music concerts in the chapel throughout the year.

MAP 1 A1 2 4 BD. DU PALAIS, 1ER 01-53-40-60-80
WWW.SAINTE-CHAPELLE.MONUMENTS-NATIONAUX.FR
HOURS: MAR.-OCT. DAILY 9:30 A.M.-6 P.M., NOV.-FEB. DAILY 9 A.M.-5 P.M.
ADMISSION: €8.50

LES ARÈNES DE LUTÈCE
A vestige of Paris's Roman past tucked into the Latin Quarter, the arena was rediscovered during construction in 1869. Once 15,000 people could watch gruesome spectacles here; now children come to play in ancient dust.

MAP 1 E6 26 ACCESS VIA RUE MONGE AND RUE DE NAVARRE, 5E
HOURS: SPRING/SUMMER DAILY 9 A.M.-9:30 P.M., FALL/WINTER DAILY 8 A.M.-5:30 P.M.
ADMISSION: FREE

PANTHÉON
Louis XV's Greek-style church was transformed during the French Revolution into a temple dedicated to the greats of French history, such as Voltaire, Victor Hugo, and Pierre and Marie Curie. Currently undergoing a facelift slated for completion in 2022, it's open to visitors throughout the construction.

MAP 1 F3 28 PL. DU PANTHÉON, 5E 01-44-32-18-00
WWW.PANTHEON.MONUMENTS-NATIONAUX.FR
HOURS: APR.-SEPT. DAILY 10 A.M.-6:30 P.M., OCT.-MAR. DAILY 10 A.M.-6 P.M.
ADMISSION: €7.50

RUE MOUFFETARD
One of the oldest market streets in Paris, Mouffetard is lined with cafés, cheap restaurants, clothing shops, gourmet-food boutiques, and market stalls every day

4 MOON MAP GUIDE

TWO WAYS TO NAVIGATE

1. Scan the map to see what listings are in the area you want to explore. Use the directory to find out the name and page number for each listing.

2. Read the listings to find the specific place you want to visit. Use the map information at the bottom of each listing to find the listing's exact location.

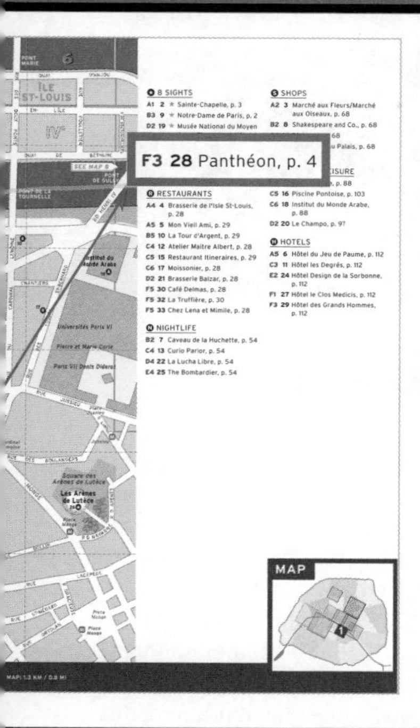

MAP KEY

Major Sights ★

Metro Stop Ⓜ

Shopping District

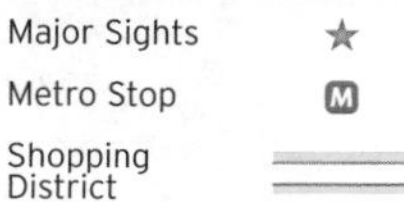

Stairs

Pedestrian Street

Adjacent Map Boundaries

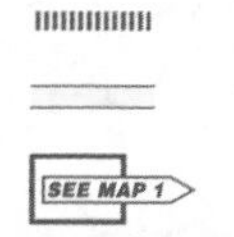

SECTION ICONS

- SIGHTS
- RESTAURANTS
- NIGHTLIFE
- SHOPS
- ARTS AND LEISURE
- HOTELS

SIGHTS

but Monday. On Sundays at Place de la Contrescarpe, open-air waltzing with a live accordionist draws locals.

MAP 1 F5 31 RUE MOUFFETARD BTWN. PL. DE LA CONTRESCARPE AND RUE CENSIER, 5E

PANTHÉON

Louis XV's Greek-style church was transformed during the French Revolution into a temple dedicated to the greats of French history, such as Voltaire, Victor Hugo, and Pierre and Marie Curie. Currently undergoing a facelift slated for completion in 2022, it's open to visitors throughout the construction.

MAP 1 F3 28 PL. DU PANTHÉON, 5E 01-44-32-18-00
WWW.PANTHEON.MONUMENTS-NATIONAUX.FR
HOURS: APR.-SEPT. DAILY 10 A.M.-6:30 P.M., OCT.-MAR. DAILY

Use the **MAP NUMBER, COLOR GRID COORDINATES,** and **BLACK LOCATOR NUMBER** to find the exact location of every listing in the book.

INTRODUCTION TO PARIS

For centuries Paris has been known as the City of Light, the City of Romance, and even the Most Beautiful City in the World. And, as many visitors to this popular tourist destination would probably agree, the nicknames endure simply because they're true. But no phrase could ever adequately describe the complex character and dramatic extremes of a city that combines sophistication and relaxation, delicacy and debauchery, chic neighborhoods and bawdy boutiques, royal promenades and frenzied shopping streets, ultramodern museums and flamboyantly Gothic cathedrals.

In this dense, congested home to 2.2 million, the high cost of living, traffic snarls, and infamous bureaucracy can wear down even the hardiest local. The legendary grumpiness of Parisian waiters can sometimes even seem merited. Still, Paris's allure remains. In fact, its imperfections reveal Paris as a profoundly down-to-earth place despite its larger-than-life reputation. Couples kiss on park benches while gray-haired grandmothers feed pigeons. People meet on the steps of the Opéra Garnier and sunbathe at the foot of the Tour Eiffel. An appreciation for the little pleasures of life takes precedence.

Paris is famous the world over for the love of good food enjoyed at leisure, the primacy of fashion and people-watching, and the strict social graces that structure daily life. Despite inroads by fast food, Parisians still prefer to spend their Sunday mornings at the market

GETTING AROUND

Paris's efficient public transportation system is one of the best in the world. An intricate network comprising buses, 14 Métro lines, five regional RER trains, and an elaborate tram service makes it a cinch to get around town without the burden of a rental car. Even with the unfortunate frequency of personnel strikes, minimal service is always guaranteed. Its only *point noir* (problem), regularly called into question by Parisians tired of running for the last Métro at 12:45 A.M. like urban Cinderellas, is the lack of 24-hour service. Finding a taxi at 2 A.M. on a Saturday night requires patience, especially if it's raining. As a last resort, night owls can try cramming aboard one of the few Noctambus night buses, which circulate hourly between 1 A.M. and 5 A.M., or pay by credit card to borrow a Vélib', the popular self-access bicycle rental system with terminals throughout Paris and the close suburbs.

Although the availability of public transport eases the stress of getting from place to place, be sure to take some time to walk around. The city spirals outward like a *coquille d'escargot* (snail's shell) into 20 unique districts called arrondissements. Each of these mini villages has its own unique flavor, and is best explored on foot. You can walk from one museum to another beginning in the 1st arrondissement at Notre-Dame, past manicured parks, colonnaded courtyards, chic boutiques, and buzzing cafés all the way to Père Lachaise cemetery in the 20th, to get a real taste of Parisian life at street level.

jockeying for the best roasted chicken or stinkiest Camembert.

The same zest inspires style mavens, forever cultivating Le Look – a person's total style that's more about knowing what's flattering than what's trendy. The urban crunch that serves the fashion-forward also makes the rules of propriety and courtesy critically important to all Parisians. These little gestures act both as a nod to the past and as a social password. Every conversation should begin with *"bonjour,"* whether you're buying bread or an Hermès scarf. And everyone has the right to be addressed as Monsieur or Madame. Do as the Parisians do, and you'll receive the same courtesies in return.

MULTICULTURAL PARIS

Cosmopolitan in every sense of the word, Parisians come from not only all corners of "l'Hexagone" (as France is affectionately called), but from every corner of the globe. Immigration in the early 20th century was mainly from other European countries, particularly Portugal, Spain, and Italy. But ever since the 1960s, citizens from distant territories and former French colonies have made Paris their new home.

The Belleville neighborhood and giant swaths of the 13th arrondissement are often referred to as Paris's "Chinatowns," but immigrants from Vietnam and Cambodia make up a good part of those populations, too. Sandwiched between the Louvre and Opéra Garnier lies rue Ste-Anne, home to dozens of Japanese noodle restaurants, Korean grocery stores, and upscale boutiques vending goods from Asia. On the eastern slope of Montmartre, the Château Rouge quarter has the bustle and visual effect of a West African market day. Down the hill in the direction of the Gare du Nord, colorful sari shops, enticing aromas, and hypnotic South Asian music will have you thinking you've wandered onto a Bollywood movie set.

With this combination of imperial grandeur and local air, Paris owes its sheer beauty not only to its material charm, but also to its approach to a civilized and refined way of life. It's no wonder that the city has been adopted over the centuries by so many artists and thinkers – and continues to hold an idealized place in many a traveler's imagination.

HISTORY

This grand city started off as a settlement of a Gallic fishing tribe known as the Parisii on an island in the Seine River. During the Roman Empire, it became an important city called Lutetia (or Lutèce, in French) – vestiges from the Roman era can still be found on the Left Bank.

After the fall of the Holy Roman Empire and subsequent invasions by barbarian tribes, Paris discovered Christianity. Clovis became its first Catholic king in A.D. 500, establishing the city as the capital of the slowly expanding French kingdom. Despite Europe's wars and plagues, Paris prospered throughout the medieval and Renaissance eras. With the Age of Enlightenment, Parisians rebelled against the supremacy of the clergy and nobility, resulting in the French Revolution of 1789 and the end of the French monarchy.

A chaotic procession of democratic presidents, constitutional monarchs, and two ambitious emperors marked the 19th century. The first emperor, Napoléon Bonaparte, crowned himself in 1804 and embarked on an ambitious military campaign that would result in his 1815 abdication and exile. Bonaparte's nephew followed suit as Napoléon III in 1850 and is credited with transforming Paris into a modern city by annexing villages such as Montmartre and tearing through the old medieval streets with tree-lined boulevards and parks. The 1870 Franco-Prussian war brought an end to his rule, and after a bloody civil conflict known as the Commune, Paris settled on its current system of democratic republicanism.

The 20th century began with the 1900 World's Fair construction of belle époque monuments such as the Tour Eiffel, Grand Palais, and Gare d'Orsay. After the casualties of the Great War and the Nazi occupation during World War II, Paris took a while to recover: It wouldn't be until the 1970s that it would finally take on the challenges of modernizing the city while preserving its historic architectural treasures.

Today, the city's metamorphosis continues with extensive public works projects, major museum revamps, improved and expanded mass transit systems, and nonstop beautification projects. Paris has never looked so good or run so smoothly, thanks to two-term mayor Bertrand Delanoë, whose progressive agenda and strident efforts to keep Paris on the cutting edge will be remembered long after his 2014 retirement. There's never been a better time to visit – or fall under the spell of – the City of Light.

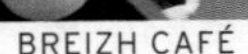

BREIZH CAFÉ MARCHÉ AUX FLEURS SACRÉ-COEUR

THE BEST OF PARIS

Paris offers so many dazzling sights that it's hard to know where to start. A day in this city could include gazing at some of the world's most famous works of art, browsing street markets, and people-watching in manicured gardens. Here is one way to visit some of the city's many monuments, and to get a taste of the way the locals live while you're at it.

① The Marais is the ideal *quartier* to begin your tour of Paris. At breakfast hot spot **Breizh Café (p. 42),** the traditional Breton crêpes and galettes provide the fuel needed to tackle the stairs at the legendary **Notre-Dame de Paris (p. 2).** Get a gargoyle's-eye view of Paris from the north tower.

② Stroll through the colorful **Marché aux Fleurs (p. 68)** at Place Louis Lépine – you'll feel like you're walking through a painting since this flower market has been depicted in so many.

③ Your last stop on the island is tiny **Sainte-Chapelle (p. 3),** for a look at its kaleidoscope of 50-foot-tall stained-glass windows.

④ Follow the **Pont Neuf (p. 7)** across the Seine and walk through the St-Germain-des-Prés district en route to the **Musée d'Orsay (p. 9).** Here, you'll find Impressionist and post-Impressionist artwork by Degas, Rodin, and Monet. For lunch, the museum has two cafés and a beautiful belle époque restaurant.

⑤ The pedestrian Pont Solferino takes you across the Seine and to the **Jardin des Tuileries (p. 13),** where the many chairs dotted around the formal French gardens make for great people-watching, especially during Fashion Week.

6 Head toward the glass pyramid marking the entrance to the **Musée du Louvre (p. 15).** It would be impossible to see everything in one quick trip, but its three most celebrated works – the *Mona Lisa, Winged Victory,* and *Venus de Milo* – are conveniently located in the Denon Wing.

7 To recover from all the museum-hopping, take the Métro to St-Paul and explore more of the Marais, a maze of medieval-era streets and 17th-century mansions. Window-shop along **rue des Francs-Bourgeois (p. 81),** where trendy stores offer jewelry, home furnishings, and gift items.

8 Make your way to the **Tour Eiffel (p. 11),** by Métro or taxi, as evening is the best time to see it. Take the elevator to the top floor for panoramic views of Paris.

9 Ride the Métro to Montmartre (get off at Pigalle), a neighborhood full of hidden fountains and stairways. For dinner, choose the **Hôtel Amour (p. 47),** a friendly and romantic restaurant hideaway.

10 Finish off the day on the stairs leading up to **La Basilique Sacré-Coeur de Montmartre (p. 20).** From these steps you can see all of Paris before you, a sparkling City of Light.

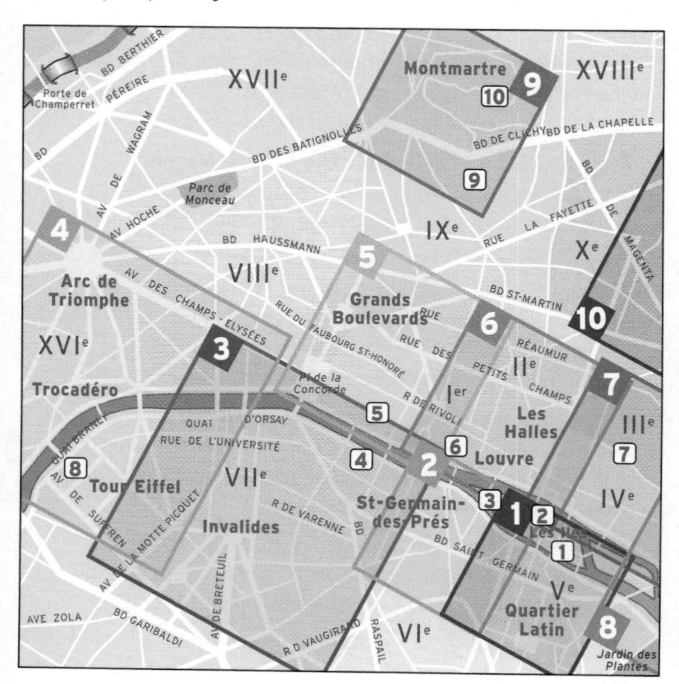

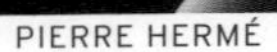

PIERRE HERMÉ

MARIAGE FRÈRES

EPICURE

PARIS
FOR FOODIES

Parisians love food and can talk about it endlessly: Who makes the best bread and vends the finest fruit; what to serve and how to prepare it; and what wine is best served with what. So it's no wonder that for many travelers, a trip to Paris couldn't be complete without planning in advance your restaurant excursions and several pilgrimages to the local *commerçants* (shopkeepers) who run the best gourmet boutiques in the city.

① French bakeries are most active in the wee hours of the morning, so stop at **Poilâne (p. 70)** to stock up on their famous crusty sourdough breads. One of their delicious *pains au chocolat* (chocolate pastries) will also make a memorable breakfast on the go.

② Nearby is **La Grande Epicerie du Bon Marché (p. 71),** with food products from around the world. This is your one-stop shop for gourmet goodies to tote home to friends and family.

③ A walk up boulevard St-Germain takes you to **Debauve et Gallais (p. 71),** one of Paris's most distinguished *chocolateries* (chocolate makers). Bring your best manners for the chance to taste before you buy.

④ Several blocks away is **Barthélemy (p. 70),** a fragrant *fromagerie* (cheese shop) with a celebrity clientele. It's revered for its excellent selection of artisanal cheeses from every corner of France.

⑤ Make a reservation for lunch at **KGB (p. 31),** one of Paris's hottest restaurants. Lunch here is a less expensive way to enjoy chef Yariv Berrebi's creative cuisine.

6 Inspired to do your own cooking? A visit to **E. Dehillerin (p. 78)** is a must to stock up on professionally rated kitchen accoutrements.

7 Take the Métro to Hôtel de Ville for teatime at **Mariage Frères (p. 81).** Choose from the wall of *thés:* green, black, and delicate white teas from across the globe. Afterwards, visit the Musée du Thé (Tea Museum) on the second floor; the ancient tea boxes from China are stunning.

8 Walk back to the Métro and exit at Concorde. Walk up the Rue Royale to **Lavinia (p. 75),** one of the best wine boutiques in the city. Thousands of vintages, many classics, are on hand. There is also an ingenious system to taste different wines for *l'heure de l'apéro* (aperitif time).

9 Finish the day's foodie festivities with an indulgently awe-inspiring dinner at **Epicure (p. 50)** in Le Bristol Paris hotel, one of the best haute cuisine tables of the moment.

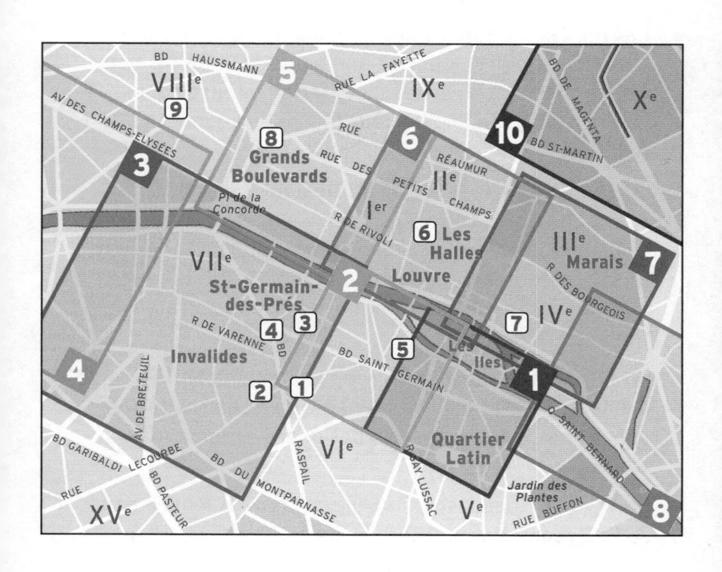

CITÉ DE LA MODE ET DU DESIGN

MUSÉE DES ARTS DÉCORATIFS

JARDIN DES TUILERIES

PARIS
FOR FASHIONISTAS

The City of Light's well-earned reputation as the culinary and culture capital of the world might be eclipsed by another delicious point of renown: Fashion. The most swoon-worthy names on the sartorial scene – Dior, Lanvin, Saint-Laurent, Chanel – launched their careers here, and the prêt-a-porter and haute couture fashion weeks consume style-watchers for an intense couple of weeks each year. Slip on your red-soled Louboutins and follow the fashion trail.

1 **The Cité de la Mode et du Design** (34 quai d'Austerlitz, 13E, 01-76-77-25-30, www.paris-docks-en-seine.fr) is a unique mélange of nightclub **(Wanderlust, p. 61),** restaurant, and fashion school (Institut Français de la Mode) that hosts rotating art exhibits on stylish themes.

2 After a long closure for renovations, the **Musée Galliera (p. 91)** finally reopened with a splashy retrospective of French-Algerian designer Azzedine Alaïa's works.

3 The Marc Jacobs-Louis Vuitton show at **Musée des Arts Décoratifs (p. 92)** drew epic crowds; whether they'll turn out for the Dries Van Noten exhibit remains to be seen.

4 The pretty people all seem to live on **rue du Faubourg St-Honoré (p. 77),** a long stretch of street that calls some of the iconic names in fashion home.

5 Stand in line for a chance to ogle the wares on offer at **Louis Vuitton's (p. 73)** flagship store.

6 The best people-watching in Paris during the fashion shows is at the **Jardin des Tuileries (p. 13),** an art-filled park in the heart of Paris. Pull one of the ubiquitous green chairs up to the fountain in the Grande Carré and spend an afternoon spotting famous faces.

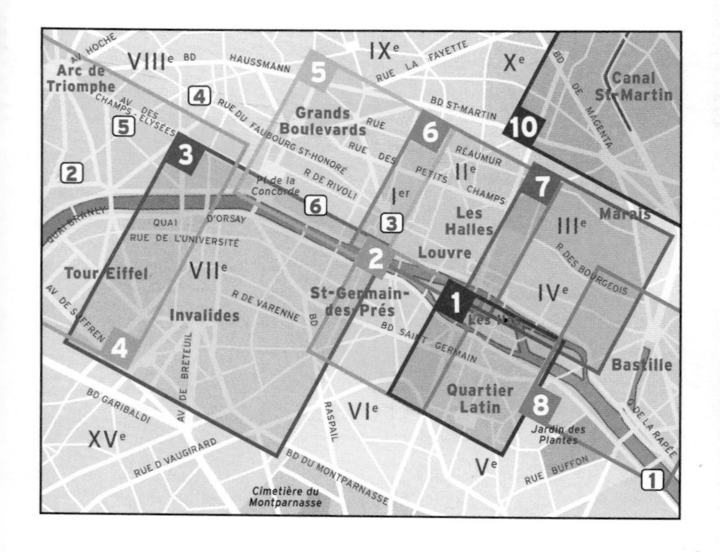

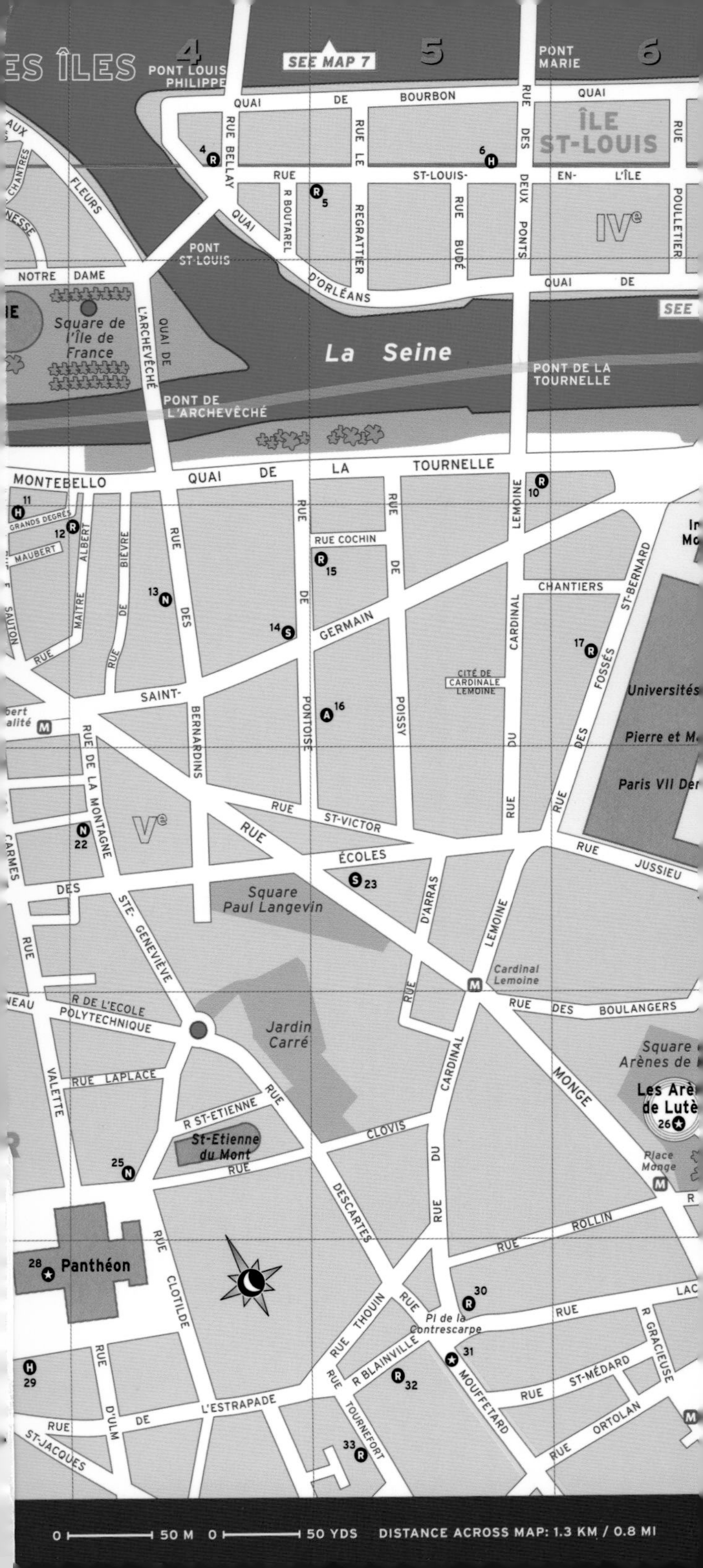

4
5
6
SEE MAP 7
PONT LOUIS PHILIPPE
PONT MARIE
QUAI DE BOURBON
QUAI
ÎLE ST-LOUIS
RUE BELLAY
RUE LE REGRATTIER
RUE DES DEUX PONTS
RUE ST-LOUIS-EN-L'ÎLE
R BOUTAREL
RUE BUDÉ
RUE POULLETIER
IVe
QUAI D'ORLÉANS
QUAI DE
PONT ST-LOUIS
FLEURS
CHANTRES
NOTRE DAME
Square de l'Île de France
QUAI DE L'ARCHEVÊCHÉ
La Seine
PONT DE LA TOURNELLE
PONT DE L'ARCHEVÊCHÉ
SEE
MONTEBELLO
QUAI DE LA TOURNELLE
GRANDS DEGRÉS
MAUBERT
RUE MAITRE ALBERT
RUE DE BIEVRE
RUE DES BERNARDINS
RUE DE PONTOISE
RUE COCHIN
RUE DE POISSY
RUE DU CARDINAL LEMOINE
CHANTIERS
RUE DES FOSSÉS ST-BERNARD
SAINT-GERMAIN
CITÉ DE CARDINALE LEMOINE
Universités Pierre et M
Paris VII Der
RUE ST-VICTOR
RUE DE LA MONTAGNE STE-GENEVIÈVE
Ve
RUE DES ÉCOLES
RUE JUSSIEU
CARMES
Square Paul Langevin
RUE D'ARRAS
Cardinal Lemoine
RUE DES BOULANGERS
R DE L'ECOLE POLYTECHNIQUE
Jardin Carré
RUE MONGE
Square Arènes de
Les Arè de Luté
RUE VALETTE
RUE LAPLACE
R ST-ETIENNE
RUE CLOVIS
St-Etienne du Mont
RUE DESCARTES
Place Monge
RUE ROLLIN
Panthéon
RUE CLOTILDE
RUE THOUIN
Pl de la Contrescarpe
RUE LACÉPÈDE
R GRACIEUSE
RUE BLAINVILLE
RUE MOUFFETARD
RUE ST-MÉDARD
RUE D'ULM
RUE DE L'ESTRAPADE
RUE TOURNEFORT
RUE ORTOLAN
RUE ST-JACQUES
0 50 M 0 50 YDS DISTANCE ACROSS MAP: 1.3 KM / 0.8 MI

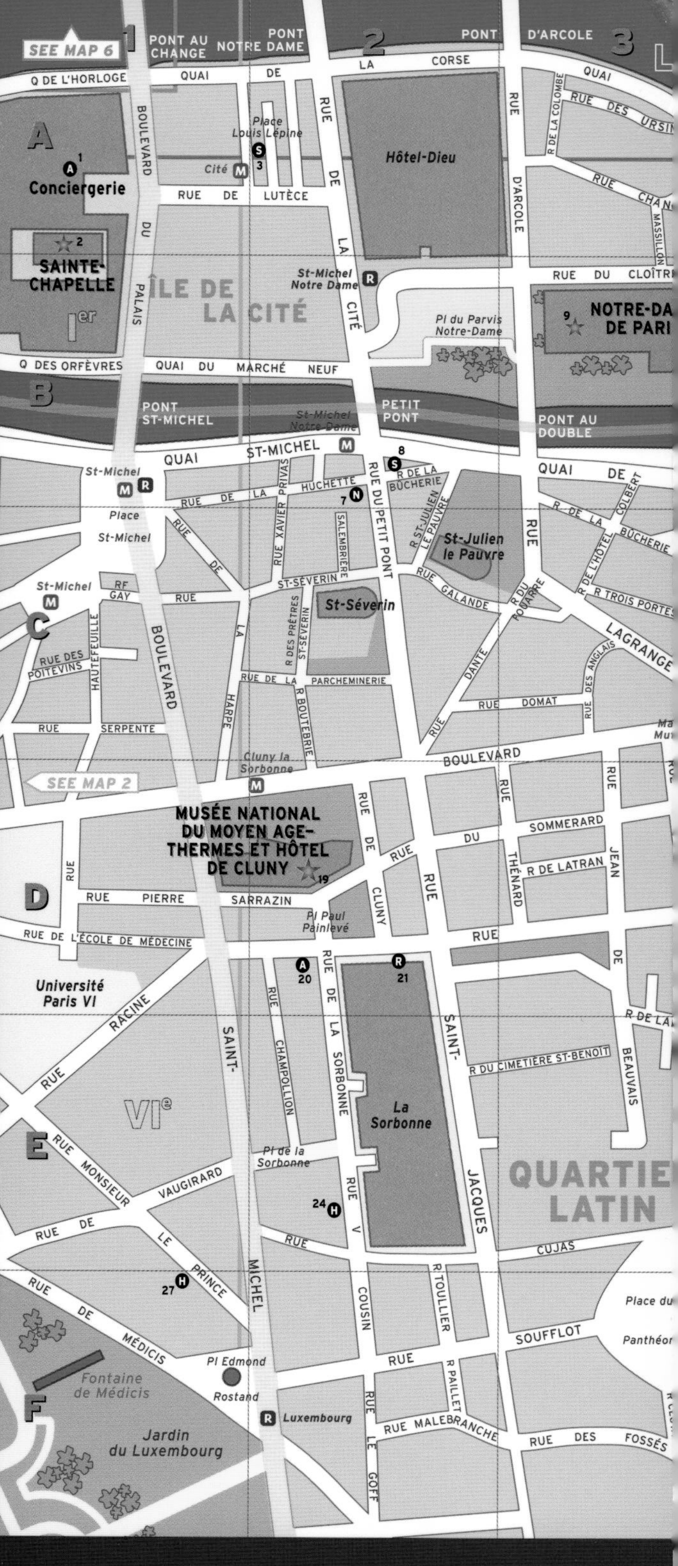

MAP 1 QUARTIER LATIN/LES ÎLES

QUARTIER LATIN/ LES ÎLES

First developed by the Gallo-Romans, Île de la Cité, Île St-Louis, and the Latin Quarter are the oldest districts in Paris. During the Middle Ages, French kings built the sights that the islands are known for today: Notre-Dame Cathedral, St-Louis en l'Île church, the Conciergerie, and the Palais de la Cité's private Sainte-Chapelle. On the Left Bank, monasteries and the Sorbonne attracted students from all over Europe whose only common language was Latin, giving the area its "Latin Quarter" moniker. In the 20th century this student-dominated center of bohemianism and radicalism was the starting point of the May 1968 riots that resulted in a nationwide workers' strike.

Today, tourism and fast food have invaded much of the Quartier Latin, particularly around the boulevard St-Michel and rue de la Huchette. But its narrow cobblestone streets are still worth exploring. Major sights include the world-famous Musée de Cluny medieval museum, the Institut du Monde Arabe center for Arabic arts, and the imposing Panthéon, a monument to France's heroes, such as Voltaire and Victor Hugo. For shopping, don't miss the rue Mouffetard market street immortalized in Ernest Hemingway's *A Moveable Feast* or the upscale gift boutiques of the adorable, untouched-by-time Île St-Louis.

★ 8 SIGHTS

A1 2 ★ Sainte-Chapelle, p. 3
B3 9 ★ Notre-Dame de Paris, p. 2
D2 19 ★ Musée National du Moyen Age – Thermes et Hôtel de Cluny, p. 2
E6 26 Les Arènes de Lutèce, p. 3
F3 28 Panthéon, p. 4
F5 31 Rue Mouffetard, p. 4

R RESTAURANTS

A4 4 Brasserie de l'Isle St-Louis, p. 28
A5 5 Mon Vieil Ami, p. 29
B5 10 La Tour d'Argent, p. 29
C4 12 Atelier Maitre Albert, p. 28
C5 15 Restaurant Itineraires, p. 29
C6 17 Moissonier, p. 28
D2 21 Brasserie Balzar, p. 28
F5 30 Café Delmas, p. 28
F5 32 La Truffière, p. 30
F5 33 Chez Lena et Mimile, p. 28

N NIGHTLIFE

B2 7 Caveau de la Huchette, p. 54
C4 13 Curio Parlor, p. 54
D4 22 La Lucha Libre, p. 54
E4 25 The Bombardier, p. 54

S SHOPS

A2 3 Marché aux Fleurs/Marché aux Oiseaux, p. 68
B2 8 Shakespeare and Co., p. 68
C4 14 Diptyque, p. 68
D5 23 Le Bonbon au Palais, p. 68

A ARTS AND LEISURE

A1 1 Conciergerie, p. 88
C5 16 Piscine Pontoise, p. 103
C6 18 Institut du Monde Arabe, p. 88
D2 20 Le Champo, p. 97

H HOTELS

A5 6 Hôtel du Jeu de Paume, p. 112
C3 11 Hôtel les Degrés, p. 112
E2 24 Hôtel Design de la Sorbonne, p. 112
F1 27 Hôtel le Clos Medicis, p. 112
F3 29 Hôtel des Grands Hommes, p. 112

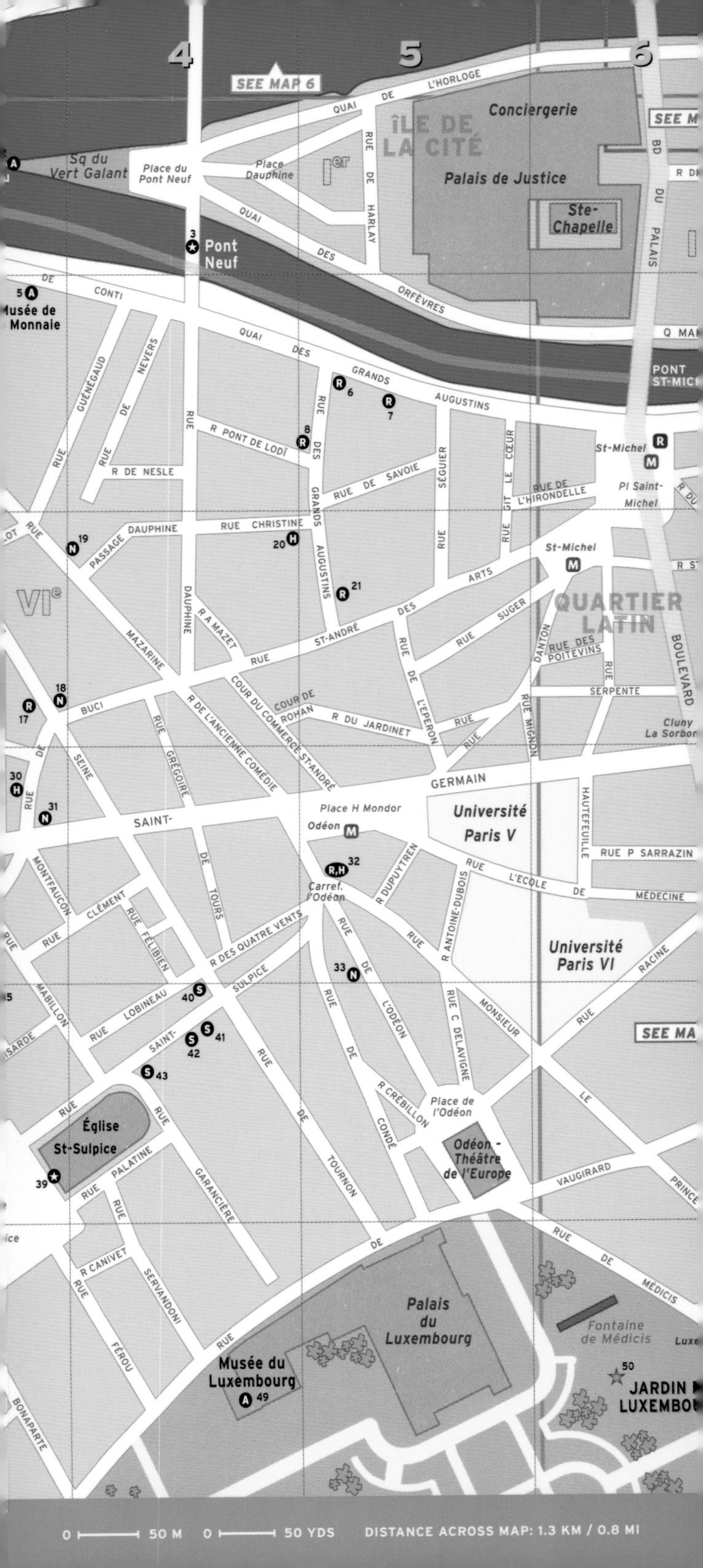
4
5
6
SEE MAP 6
Conciergerie
ÎLE DE LA CITÉ
Palais de Justice
Ste-Chapelle
Place du Pont Neuf
Place Dauphine
Sq du Vert Galant
Pont Neuf
Musée de Monnaie
QUAI DE L'HORLOGE
QUAI DES ORFÈVRES
QUAI DE CONTI
QUAI DES GRANDS AUGUSTINS
RUE DE HARLAY
BD DU PALAIS
PONT ST-MICHEL
St-Michel
Pl Saint-Michel
QUARTIER LATIN
VIe
RUE GUÉNÉGAUD
RUE DE NEVERS
R DE NESLE
R PONT DE LODI
RUE DES GRANDS AUGUSTINS
RUE DE SAVOIE
RUE SÉGUIER
RUE GIT LE CŒUR
RUE DE L'HIRONDELLE
RUE CHRISTINE
PASSAGE DAUPHINE
RUE DAUPHINE
RUE MAZARINE
R A MAZET
RUE ST-ANDRÉ DES ARTS
RUE SUGER
RUE DES POITEVINS
RUE DANTON
RUE SERPENTE
BOULEVARD
Cluny La Sorbonne
BUCI
COUR DE ROHAN
COUR DU COMMERCE ST-ANDRÉ
R DU JARDINET
RUE DE L'EPERON
RUE MIGNON
R DE L'ANCIENNE COMÉDIE
RUE GRÉGOIRE DE TOURS
RUE DE SEINE
SAINT-GERMAIN
Place H Mondor
Odéon
Université Paris V
HAUTEFEUILLE
RUE P SARRAZIN
RUE DE L'ECOLE DE MÉDECINE
Carref. l'Odéon
R DUPUYTREN
R ANTOINE-DUBOIS
Université Paris VI
RUE RACINE
SEE MAP
RUE MONTFAUCON
RUE CLÉMENT
RUE FÉLIBIEN
R DES QUATRE VENTS
RUE DE L'ODÉON
RUE C DELAVIGNE
RUE MONSIEUR LE PRINCE
RUE MABILLON
RUE LOBINEAU
RUE SAINT-SULPICE
RUE DE CONDÉ
R CRÉBILLON
Place de l'Odéon
Odéon - Théâtre de l'Europe
VAUGIRARD
RUE DE TOURNON
Église St-Sulpice
RUE PALATINE
RUE GARANCIÈRE
RUE SERVANDONI
R CANIVET
RUE FÉROU
RUE DE MÉDICIS
Palais du Luxembourg
Musée du Luxembourg
Fontaine de Médicis
JARDIN DU LUXEMBOURG
BONAPARTE
0 50 M 0 50 YDS DISTANCE ACROSS MAP: 1.3 KM / 0.8 MI

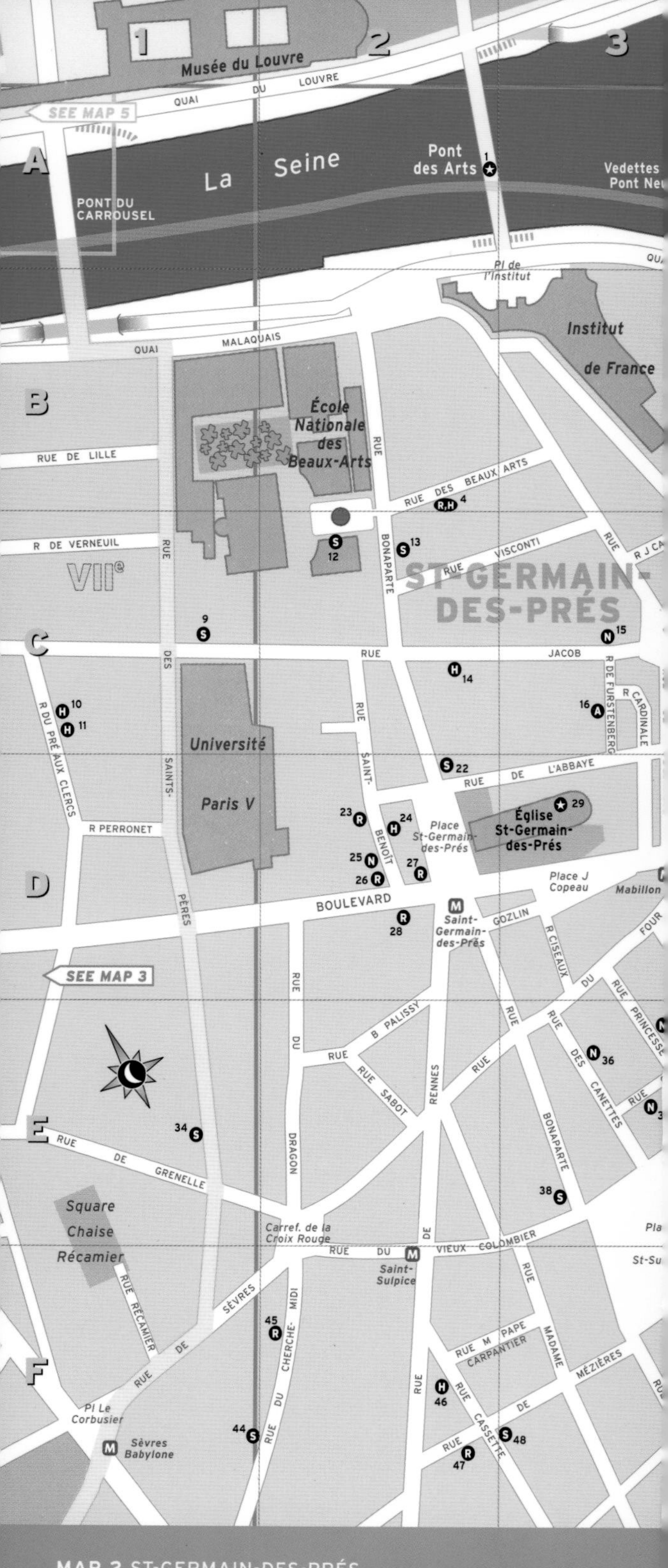
Musée du Louvre
QUAI DU LOUVRE
SEE MAP 5
La Seine
Pont des Arts
Vedettes Pont Neuf
PONT DU CARROUSEL
Pl de l'Institut
Institut de France
QUAI MALAQUAIS
École Nationale des Beaux-Arts
RUE DE LILLE
RUE DES BEAUX ARTS
R DE VERNEUIL
RUE VISCONTI
RUE BONAPARTE
ST-GERMAIN-DES-PRÉS
VIIe
RUE JACOB
RUE DES SAINTS-PÈRES
R DU PRÉ AUX CLERCS
Université Paris V
R DE FURSTENBERG
R CARDINALE
RUE SAINT-BENOÎT
RUE DE L'ABBAYE
R PERRONET
Place St-Germain-des-Prés
Église St-Germain-des-Prés
Place J Copeau
Mabillon
BOULEVARD
Saint-Germain-des-Prés
GOZLIN
R CISEAUX
RUE DU FOUR
SEE MAP 3
RUE DU DRAGON
B PALISSY
RUE SABOT
RUE DE RENNES
RUE PRINCESSE
RUE DES CANETTES
RUE BONAPARTE
RUE DE GRENELLE
Square Chaise Récamier
Carref. de la Croix Rouge
RUE DU VIEUX COLOMBIER
Saint-Sulpice
St-Su
RUE MADAME
RUE RÉCAMIER
RUE DE SÈVRES
RUE DU CHERCHE-MIDI
RUE M PAPE CARPANTIER
RUE CASSETTE
RUE DE MÉZIÈRES
Pl Le Corbusier
Sèvres Babylone
A
B
C
D
E
F
1
2
3

ST-GERMAIN-DES-PRÉS

The St-Germain-des-Prés district, on the north end of the 6th arrondissement, is named for one of the oldest churches in Paris, which is the only remaining remnant of a vast Benedictine abbey destroyed during the Revolution. From the early 1900s to the 1970s, the neighborhood attracted legendary writers and intellectuals like Jean-Paul Sartre and Simone de Beauvoir, along with artists like Pablo Picasso, Modigliani, and Man Ray, who converged in famous jazz clubs and cafés like Les Deux Magots and the Café de Flore.

Since the 1990s, St-Germain-des-Prés has become more trendy, with fashion boutiques replacing bookshops; however, the Parisian literati and thinkers of today continue to frequent this hallowed ground. Art galleries and interior decorating shops line the streets around the École Nationale des Beaux-Arts (School of Fine Arts), while farther east, fruit stalls, gourmet food stores, and sidewalk cafés make rue de Buci perfect for people-watching. But the district has not become all retail therapy: Escape the crowds at the romantic Jardin du Luxembourg, a formal French garden of tree-lined gravel alleys, sculpted fountains, and elaborate floral displays.

SIGHTS

- A2 **1** Pont des Arts, p. 6
- A4 **3** Pont Neuf, p. 7
- D3 **29** Église Saint-Germain-des-Prés, p. 6
- E3 **39** Église Saint-Sulpice, p. 6
- F6 **50** ★ Jardin du Luxembourg, p. 5

RESTAURANTS

- B2 **4** Le Restaurant, p. 32
- B5 **6** Lapérouse, p. 31
- B5 **7** Fogón, p. 31
- B5 **8** Le Relais Louis XIII, p. 32
- C3 **17** Cosi, p. 30
- C5 **21** KGB, p. 31
- D2 **23** Le Relais de l'Entrecôte, p. 32
- D2 **26** Café de Flore, p. 30
- D2 **27** Les Deux Magots, p. 31
- D2 **28** Brasserie Lipp, p. 30
- D5 **32** Le Comptoir du Relais, p. 30
- F2 **45** La Cuisine de Bar, p. 30
- F2 **47** Pizza Chic, p. 32

NIGHTLIFE

- C3 **15** L'Echelle de Jacob, p. 55
- C3 **18** Bar du Marché, p. 54
- C4 **19** Prescription Cocktail Club, p. 55
- D2 **25** Le Montana, p. 55
- D3 **31** La Rhumerie, p. 55
- D5 **33** Le Dix Bar, p. 55
- E3 **35** Castel, p. 54
- E3 **36** Chez Georges, p. 54
- E3 **37** Le Pousse-au-Crime, p. 55

SHOPS

- C1 **9** Adelline, p. 68
- C2 **12** Mona, p. 69
- C2 **13** Ladurée Beauté, p. 69
- D2 **22** Assouline, p. 68
- E1 **34** Paul & Joe, p. 70
- E3 **38** Pierre Hermé, p. 70
- E4 **40** Cire Trudon, p. 69
- E4 **41** Marie Mercié, p. 69
- E4 **42** Vanessa Bruno, p. 70
- E4 **43** Maison de Famille, p. 69
- F1 **44** Poilâne, p. 70
- F3 **48** La Cerise sur le Chapeau, p. 68

ARTS AND LEISURE

- A3 **2** Vedettes du Pont Neuf, p. 103
- B3 **5** Musée de la Monnaie, p. 88
- C3 **16** Musée National Eugène Delacroix, p. 89
- F4 **49** Musée du Luxembourg, p. 88

HOTELS

- B2 **4** L'Hôtel, p. 112
- C1 **10** Hôtel Saint Thomas d'Aquin, p. 113
- C1 **11** Hôtel Saint Vincent, p. 114
- C2 **14** Hôtel des Marronniers, p. 113
- C4 **20** Relais Christine, p. 114
- D2 **24** Hôtel Bel Ami, p. 113
- D3 **30** Artus, p. 112
- D5 **32** Hôtel Relais St-Germain, p. 113
- F2 **46** Hôtel de l'Abbaye St-Germain, p. 113

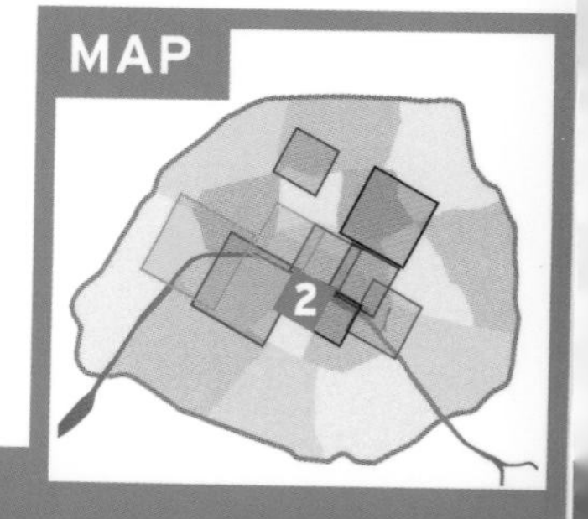

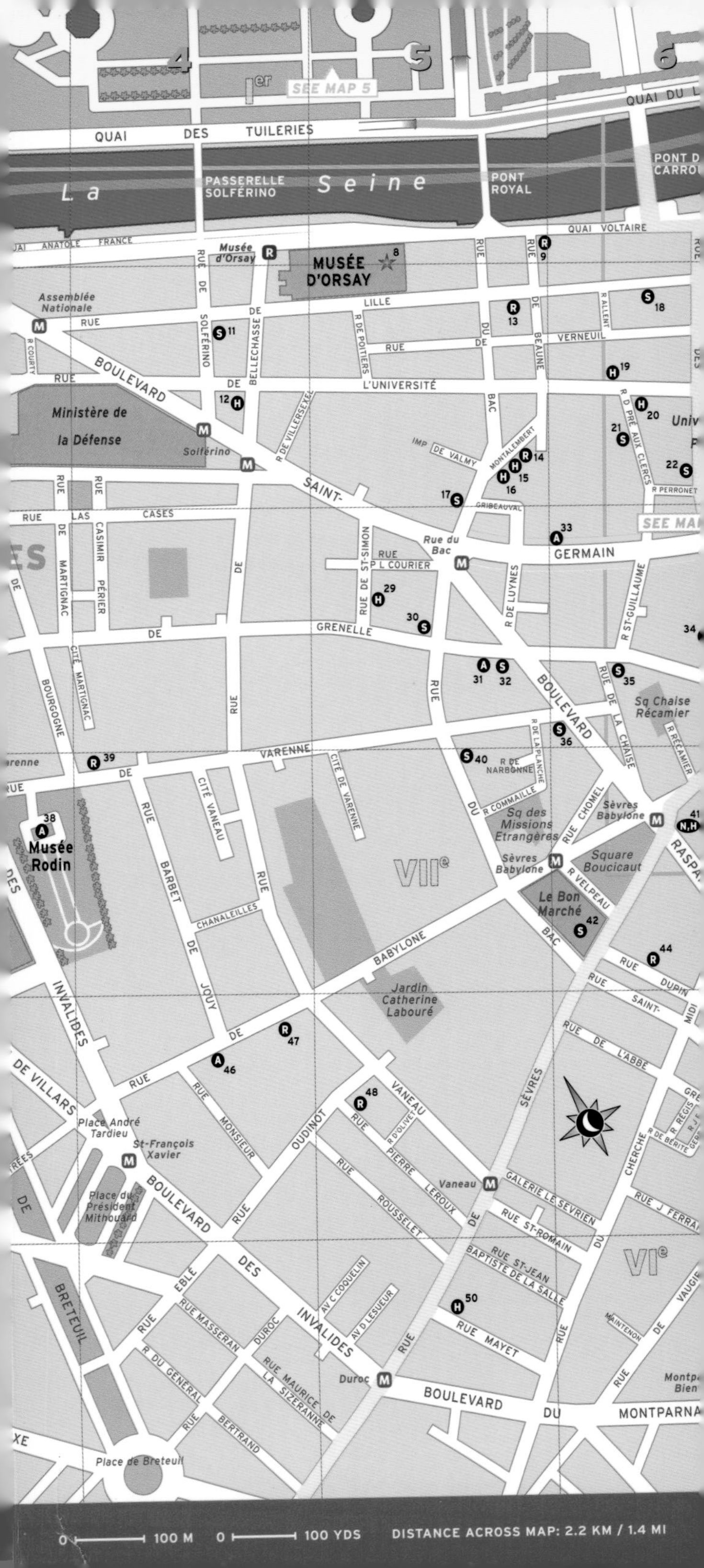

SEE MAP 5
Ier
QUAI DES TUILERIES
QUAI DU L
La Seine
PASSERELLE SOLFÉRINO
PONT ROYAL
PONT D CARROU
QUAI VOLTAIRE
QUAI ANATOLE FRANCE
Musée d'Orsay
MUSÉE D'ORSAY
Assemblée Nationale
RUE DE LILLE
RUE DE SOLFÉRINO
RUE DE BELLECHASSE
R DE POITIERS
RUE DU BAC
RUE DE BEAUNE
RUE DE VERNEUIL
R ALLENT
BOULEVARD SAINT-GERMAIN
RUE DE L'UNIVERSITÉ
R COURTY
Ministère de la Défense
Solférino
R DE VILLERSEXEL
IMP DE VALMY
MONTALEMBERT
R D PRÉ AUX CLERCS
Univ
R PERRONET
SEE MA
GRIBEAUVAL
Rue du Bac
RUE LAS CASES
RUE DE MARTIGNAC
RUE CASIMIR PÉRIER
RUE DE ST-SIMON
RUE P L COURIER
R DE LUYNES
R ST-GUILLAUME
RUE DE GRENELLE
RUE DE BOURGOGNE
CITÉ MARTIGNAC
Sq Chaise Récamier
R RÉCAMIER
RUE DE LA CHAISE
R DE LA PLANCHE
R DE NARBONNE
R COMMAILLE
RUE DE VARENNE
CITÉ DE VARENNE
CITÉ VANEAU
RUE BARBET DE JOUY
RUE CHOMEL
Sèvres Babylone
Sq des Missions Etrangères
Square Boucicaut
R VELPEAU
RASPA
Musée Rodin
VIIe
CHANALEILLES
RUE DE BABYLONE
Le Bon Marché
Jardin Catherine Labouré
RUE DUPIN
RUE SAINT-
MIDI
RUE DE L'ABBÉ GRÉGOIRE
RUE DE SÈVRES
BOULEVARD DES INVALIDES
RUE DE VILLARS
RUE MONSIEUR
RUE OUDINOT
RUE VANEAU
R D'OLIVET
RUE PIERRE LEROUX
R RÉGIS
R DE BÉRITE
R J F
Place André Tardieu
St-François Xavier
Place du Président Mithouard
RUE ROUSSELET
Vaneau
GALERIE LE SEVRIEN
RUE CHERCHE MIDI
RUE J FERRA
RUE ST-ROMAIN
RUE ST-JEAN BAPTISTE DE LA SALLE
VIe
BRETEUIL
RUE EBLÉ
AV C COQUELIN
AV D LESUEUR
RUE MASSERAN
RUE DUROC
RUE MAYET
MAINTENON
RUE DE VAUGI
Montp Bien
R DU GÉNÉRAL BERTRAND
RUE MAURICE DE LA SIZERANNE
Duroc
BOULEVARD DU MONTPARNA
Place de Breteuil
0 100 M 0 100 YDS
DISTANCE ACROSS MAP: 2.2 KM / 1.4 MI

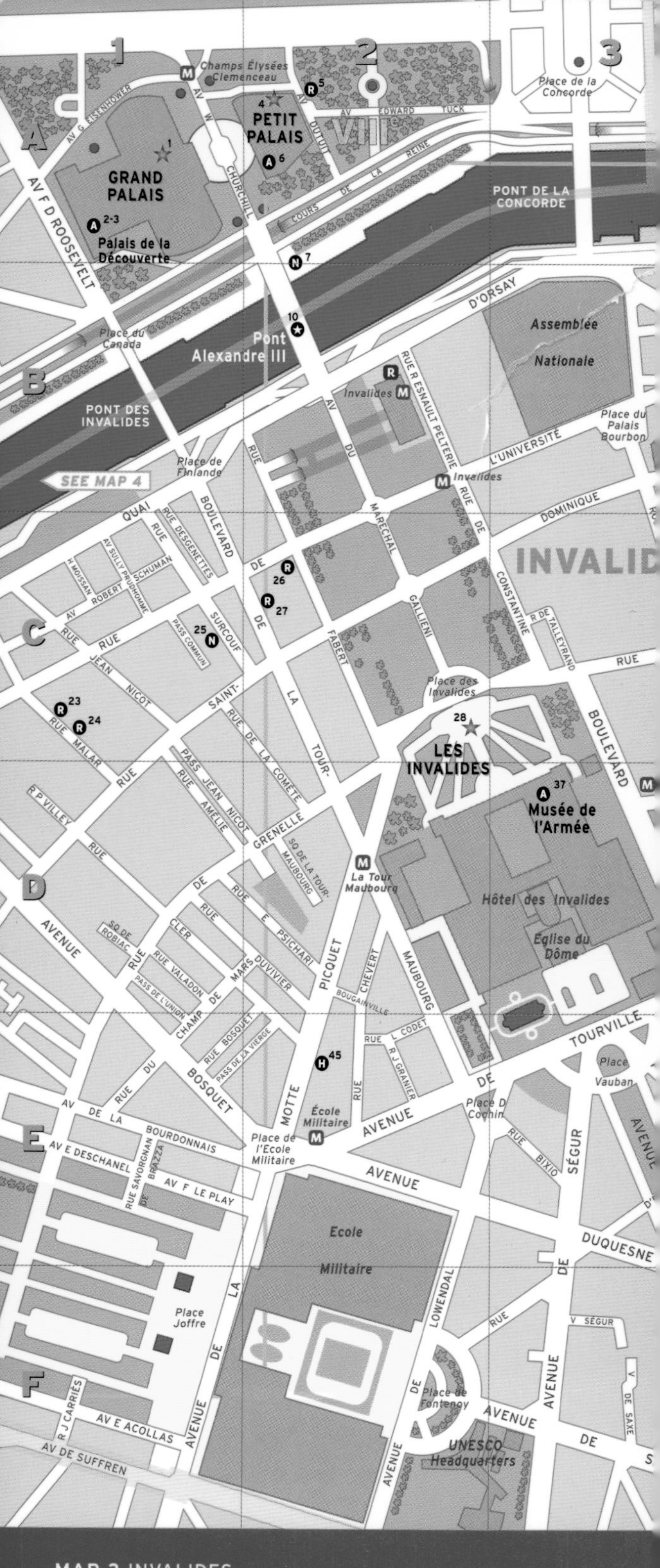

GRAND PALAIS
Palais de la Découverte
PETIT PALAIS
Champs Élysées Clemenceau
Place de la Concorde
PONT DE LA CONCORDE
Pont Alexandre III
PONT DES INVALIDES
Place du Canada
Assemblée Nationale
Place du Palais Bourbon
Invalides
Place de Finlande
SEE MAP 4
INVALID
Place des Invalides
LES INVALIDES
Musée de l'Armée
Hôtel des Invalides
Église du Dôme
La Tour Maubourg
École Militaire
Place de l'École Militaire
Place Vauban
Place Joffre
Ecole Militaire
Place de Fontenoy
UNESCO Headquarters
Place Cochin

INVALIDES

The diamond-shaped 7th arrondissement houses the wealthiest part of the Left Bank, where government offices and foreign embassies occupy many opulent town houses. Its wide avenues offer perfectly aligned views of landmarks and refreshing open spaces. Manicured gardens and bronze cannons surround its most imposing monument, the Hôtel des Invalides, built by Louis XIV as a refuge for wounded and retired soldiers. Beneath the golden Église du Dôme lies the tomb of Emperor Napoléon I. Next door is the aristocratic Hôtel Biron, an 18th-century mansion housing the Musée Rodin and a romantic sculpture garden.

Overlooking the Seine is the Musée d'Orsay, the former belle époque train station transformed into the museum for French Impressionist and post-Impressionist arts. The grand complex in the shadow of the Tour Eiffel is the École Militaire, the still-active military academy where Napoléon trained as an officer. The charming rue Cler street market brings together a mix of food shops, cafés, and open-air stalls. For high-fashion shopping, follow the chic Parisiennes to the Bon Marché department store at rue de Sèvres.

SIGHTS

A1 **1** ★ Grand Palais, p. 7
A2 **4** ★ Petit Palais, p. 7
A5 **8** ★ Musée d'Orsay, p. 9
B2 **10** Pont Alexandre III, p. 10
C2 **28** ★ Les Invalides, p. 8

RESTAURANTS

A2 **5** Ledoyen, p. 35
A5 **9** Le Voltaire, p. 35
B5 **13** Le Bistrot de Paris, p. 33
B5 **14** L'Atelier de Joel Robuchon, p. 33
C1 **23** L'Affriolé, p. 32
C1 **24** Chez l'Ami Jean, p. 33
C2 **26** Le Divellec, p. 34
C2 **27** Il Vino, p. 35
D4 **39** L'Arpège, p. 33
D6 **43** Hélène Darroze, p. 34
D6 **44** L'Epi Dupin, p. 34
E4 **47** Coutume Café, p. 34
E5 **48** Aida, p. 32

NIGHTLIFE

A2 **7** Le Showcase, p. 56
C1 **25** The Club, p. 56
D6 **41** Bar du Lutetia, p. 56

SHOPS

B4 **11** 1 Et 1 Font 3, p. 71
B5 **17** Prince Jardinier and Maison Deyrolle, p. 72
B6 **18** Librairie Studio 7L, p. 71
B6 **21** Les Prairies de Paris, p. 72
B6 **22** Debauve et Gallais, p. 71
C5 **30** Bonton, p. 71
C5 **32** Barthélemy, p. 70
C6 **34** Sabbia Rosa, p. 72
C6 **35** Editions de Parfum Frédéric Malle, p. 71
C6 **36** Sentou, p. 72
D5 **40** La Pâtisserie des Rêves, p. 71
D6 **42** La Grande Epicerie du Bon Marché, p. 71
E6 **49** Moda, p. 71

ARTS AND LEISURE

A1 **2** Galeries Nationales du Grand Palais, p. 89
A1 **3** Palais de la Découverte, p. 90
A2 **6** Musée des Beaux-Arts de la Ville de Paris, p. 89
C5 **31** Musée Maillol – Fondation Dina Vierny, p. 90
C6 **33** Musée des Lettres et Manuscrits, p. 89
D3 **37** Musée de l'Armée, p. 89
D3 **38** Musée Rodin, p. 90
E4 **46** La Pagode, p. 97

HOTELS

B4 **12** Hôtel le Bellechasse, p. 114
B5 **15** Le Montalembert, p. 115
B5 **16** Hôtel Pont Royal, p. 115
B6 **19** Hôtel de L'Université, p. 114
B6 **20** Hôtel Lenox, p. 115
C5 **29** Hôtel Duc de St-Simon, p. 114
D6 **41** Hôtel Lutetia, p. 115
E2 **45** Le Walt, p. 116
F5 **50** Hôtel Mayet, p. 115

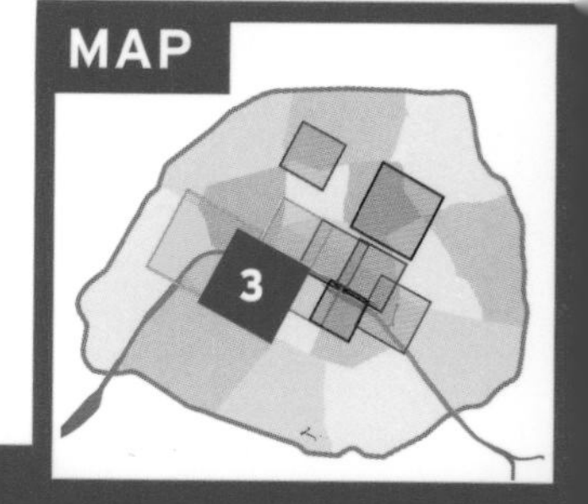

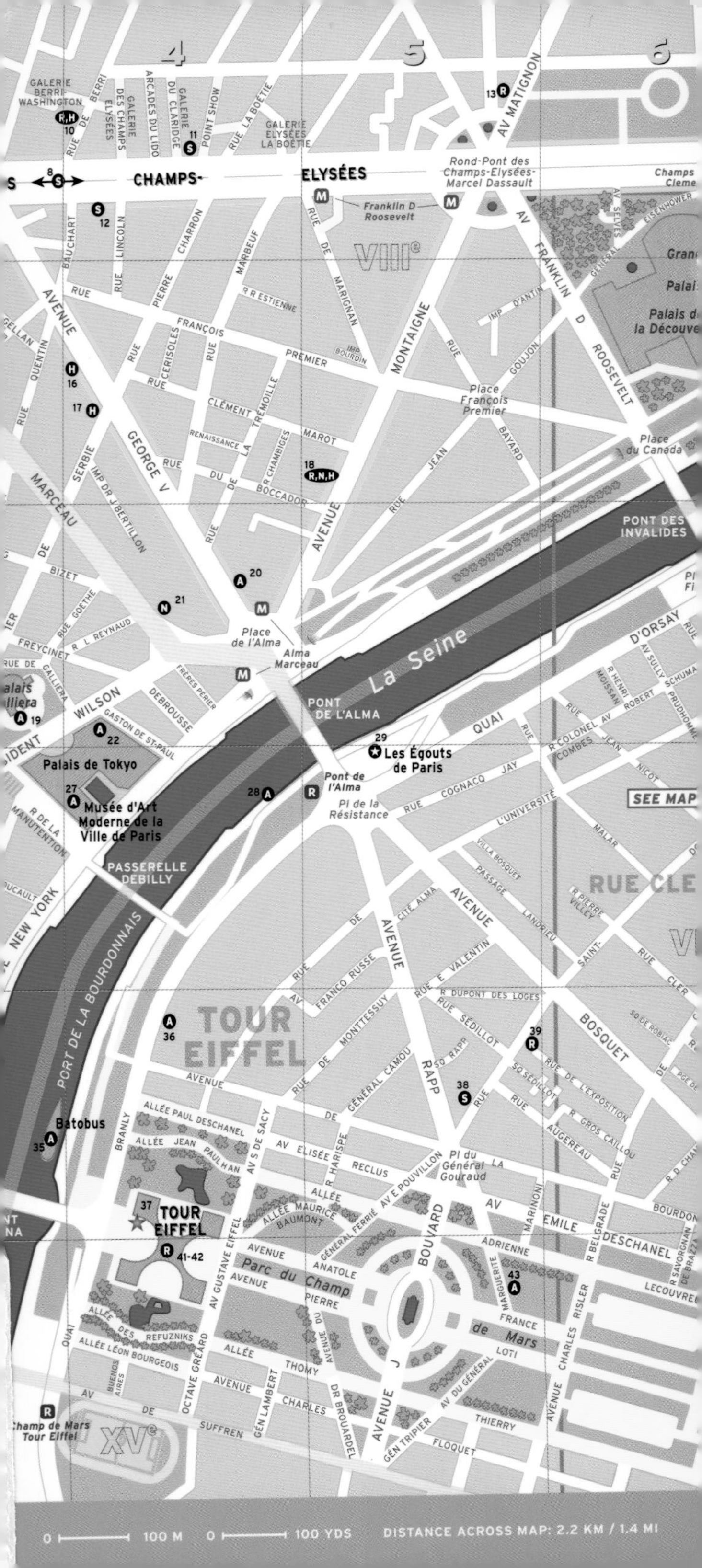
CHAMPS-ELYSÉES
Rond-Pont des Champs-Elysées-Marcel Dassault
Franklin D Roosevelt
VIII
La Seine
PONT DE L'ALMA
Place de l'Alma
Alma Marceau
Palais de Tokyo
Musée d'Art Moderne de la Ville de Paris
PASSERELLE DEBILLY
Les Égouts de Paris
Pont de l'Alma
Pl de la Résistance
SEE MAP
TOUR EIFFEL
Batobus
Parc du Champ de Mars
Champ de Mars Tour Eiffel
XV
0 100 M 0 100 YDS DISTANCE ACROSS MAP: 2.2 KM / 1.4 MI

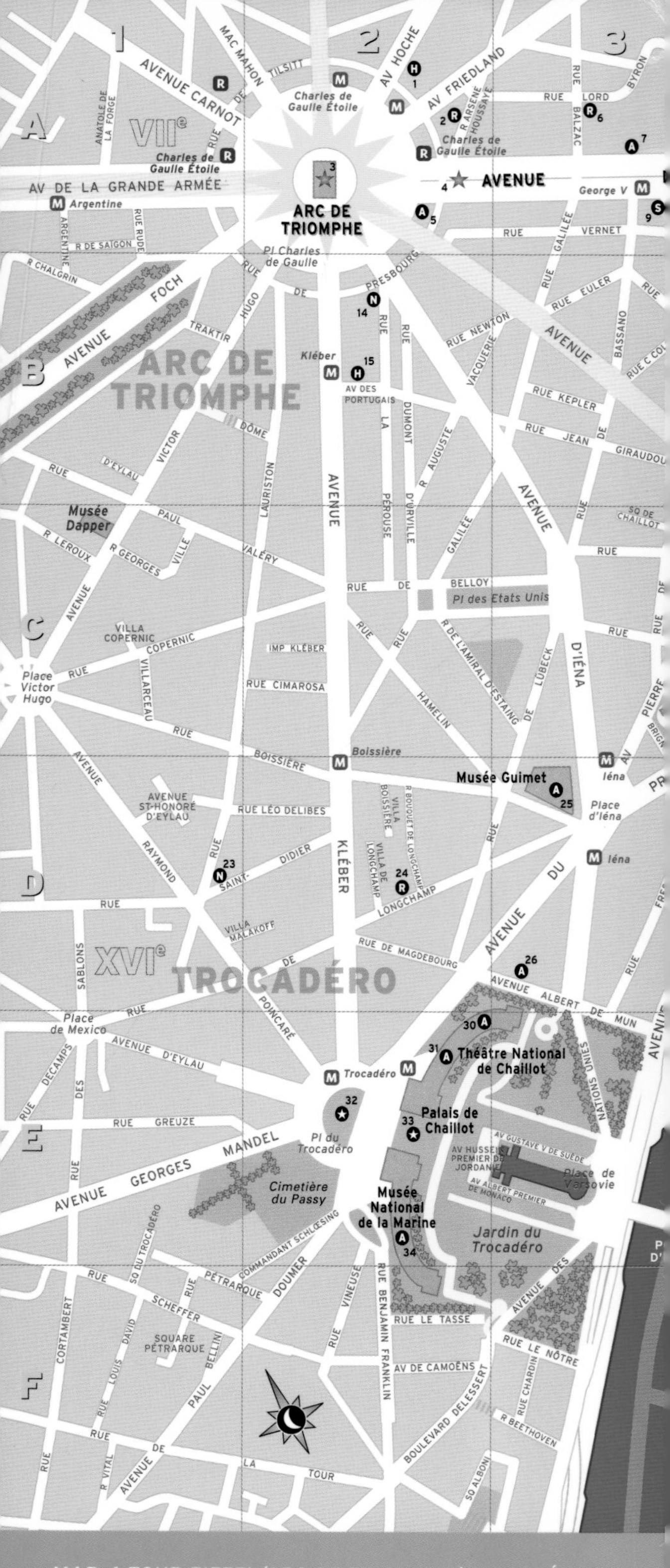

ARC DE TRIOMPHE
Charles de Gaulle Étoile
Pl Charles de Gaulle
AV DE LA GRANDE ARMÉE
AVENUE CARNOT
AVENUE FOCH
AV HOCHE
AV FRIEDLAND
Kléber
Boissière
Iéna
Trocadéro
George V
Argentine
Musée Dapper
Musée Guimet
Place d'Iéna
Place Victor Hugo
Place de Mexico
Pl des Etats Unis
Pl du Trocadéro
Cimetière du Passy
Théâtre National de Chaillot
Palais de Chaillot
Musée National de la Marine
Jardin du Trocadéro
Place de Varsovie
AVENUE GEORGES MANDEL
AVENUE KLÉBER
AVENUE D'IÉNA
AVENUE ALBERT DE MUN
AVENUE VICTOR HUGO
AVENUE RAYMOND POINCARÉ
RUE BENJAMIN FRANKLIN
BOULEVARD DELESSERT
TROCADÉRO
XVIe
VIIIe

TOUR EIFFEL/ARC DE TRIOMPHE/TROCADÉRO

The western expanse of the capital represents the height of Parisian pomp and glitz. Constructed in the 19th century, Napoléon's magnificent military monument, the Arc de Triomphe, stands as a cornerstone of this area. It is the hub of 12 radiating avenues, including the famous Champs-Elysées. This tree-lined avenue of upscale shops and fast food chains joins with avenues George V and Montaigne to make up the Golden Triangle, home to top couture houses.

Beyond, the posh 16th arrondissement is a haven for art lovers, with the Musée Guimet of Asian arts, the Palais de Tokyo's contemporary art lab, and the Musée de la Mode's historic fashion collection. The vast esplanade of the neoclassical Palais de Chaillot is the best place to admire the city's most beloved monument, the Tour Eiffel, framed by the shooting water cannons of the Trocadéro gardens.

GRANDS BOULEVARDS

First created when Louis XIV converted the city's 17th-century fortifications into wide promenades, boulevards really came of age in the 19th century, when they replaced the choked alleys of medieval Paris. Branching out from the Opéra Garnier and the Place de la Madeleine, the Grands Boulevards became the stomping grounds of the fashionable bourgeoisie. Today these roads remain popular among shopaholics undeterred by the constant stream of noisy traffic. Behind Charles Garnier's majestic opera house, on the boulevard Haussmann, are two of the city's grandest department stores, Printemps and Galeries Lafayette. Down boulevard de la Madeleine, the Greek temple-turned-church of the same name is surrounded by gourmet food and chocolate shops like Fauchon and Hédiard. Mouths will water at window dressings on the Place Vendôme, land of ritzy jewelers, and along rue St-Honoré, where fashionistas with fat wallets chase the latest trends.

Escape commercial temptation at the Jardin des Tuileries, where you can enjoy a bucolic stroll beneath the plane trees or participate in the ultimate Paris activity: people-watching. The sport can continue into the evening as the brasseries and cafés around the Opéra Garnier fill with a lively post-theater crowd.

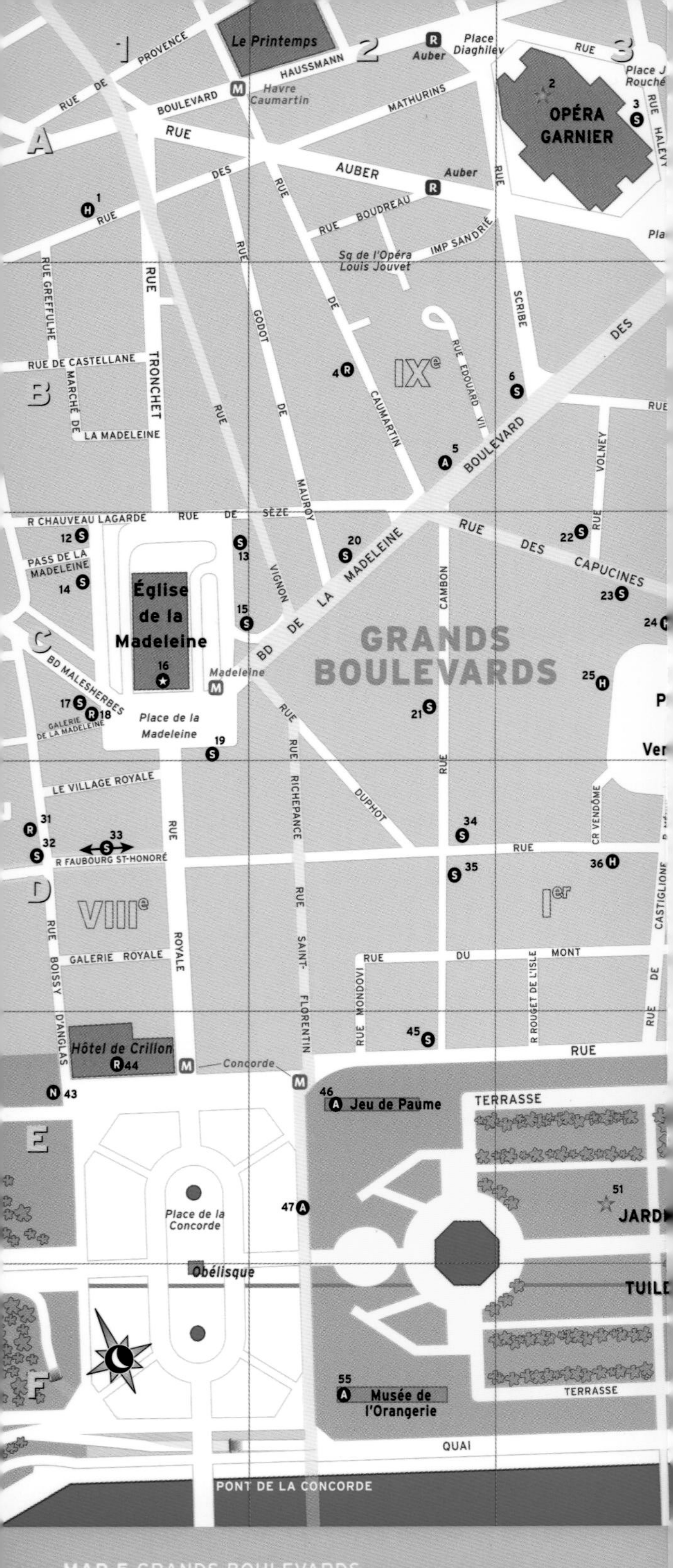

Le Printemps
Opéra Garnier
Église de la Madeleine
Place de la Madeleine
Grands Boulevards
IXe
VIIIe
Ier
Hôtel de Crillon
Jeu de Paume
Place de la Concorde
Obélisque
Musée de l'Orangerie
Pont de la Concorde
Boulevard Haussmann
Rue Auber
Rue Tronchet
Rue Caumartin
Boulevard des Capucines
Rue Royale
R Faubourg St-Honoré
Rue Saint-Florentin
Rue de Rivoli
Quai
Terrasse

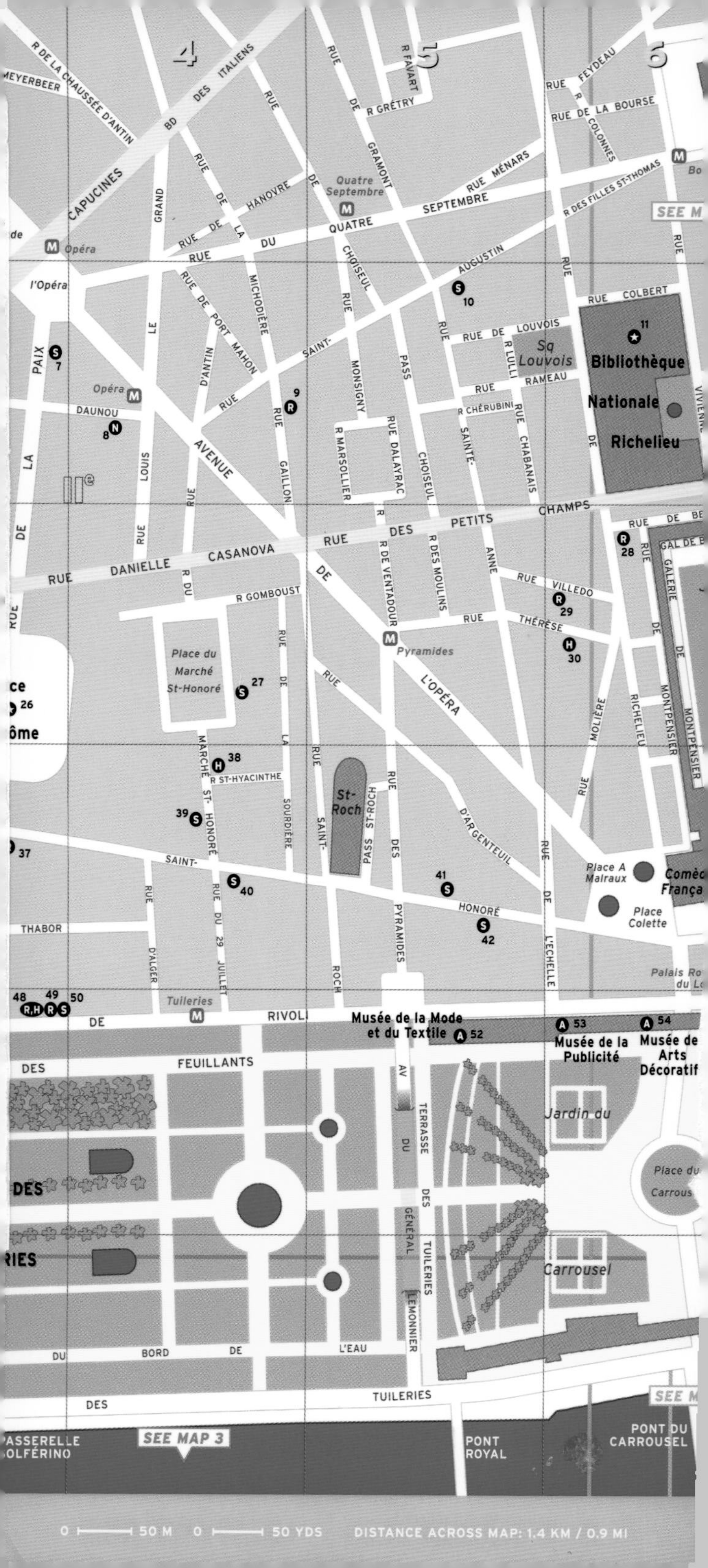

4
5
6
R DE LA CHAUSSÉE D'ANTIN
MEYERBEER
BD DES ITALIENS
CAPUCINES
RUE
R FAVART
R GRÉTRY
RUE DE GRAMONT
RUE FEYDEAU
R COLONNES
RUE DE LA BOURSE
GRAND
RUE DE HANOVRE
Quatre Septembre
RUE MÉNARS
SEPTEMBRE
R DES FILLES ST-THOMAS
SEE M
Opéra
l'Opéra
RUE DU QUATRE
RUE DE LA MICHODIÈRE
RUE DE CHOISEUL
RUE
AUGUSTIN
10
RUE COLBERT
RUE DE LOUVOIS
11
Sq Louvois
Bibliothèque Nationale Richelieu
PAIX
7
LE
RUE DE PORT MAHON
D'ANTIN
SAINT-
MONSIGNY
PASS
R LULLI
RAMEAU
RUE
VIVIENNE
9
RUE GAILLON
R CHÉRUBINI
RUE CHABANAIS
Opéra
DAUNOU
8
LA
LOUIS
AVENUE
R MARSOLLIER
RUE DALAYRAC
CHOISEUL
SAINTE-
DE
RUE
RUE
CHAMPS
DES PETITS
RUE DE BE
28
GAL DE B
DE
RUE DANIELLE CASANOVA
RUE
R DU
R GOMBOUST
DE
R DE VENTADOUR
R DES MOULINS
ANNE
RUE VILLEDO
29
GALERIE
RUE THÉRÈSE
30
Place du Marché St-Honoré
27
Pyramides
L'OPÉRA
RUE DE LA SOURDIÈRE
MOLIÈRE
RICHELIEU
DE MONTPENSIER
MONTPENSIER
ce
26
ôme
38
MARCHÉ ST-HONORÉ
R ST-HYACINTHE
39
RUE SAINT-ROCH
St-Roch
PASS ST-ROCH
RUE DES PYRAMIDES
D'ARGENTEUIL
RUE
37
SAINT-
40
41
RUE DE L'ECHELLE
Place A Malraux
Comédie Française
HONORÉ
42
Place Colette
THABOR
RUE D'ALGER
RUE DU 29 JUILLET
Palais Royal du Louvre
48
49
50
Tuileries
DE
RIVOLI
Musée de la Mode et du Textile
52
53
Musée de la Publicité
54
Musée des Arts Décoratifs
DES
FEUILLANTS
AV DU GÉNÉRAL LEMONNIER
TERRASSE DES TUILERIES
Jardin du Carrousel
Place du Carrousel
DES
RIES
DU
BORD
DE
L'EAU
DES
TUILERIES
SEE M
PASSERELLE SOLFÉRINO
SEE MAP 3
PONT ROYAL
PONT DU CARROUSEL
0 50 M 0 50 YDS
DISTANCE ACROSS MAP: 1.4 KM / 0.9 MI

✪ SIGHTS

A2 **3** ★ Arc de Triomphe, p. 11
A2 **4** ★ Champs-Elysées, p. 11
D5 **29** Les Égouts de Paris, p. 12
E2 **32** Trocadéro, p. 13
E2 **33** Palais de Chaillot, p. 12
E4 **37** ★ Tour Eiffel, p. 11

Ⓡ RESTAURANTS

A2 **2** Chiberta, p. 35
A3 **6** Pierre Gagnaire, p. 37
A4 **10** La Table du Lancaster, p. 37
A5 **13** Market, p. 36
B5 **18** Alain Ducasse au Plaza Athénée, p. 35
D2 **24** Jamin, p. 36
E5 **39** La Fontaine de Mars, p. 36
F4 **41** 58 Tour Eiffel, p. 35
F4 **42** Le Jules Verne, p. 36

Ⓝ NIGHTLIFE

B2 **14** Sir Winston, p. 57
B5 **18** Le Bar du Plaza Athénée, p. 56
C4 **21** Le Baron, p. 57
D1 **23** Le Dokhan's Bar, p. 57

Ⓢ SHOPS

A3 **8** Champs-Elysées, p. 72
A3 **9** Louis Vuitton, p. 73
A4 **11** Guerlain, p. 72
A4 **12** Ladurée, p. 73
E5 **38** Grégory Renard Chocolatier: Cacao et Macarons, p. 72
E6 **40** Rue Cler, p. 73

Ⓐ ARTS AND LEISURE

A2 **5** I Heart Hanif Cabs, p. 103
A3 **7** Le Lido, p. 97
C3 **19** Musée Galliera (Musée de la Mode de La Ville de Paris), p. 91
C4 **20** Le Crazy Horse, p. 97
C4 **22** Palais de Tokyo – Site de Création Contemporaine, p. 91
D3 **25** Musée Guimet, p. 91
D3 **26** Aquarium du Trocadéro, p. 90
D4 **27** Musée d'Art Moderne de la Ville de Paris, p. 91
D4 **28** Bateaux-Mouches, p. 103
E2 **30** Musée de l'Homme, p. 91
E2 **31** Théâtre National de Chaillot, p. 98
E2 **34** Musée National de la Marine, p. 91
E3 **35** Batobus, p. 103
E4 **36** Musée du Quai Branly, p. 91
F5 **43** Les Marionnettes du Champs de Mars, p. 97

Ⓗ HOTELS

A2 **1** Le Royal Monceau – Raffles Paris, p. 116
A4 **10** Hôtel Lancaster, p. 116
B2 **15** Hôtel Raphael, p. 116
B4 **16** Four Seasons George V, p. 116
B4 **17** Hôtel de Sers, p. 116
B5 **18** Hôtel Plaza Athénée, p. 116

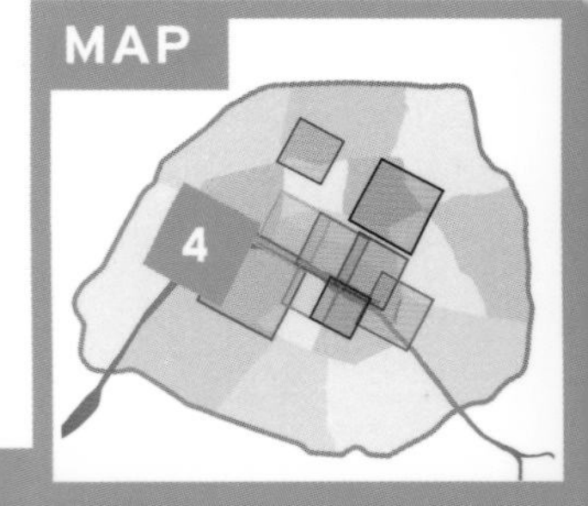

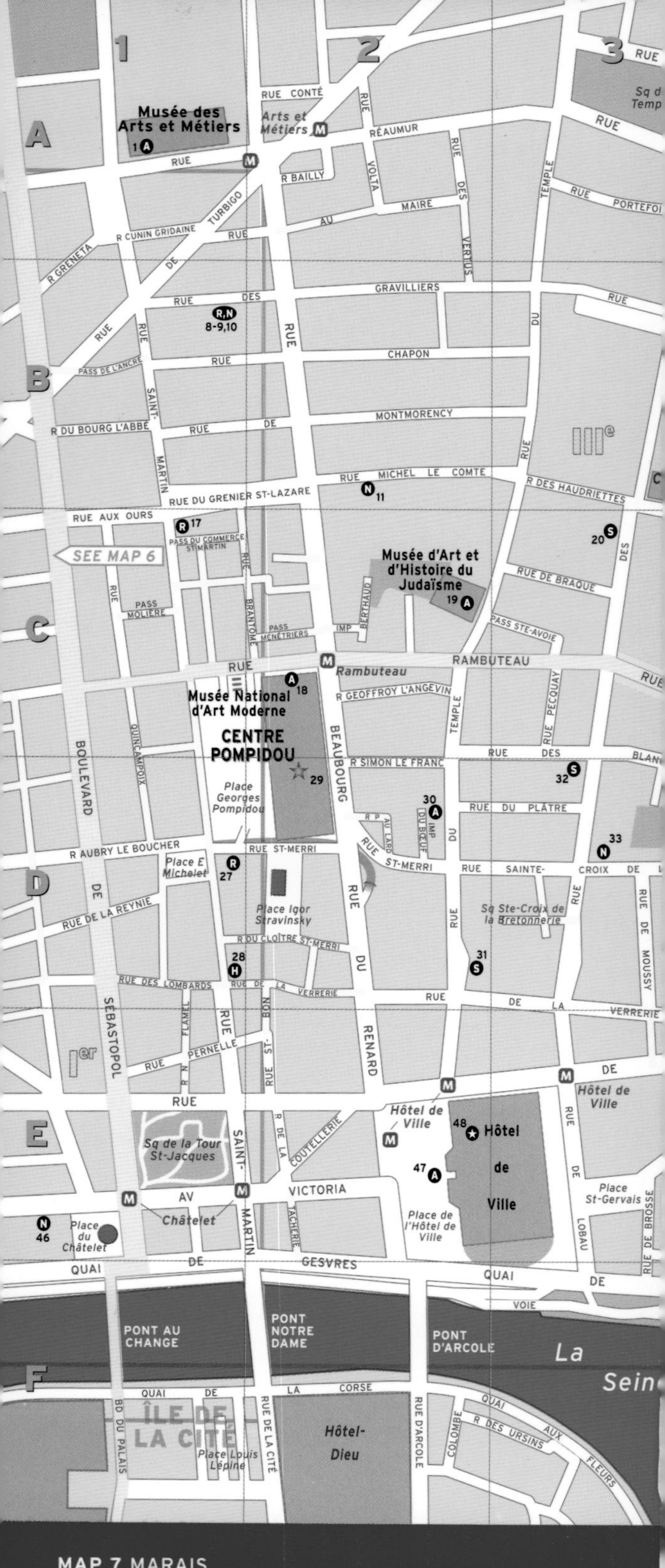
Musée des Arts et Métiers
Arts et Métiers
Musée d'Art et d'Histoire du Judaïsme
Musée National d'Art Moderne
CENTRE POMPIDOU
Place Georges Pompidou
Rambuteau
Place Igor Stravinsky
Sq de la Tour St-Jacques
Châtelet
Place du Châtelet
Hôtel de Ville
Place de l'Hôtel de Ville
Place St-Gervais
Sq Ste-Croix de la Bretonnerie
PONT AU CHANGE
PONT NOTRE DAME
PONT D'ARCOLE
La Seine
ÎLE DE LA CITÉ
Hôtel-Dieu
Place Louis Lépine
SEE MAP 6

MARAIS

A web of narrow streets bursting with mansions, museums, and secret gardens, the Marais preserves much of the best Renaissance architecture in Paris. Originally a swamp (*marais* is French for marsh), it became the epicenter of French aristocracy in 1605 with the construction of the Place des Vosges. After Louis XIV moved the court to Versailles, the Marais declined and degenerated into a slum. Ambitious restoration work in the late 1960s brought the neighborhood back to its former glory. Many of its mansions, or *hôtels particuliers,* have been converted into museums, such as the Musée Carnavalet and the Musée National Picasso, which is slated to re-open after a multi-year renovation project. Centre Pompidou adds some new architecture to the mix with its bold, striking design.

The Marais is one of Paris's most vibrant neighborhoods. The rue Vieille du Temple is lively night and day, lined with trendy cafés and hip clothing stores. It's also the center of gay and lesbian life in Paris, particularly along the rue Ste-Croix de la Bretonnerie. One part of the Marais that has remained fairly constant through the centuries is the Jewish Quarter, centered on rue des Rosiers. High fashion has encroached upon its synagogues and kosher delis, but the street still feels authentic.

LOUVRE/LES HALLES

Located between the Arc de Triomphe/Champs-Elysées pomp and the Marais buzz, this area balances the frenetic motion of its neighbors with the frozen grandeur of its monuments. The Musée du Louvre beckons visitors from around the world to its grand galleries. Next door, the historic theater of the Comédie Française hides within the gardens and stately arcades of the Palais Royal. Just beyond are more than a dozen 19th-century shopping arcades to explore, like the Galerie Vivienne and Passage Choiseul.

But this center is hardly static. Cross the elegant Place des Victoires to the rue Etienne Marcel for streetwise fashions and trendy cafés. Pedestrian streets surrounding the charming rue Montorgueil have become home to many of the city's hot new restaurants and nightspots. Four years into a six-year renovation project, the revamped Forum des Halles shopping district has already ditched its seedy vibe and reclaimed some of the glory it possessed in its heyday, when it was the city's central food market. (*Halle* means "covered market" in French.) If you find Les Halles' new parks, gardens, and pedestrian promenades too sedate, the nearby rue de Rivoli promises a livelier experience, every day *sauf* (except) Sunday.

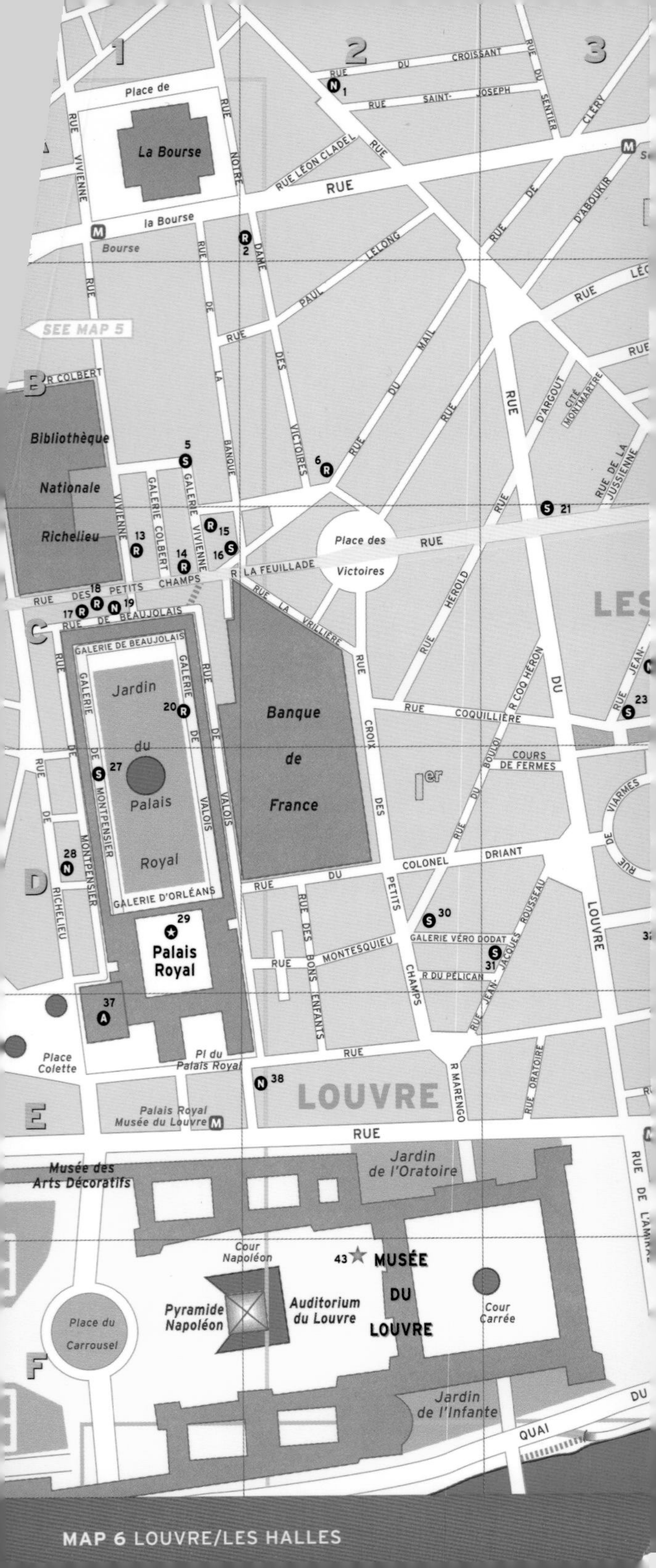
La Bourse
Bibliothèque Nationale Richelieu
Place des Victoires
Banque de France
Jardin du Palais Royal
Palais Royal
LOUVRE
Musée des Arts Décoratifs
Jardin de l'Oratoire
Cour Napoléon
Pyramide Napoléon
Auditorium du Louvre
MUSÉE DU LOUVRE
Cour Carrée
Place du Carrousel
Jardin de l'Infante
Place Colette
Pl du Palais Royal
Palais Royal Musée du Louvre
Bourse
SEE MAP 5
RUE DU CROISSANT
RUE SAINT-JOSEPH
RUE DU SENTIER
RUE LÉON CLADEL
RUE D'ABOUKIR
RUE PAUL LELONG
RUE DU MAIL
RUE DES VICTOIRES
RUE VIVIENNE
RUE DE LA BANQUE
GALERIE COLBERT
GALERIE VIVIENNE
R COLBERT
RUE DES PETITS CHAMPS
RUE DE BEAUJOLAIS
GALERIE DE BEAUJOLAIS
GALERIE DE MONTPENSIER
GALERIE DE VALOIS
GALERIE D'ORLÉANS
RUE DE VALOIS
RUE DE MONTPENSIER
RUE DE RICHELIEU
R LA FEUILLADE
RUE LA VRILLIÈRE
RUE CROIX DES PETITS CHAMPS
RUE HEROLD
R COQ HÉRON
RUE COQUILLIÈRE
COURS DE FERMES
RUE DU BOULOI
RUE DU LOUVRE
RUE DE VIARMES
RUE COLONEL DRIANT
RUE DU MONTESQUIEU
RUE DES BONS ENFANTS
GALERIE VÉRO DODAT
R DU PÉLICAN
RUE JEAN-JACQUES ROUSSEAU
R MARENGO
RUE ORATOIRE
RUE DE L'AMIRAL
RUE DE LA JUSSIENNE
CITÉ MONTMARTRE
RUE D'ARGOUT
QUAI DU
LES
Ier

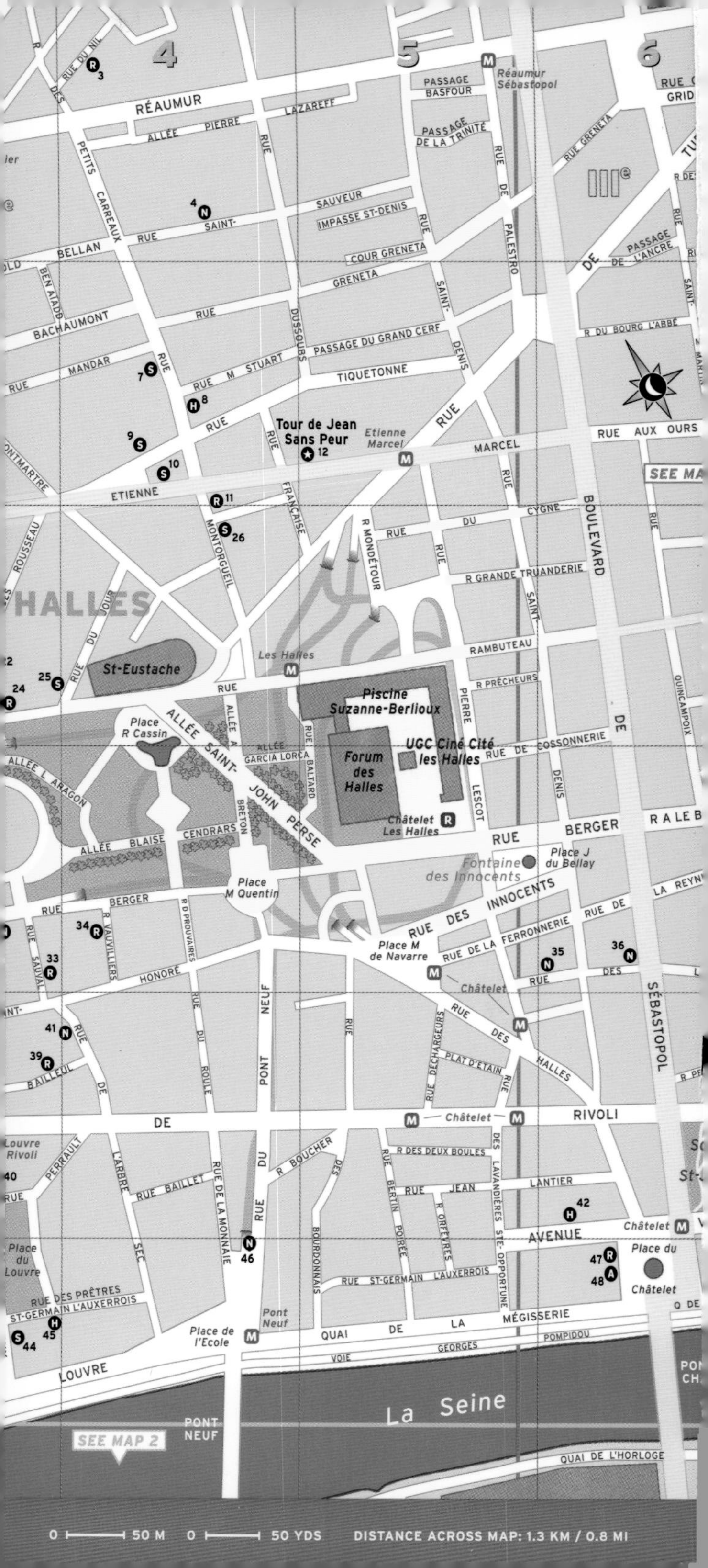
4
5
6
RÉAUMUR
ALLÉE PIERRE LAZAREFF
PASSAGE BASFOUR
Réaumur Sébastopol
PASSAGE DE LA TRINITÉ
RUE GRENETA
III e
RUE DU NIL
RUE DES PETITS CARREAUX
RUE SAINT-SAUVEUR
IMPASSE ST-DENIS
COUR GRENETA
GRENETA
BELLAN
BEN AIADD
BACHAUMONT
RUE DUSSOUBS
RUE DE PALESTRO
RUE SAINT-DENIS
PASSAGE DE L'ANCRE
R DU BOURG L'ABBÉ
MANDAR
RUE M STUART
PASSAGE DU GRAND CERF
TIQUETONNE
RUE AUX OURS
Tour de Jean Sans Peur
Etienne Marcel
RUE ETIENNE MARCEL
MONTMARTRE
FRANÇAISE
MONTORGUEIL
SEE MAP
ROUSSEAU
HALLES
R MONDÉTOUR
RUE DU CYGNE
R GRANDE TRUANDERIE
BOULEVARD DE SÉBASTOPOL
RUE DU JOUR
St-Eustache
Les Halles
RAMBUTEAU
R PRÊCHEURS
QUINCAMPOIX
Piscine Suzanne-Berlioux
Place R Cassin
ALLÉE SAINT-JOHN PERSE
ALLÉE GARCIA LORCA
RUE BALTARD
Forum des Halles
UGC Ciné Cité les Halles
RUE DE COSSONNERIE
RUE PIERRE LESCOT
ALLÉE L ARAGON
ALLÉE BLAISE CENDRARS
BRETON
Châtelet Les Halles
RUE BERGER
Place J du Bellay
Fontaine des Innocents
Place M Quentin
RUE DES INNOCENTS
LA REYNIE
R D PROUVAIRES
R VAUVILLIERS
RUE SAUVAL
HONORÉ
Place M de Navarre
RUE DE LA FERRONNERIE
RUE DES LOMBARDS
Châtelet
RUE DES HALLES
RUE DU ROULE
PONT NEUF
RUE DES DÉCHARGEURS
PLAT D'ETAIN
BAILLEUL
RUE DE RIVOLI
Louvre Rivoli
PERRAULT
L'ARBRE SEC
RUE BAILLET
RUE DE LA MONNAIE
RUE DU PONT NEUF
R BOUCHER
R DES DEUX BOULES
RUE BERTIN POIRÉE
RUE JEAN LANTIER
R ORFÈVRES
RUE DES LAVANDIÈRES STE-OPPORTUNE
AVENUE
BOURDONNAIS
Place du Louvre
RUE DES PRÊTRES ST-GERMAIN L'AUXERROIS
RUE ST-GERMAIN L'AUXERROIS
Place du Châtelet
Place de l'Ecole
Pont Neuf
QUAI DE LA MÉGISSERIE
VOIE GEORGES POMPIDOU
LOUVRE
La Seine
PONT NEUF
SEE MAP 2
QUAI DE L'HORLOGE
0 50 M
0 50 YDS
DISTANCE ACROSS MAP: 1.3 KM / 0.8 MI

SIGHTS

- A3 **2** ★ Opéra Garnier, p. 14
- B6 **11** Bibliothèque Nationale Richelieu, p. 15
- C1 **16** Église de la Madeleine, p. 15
- C3 **26** Place Vendôme, p. 15
- E3 **51** ★ Jardin des Tuileries, p. 13

RESTAURANTS

- B2 **4** Les Bacchantes, p. 37
- B4 **9** Drouant, p. 38
- C1 **18** Senderens, p. 38
- C6 **28** Verjus, p. 38
- C6 **29** Kunitoraya, p. 38
- D1 **31** Bread and Roses, p. 37
- D3 **37** Le Carré des Feuillants, p. 38
- E1 **44** Les Ambassadeurs, p. 37
- E3 **48** Restaurant le Meurice, p. 38
- E3 **49** Angelina, p. 37

NIGHTLIFE

- B4 **8** Harry's New York Bar, p. 57
- E1 **43** Buddha Bar, p. 57

SHOPS

- A3 **3** La Galerie de l'Opéra de Paris, p. 75
- B3 **6** Ateliers d'Art de France, p. 74
- B3 **7** Repetto, p. 77
- B5 **10** Workshop Issé, p. 77
- C1 **12** Hédiard, p. 75
- C1 **13** Fauchon, p. 75
- C1 **14** Maison de la Truffe, p. 75
- C1 **15** Lavinia, p. 75
- C1 **17** Au Nain Bleu, p. 76
- C1 **19** Boutique Maille, p. 74
- C2 **20** La Maison du Chocolat, p. 76
- C2 **21** Chanel, p. 74
- C3 **22** Pierre Corthay, p. 76
- C3 **23** Maître Parfumeur et Gantier, p. 76
- C4 **27** Atelier du Bracelet Parisien, p. 74
- D1 **32** Hermès, p. 75
- D1 **33** Rue du Faubourg St-Honoré, p. 77
- D2 **34** Mina Poe, p. 76
- D2 **35** Alice Cadolle, p. 73
- D4 **39** Morganne Bello, p. 76
- D4 **40** Colette, p. 75
- D5 **41** Anne Fontaine, p. 74
- D5 **42** Astier de Villatte, p. 74
- E2 **45** W. H. Smith, p. 77
- E3 **50** Galignani, p. 75

ARTS AND LEISURE

- B2 **5** L'Olympia, p. 98
- E2 **46** Jeu de Paume, p. 92
- E2 **47** Citroën Tours of Paris – 4 Roues Sous 1 Parapluie, p. 104
- E5 **52** Musée de la Mode et du Textile, p. 92
- E6 **53** Musée de la Publicité, p. 92
- E6 **54** Musée des Arts Décoratifs, p. 92
- F2 **55** Musée de l'Orangerie, p. 92

HOTELS

- A1 **1** Hôtel George Sand, p. 117
- C3 **24** Park Hyatt Paris-Vendôme, p. 118
- C3 **25** Hôtel Ritz, p. 117
- C6 **30** Hôtel Thérèse, p. 118
- D3 **36** Hôtel Costes, p. 117
- D4 **38** Hôtel des Tuileries, p. 117
- E3 **48** Hôtel le Meurice, p. 117

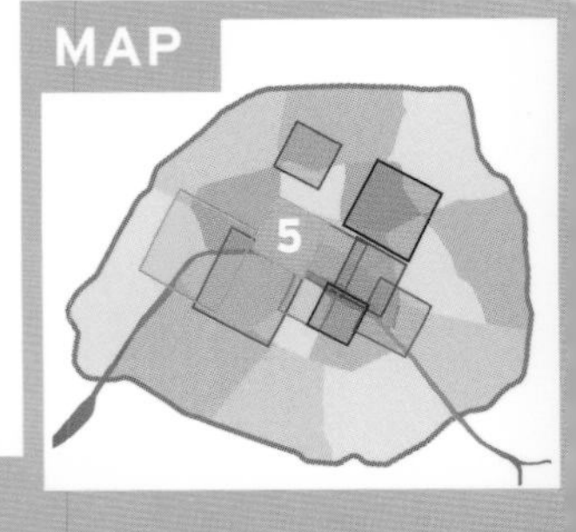

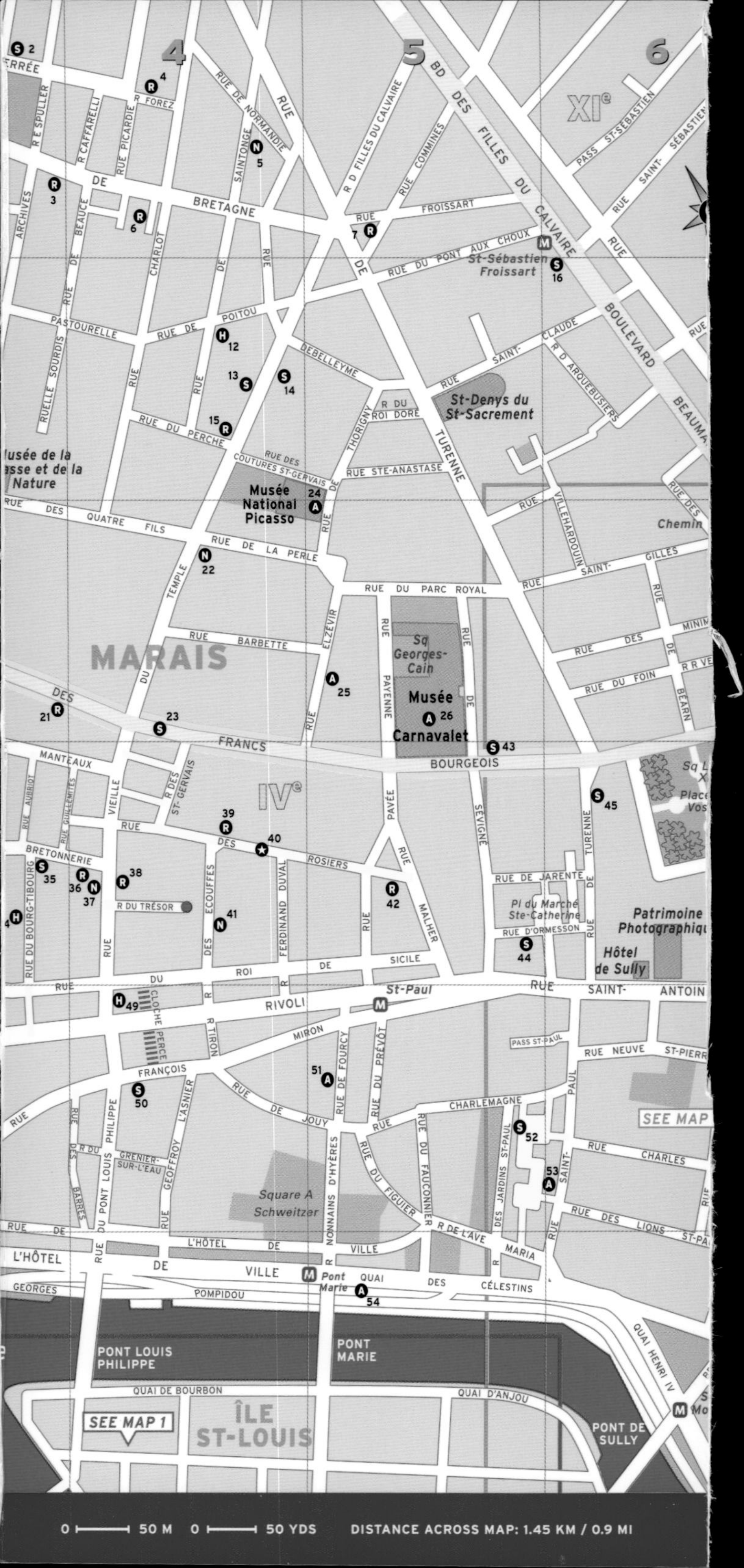

4
5
6
XIe
MARAIS
IVe
ÎLE ST-LOUIS
Musée National Picasso
Musée Carnavalet
Sq Georges-Cain
St-Denys du St-Sacrement
Square A Schweitzer
Hôtel de Sully
Patrimoine Photographique
Pl du Marché Ste-Catherine
St-Sébastien Froissart
St-Paul
Pont Marie
PONT LOUIS PHILIPPE
PONT MARIE
PONT DE SULLY
BD DES FILLES DU CALVAIRE
BOULEVARD BEAUMARCHAIS
RUE DE BRETAGNE
RUE DE TURENNE
RUE DU TEMPLE
RUE DES FRANCS BOURGEOIS
RUE DE RIVOLI
RUE SAINT-ANTOINE
RUE DES ROSIERS
RUE VIEILLE DU TEMPLE
RUE DE SÉVIGNÉ
RUE DU PARC ROYAL
RUE DES QUATRE FILS
RUE DE LA PERLE
RUE BARBETTE
RUE ELZEVIR
RUE PAYENNE
RUE PAVÉE
RUE MALHER
RUE DE SICILE
RUE DU ROI DE SICILE
RUE FRANÇOIS MIRON
RUE DE JOUY
RUE CHARLEMAGNE
RUE SAINT-PAUL
RUE DES LIONS ST-PAUL
RUE CHARLES V
RUE DE L'HÔTEL DE VILLE
QUAI DE L'HÔTEL DE VILLE
QUAI DES CÉLESTINS
QUAI HENRI IV
QUAI DE BOURBON
QUAI D'ANJOU
VOIE GEORGES POMPIDOU
RUE VIEILLE DU TEMPLE
RUE DE POITOU
RUE DE BEAUCE
RUE CHARLOT
RUE DE SAINTONGE
RUE DE NORMANDIE
RUE FROISSART
RUE DU PONT AUX CHOUX
RUE SAINT-CLAUDE
RUE SAINT-GILLES
RUE DES MINIMES
RUE DU FOIN
RUE DE BÉARN
RUE DE JARENTE
RUE D'ORMESSON
PASS ST-PAUL
RUE NEUVE ST-PIERRE
RUE DES JARDINS ST-PAUL
RUE DE L'AVE MARIA
RUE DU FIGUIER
RUE DU FAUCONNIER
RUE DU PRÉVÔT
RUE DE FOURCY
RUE DES NONNAINS D'HYÈRES
RUE GEOFFROY L'ASNIER
R DU GRENIER-SUR-L'EAU
RUE DES BARRES
RUE DU PONT LOUIS PHILIPPE
R DU TRÉSOR
RUE DES ECOUFFES
RUE FERDINAND DUVAL
RUE DU BOURG-TIBOURG
RUE DE LA VERRERIE
RUE DES BLANCS MANTEAUX
R DES GUILLEMITES
RUE AUBRIOT
R DES ST-GERVAIS
RUE DES COUTURES ST-GERVAIS
RUE DEBELLEYME
RUE DE THORIGNY
R DU ROI DORÉ
RUE STE-ANASTASE
RUE VILLEHARDOUIN
R D ARQUEBUSIERS
R D FILLES DU CALVAIRE
RUE COMMINES
PASS ST-SÉBASTIEN
RUE SAINT-SÉBASTIEN
RUE DU PERCHE
RUE DE PASTOURELLE
RUELLE SOURDIS
RUE DES ARCHIVES
R E SPULLER
R CAFFARELLI
RUE PICARDIE
R FOREZ
R DU CLOCHE PERCE
R TIRON
SEE MAP 1
SEE MAP
0 50 M 0 50 YDS DISTANCE ACROSS MAP: 1.45 KM / 0.9 MI

SIGHTS

- B5 **12** Tour de Jean Sans Peur, p. 17
- D1 **29** Palais Royal, p. 16
- F2 **43** ★ Musée du Louvre, p. 15

RESTAURANTS

- A2 **2** Saturne, p. 41
- A4 **3** Frenchie, p. 39
- B2 **6** Chez Georges, p. 39
- B4 **11** L'Escargot Montorgueil, p. 39
- C1 **13** Le Grand Colbert, p. 40
- C1 **14** Bistrot Vivienne, p. 39
- C1 **15** A Priori Thé, p. 40
- C1 **17** Le Grand Véfour, p. 40
- C1 **18** Willi's Wine Bar, p. 41
- C1 **20** Le Restaurant du Palais Royal, p. 41
- C3 **24** Au Pied de Cochon, p. 40
- D3 **33** Yam'tcha, p. 41
- D4 **34** Le Poule au Pot, p. 40
- E3 **39** Spring, p. 41
- F6 **47** Le Zimmer, p. 41

NIGHTLIFE

- A2 **1** Le Social Club, p. 59
- A4 **4** Experimental Cocktail Club, p. 58
- C1 **19** Club 18, p. 58
- C3 **22** Ballroom du Beef Club, p. 57
- D1 **28** Le Magnifique, p. 59
- D3 **32** 1979, p. 59
- D6 **35** Sunset/Sunside, p. 59
- D6 **36** Le Duc des Lombards, p. 58
- E2 **38** Cab, p. 58
- E3 **40** Le Fumoir, p. 58
- E4 **41** La Garde Robe, p. 59
- F4 **46** Kong, p. 59

SHOPS

- B1 **5** Galerie Vivienne, p. 78
- B4 **7** Stohrer, p. 79
- B4 **9** Kiliwatch, p. 79
- B4 **10** Un Après-Midi de Chien, p. 77
- C1 **16** Legrand Filles et Fils, p. 79
- C3 **21** Gas Bijoux, p. 78
- C3 **23** E. Dehillerin, p. 78
- C3 **25** Agnès B., p. 77
- C4 **26** Spa Nuxe, p. 79
- D1 **27** Didier Ludot, p. 78
- D2 **30** By Terry, p. 77
- D3 **31** Christian Louboutin, p. 78
- F3 **44** L'Artisan Parfumeur, p. 77

ARTS AND LEISURE

- E1 **37** Comédie Française (Salle Richelieu), p. 99
- F6 **48** Théâtre du Châtelet (Théâtre Musical de Paris), p. 99

HOTELS

- B4 **8** Hôtel Victoires Opéra, p. 119
- E6 **42** Hôtel Britannique, p. 118
- F3 **45** Hôtel le Relais du Louvre, p. 118

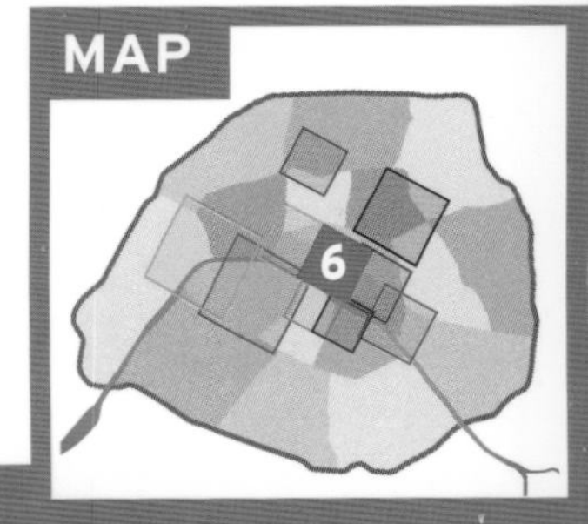

MONTMARTRE

At the turn of the 20th century, Montmartre was home to a thriving community of artists that included Van Gogh and Picasso. Today, in the famed Place du Tertre, artists with varying degrees of skill compete to sketch your portrait or sell you an "Impressionist" sunset. Although pretty, the chalky white Sacré-Coeur Basilica, which dominates the hillside, takes on the atmosphere of a crowded elevator in peak tourist season. But despite the theme-park air of the neighborhood's main attractions, the charm remains in its picturesquely steep staircases and quieter streets on the north side of the hill. This is where the grapes ripen in one of Paris's last remaining vineyards, Le Clos Montmartre, and two ancient windmills still stand on rue Lepic, not far from the Café des Deux Moulins, made famous in Jean-Pierre Jeunet's classic movie *Amélie*.

On the south side of the hill is the Pigalle district and the historic can-can cabarets that were immortalized by Toulouse-Lautrec. Today it's more seedy than racy, though the neon sex shops are slowly being replaced by more legitimate entertainment venues. Here, the Moulin Rouge endures, offering a Las Vegas-style show and overpriced food.

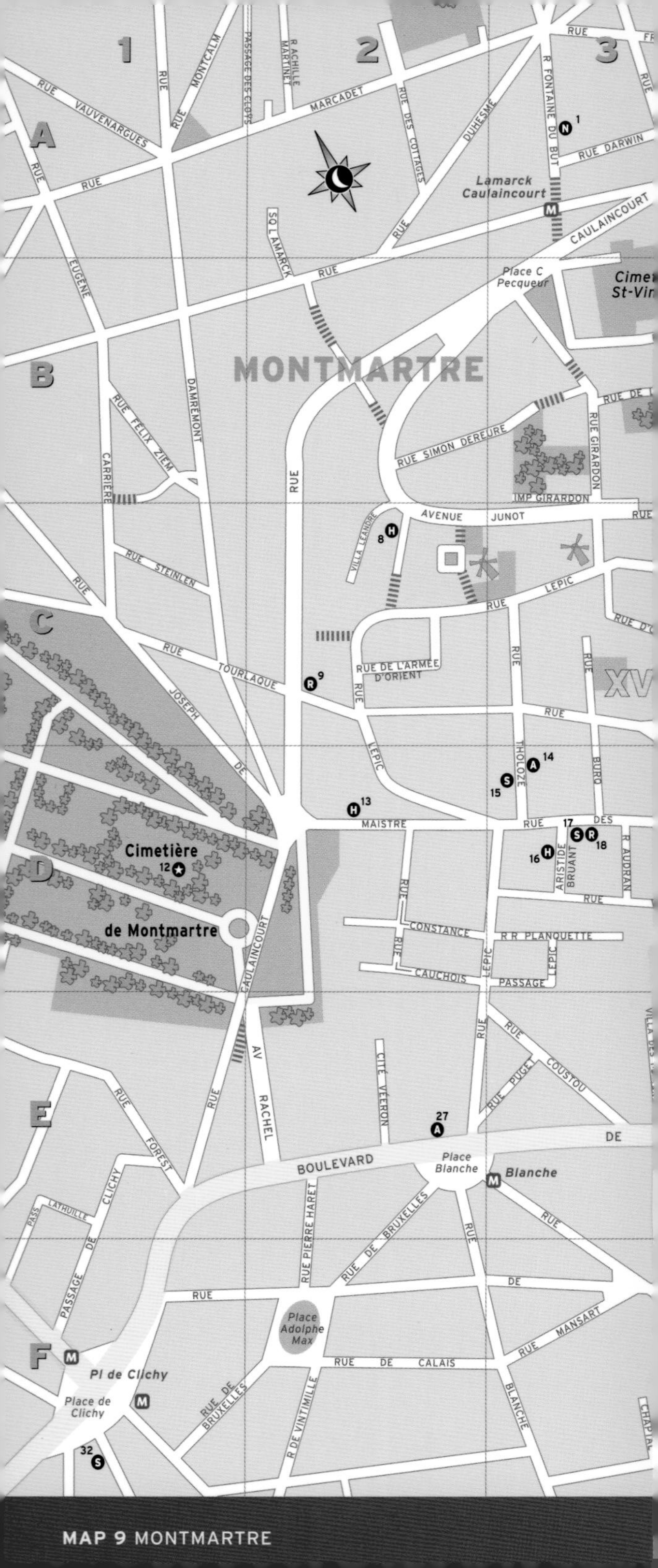
MONTMARTRE
Cimetière de Montmartre
Lamarck Caulaincourt
Place C Pecqueur
Place Blanche
Blanche
Place Adolphe Max
Pl de Clichy
Place de Clichy
Rue Marcadet
Rue Vauvenargues
Rue Caulaincourt
Rue Lepic
Avenue Junot
Rue Tholozé
Rue des Abbesses
Boulevard de Clichy
Rue Blanche
Rue de Calais
Rue Mansart
Rue de Bruxelles
Av Rachel
Rue Joseph de Maistre
Rue Damrémont
Rue Eugène Carrière
Rue Tourlaque
Rue Steinlen
Rue Félix Ziem
Rue Simon Dereure
Rue Girardon
Imp Girardon
Rue Darwin
R Fontaine du But
Rue Duhesme
Rue des Cottages
R Achille Martinet
Passage des Cloÿs
Rue Montcalm
Sq Lamarck
Villa Léandre
Rue de l'Armée d'Orient
Aristide Bruant
R Audran
Rue Burq
Rue Constance
R R Planquette
Rue Cauchois
Passage Lepic
Rue Puget
Rue Coustou
Cité Véron
Rue Forest
Rue Pierre Haret
R de Vintimille
Pass Lathuille
Passage de Clichy
Rue de Bruxelles
Chaptal
Cimetière St-Vincent
XVIII

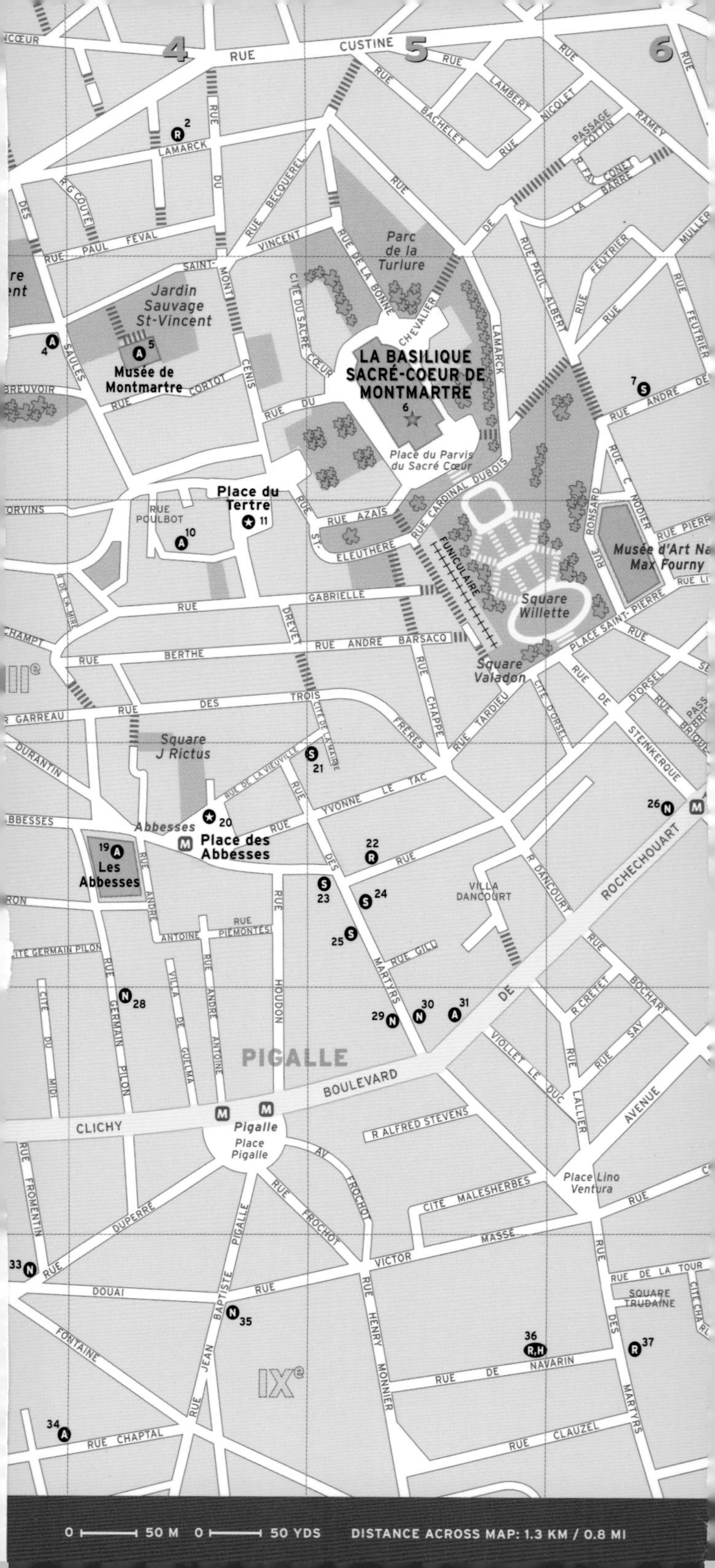

4
5
6
RUE CUSTINE
RUE LAMARCK
RUE BACHELET
RUE LAMBERT
RUE NICOLET
PASSAGE COTTIN
RUE RAMEY
RUE DE LA BARRE
RUE DU MONT CENIS
RUE BECQUEREL
RUE PAUL FEVAL
RUE ST-VINCENT
R G COUTE
RUE DES SAULES
Jardin Sauvage St-Vincent
Musée de Montmartre
RUE CORTOT
RUE DU CHEVALIER DE LA BARRE
Parc de la Turlure
RUE DE LA BONNE
CITÉ DU SACRÉ CŒUR
LA BASILIQUE SACRÉ-COEUR DE MONTMARTRE
Place du Parvis du Sacré Cœur
RUE LAMARCK
RUE PAUL ALBERT
RUE FEUTRIER
RUE MULLER
RUE ANDRÉ DEL
RUE C NODIER
RUE RONSARD
Musée d'Art Na Max Fourny
Place du Tertre
RUE POULBOT
RUE NORVINS
RUE AZAÏS
RUE ST-ELEUTHERE
RUE CARDINAL DUBOIS
FUNICULAIRE
Square Willette
PLACE SAINT-PIERRE
RUE GABRIELLE
RUE DREVET
RUE ANDRÉ BARSACQ
RUE BERTHE
Square Valadon
RUE DES TROIS FRERES
RUE CHAPPE
RUE TARDIEU
CITÉ D'ORSEL
RUE D'ORSEL
RUE DE STEINKERQUE
RUE GARREAU
RUE DURANTIN
Square J Rictus
RUE DE LA VIEUVILLE
RUE YVONNE LE TAC
Abbesses
Place des Abbesses
RUE DES ABBESSES
Les Abbesses
RUE ANDRÉ ANTOINE
RUE PIEMONTÉSI
RUE HOUDON
RUE DES MARTYRS
RUE GILL
R DANCOURT
VILLA DANCOURT
BOULEVARD DE ROCHECHOUART
RUE BOCHART
R CRETET
RUE SAY
CITÉ GERMAIN PILON
RUE GERMAIN PILON
VILLA DE GUELMA
CITÉ DU MIDI
PIGALLE
BOULEVARD CLICHY
Pigalle
Place Pigalle
VIOLLET LE DUC
RUE LALLIER
AVENUE
R ALFRED STEVENS
AV FROCHOT
RUE FROCHOT
Place Lino Ventura
CITÉ MALESHERBES
RUE MASSE
RUE VICTOR
RUE DUPERRÉ
RUE FROMENTIN
RUE DOUAI
RUE JEAN BAPTISTE PIGALLE
RUE HENRY MONNIER
RUE DE LA TOUR
SQUARE TRUDAINE
RUE DES MARTYRS
RUE FONTAINE
RUE DE NAVARIN
IXe
RUE CHAPTAL
RUE CLAUZEL
0 50 M 0 50 YDS
DISTANCE ACROSS MAP: 1.3 KM / 0.8 MI

SIGHTS

A1 **2** Place des Vosges, p. 19
B5 **23** Marche d'Aligre, p. 19
F2 **31** Jardin des Plantes, p. 19

RESTAURANTS

A3 **3** Café de l'Industrie, p. 45
A5 **6** Rino, p. 45
B2 **11** Bofinger, p. 45
B4 **14** Le Café du Passage, p. 45
B4 **18** Assaporare, p. 44
B5 **20** Blé Sucré, p. 45
B5 **21** La Gazzetta, p. 45
B5 **22** Le Baron Rouge, p. 44
B6 **24** Le Siffleur de Ballons, p. 46
C5 **27** Sardegna a Tavola, p. 46
D5 **29** Le Train Bleu, p. 46

NIGHTLIFE

A6 **7** Le Réservoir, p. 61
A6 **9** Red House, p. 61
B5 **19** Bottle Shop, p. 61
C5 **28** Le Viaduc Café, p. 61
F5 **32** Wanderlust, p. 61

SHOPS

A3 **4** Le Chocolat Alain Ducasse, p. 82
A6 **8** Lilli Bulle, p. 82
B4 **13** Isabel Marant, p. 82
B4 **15** Muji, p. 82
B4 **16** Caravane Chambre 19, p. 82
B4 **17** Louison, p. 82
C4 **25** Viaduc des Arts, p. 82

ARTS AND LEISURE

B2 **10** Maison de Victor Hugo, p. 94
B3 **12** Opéra National de Paris Bastille, p. 100
C5 **26** Promenade Plantée, p. 105
E2 **30** Dancing on the Square Tino Rossi, p. 105

HOTELS

A1 **1** Le Pavillon de La Reine, p. 119

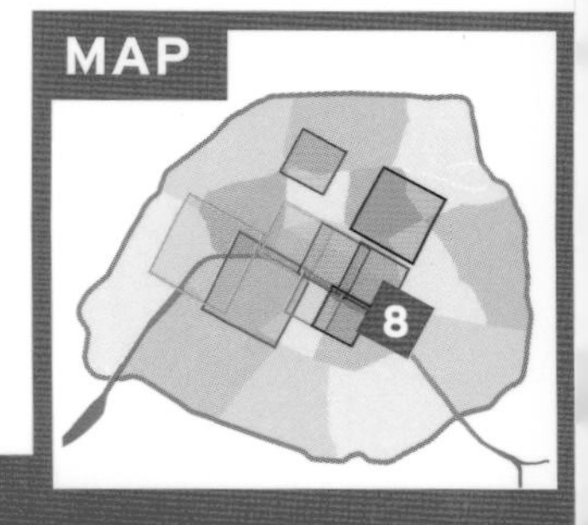

CANAL ST-MARTIN

This fun and funky neighborhood takes its name from the murky-green, 4.5-kilometer waterway that connects the Seine to the Canal de l'Ourcq in northeast Paris. Constructed at Napoléon I's behest beginning in 1804, the canal hit its heyday during the industrial revolution, when factories, mills, and workshops mushroomed along its banks. Today, the local industry veers toward trendy boutiques, outdoor cafés, and artists' ateliers, and the working-class population has been supplanted by young hipsters and bobos wielding *poussettes* (strollers).

The neighborhood hums with life year-round, but it bursts into animated Technicolor during the summer months, when the canal's cobbled banks morph into a public picnic zone, shaded by a verdant canopy of old plane trees. Private barges and tourist boats still ply the waterway, passing underground and up again, through nine functioning locks from end to end. On Sundays, Quai Valmy and Quai Jemmapes close to car traffic, and the elbow of the canal turns into an all-ages playground.

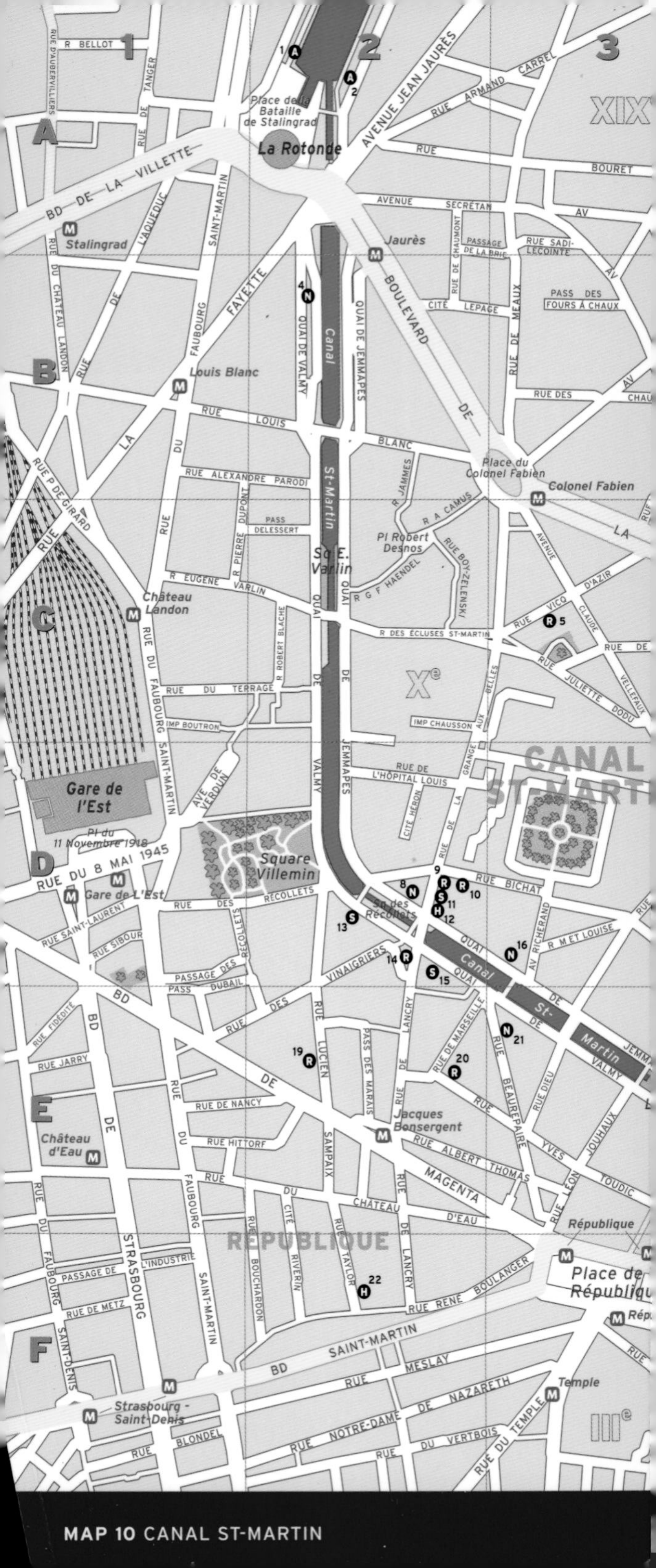

MAP 10 CANAL ST-MARTIN

Place des Vosges
Chemin Vert
Bastille
Place de la Bastille
Colonne de Juillet
SEE MAP 7
SEE MAP 1
Basin de l'Arsenal
Sully Morland
ÎLE ST-LOUIS
Square Bary
PONT DE SULLY
QUAI SAINT-BERNARD
QUAI HENRI IV
BOULEVARD HENRI IV
BOULEVARD BEAUMARCHAIS
BOULEVARD RICHARD LENOIR
BOULEVARD BOURDON
BOULEVARD MORLAND
RUE ST-ANTOINE
RUE DE SULLY
RUE DES FRANCS BOURGEOIS
R DU PAS DE LA MULE
RUE DE BIRAGUE
RUE DE TURENNE
RUE DES TOURNELLES
RUE ST-PAUL
RUE CHARLES V
RUE DES LIONS ST-PAUL
QUAI DES CÉLESTINS
RUE CUVIER
RUE JUSSIEU
Jardin des Plantes

BASTILLE

Nothing remains of the Bastille prison, stormed by the revolutionary mob on July 14, 1789, but Place de la Bastille still has a revolutionary kick; it's the starting point for most of Paris's modern-day *grèves* (strikes) and *manifestations* (public gatherings). The modern Opéra National de Paris Bastille, inaugurated on the 1989 Bastille Day Bicentennial, overlooks the square's Colonne de Juillet, built to commemorate the 1830 revolutionaries and a rallying point for political demonstrations.

Nearby, the rue de Lappe and rue de la Roquette reverberate with student nightlife venues blaring salsa and techno. Just past the famous woodworking workshops in the faubourg of St-Antoine you'll find the lively open-air market Marché d'Aligre and the high-end galleries of the Viaduc des Arts, located under the arcades of the Promenade Plantée's elevated garden trail.

Across the river, the beloved Jardin des Plantes holds, as its name suggests, numerous varieties of plants and trees. Summer is a particularly fun time for this area, when the Square Tino Rossi hosts open-air dancing every night.

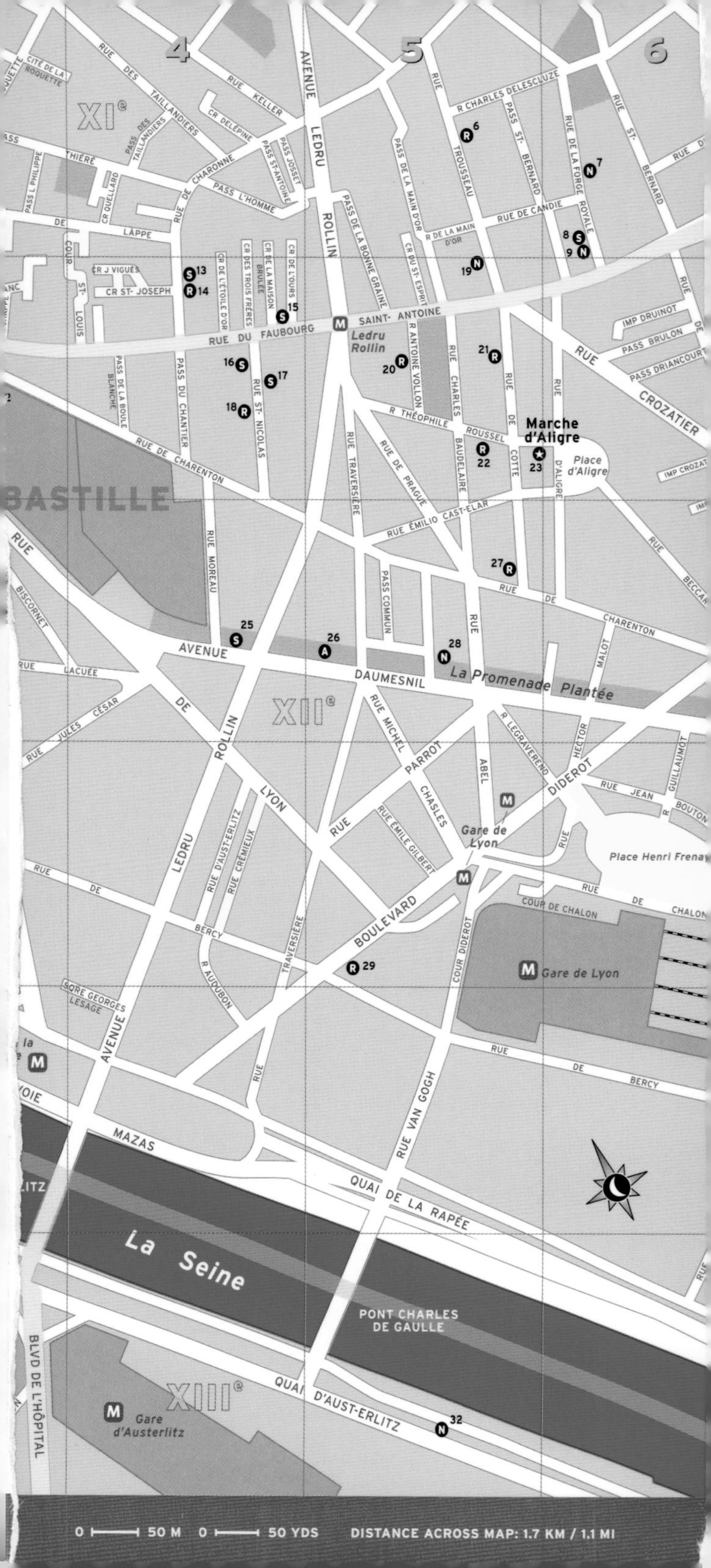

4
5
6
XIe
XIIe
XIIIe
BASTILLE
AVENUE LEDRU ROLLIN
RUE DES TAILLANDIERS
RUE KELLER
CR DELÉPINE
PASS DES TAILLANDIERS
PASS ST-ANTOINE
PASS JOSSET
RUE DE CHARONNE
PASS L'HOMME
PASS L PHILIPPE
CR QUELLARD
RUE DE LAPPE
COUR ST-LOUIS
CR J VIGUÈS
CR ST-JOSEPH
CR DE L'ÉTOILE D'OR
CR DES TROIS FRÈRES
CR DE LA MAISON BRULÉE
CR DE L'OURS
PASS DE LA BONNE GRAINE
PASS DE LA MAIN D'OR
R DE LA MAIN D'OR
CR DU ST-ESPRIT
RUE TROUSSEAU
R CHARLES DELESCLUZE
PASS ST-BERNARD
RUE DE LA FORGE ROYALE
RUE ST-BERNARD
RUE DE CANDIE
RUE DU FAUBOURG SAINT-ANTOINE
Ledru Rollin
IMP DRUINOT
PASS BRULON
PASS DRIANCOURT
RUE CROZATIER
R ANTOINE VOLLON
RUE CHARLES BAUDELAIRE
RUE DE COTTE
RUE D'ALIGRE
R THÉOPHILE ROUSSEL
Marche d'Aligre
Place d'Aligre
IMP CROZATIER
PASS DE LA BOULE BLANCHE
PASS DU CHANTIER
RUE ST-NICOLAS
RUE DE CHARENTON
RUE TRAVERSIÈRE
RUE DE PRAGUE
RUE ÉMILIO CAST-ELAR
RUE MOREAU
PASS COMMUN
RUE BECCARIA
RUE DE CHARENTON
RUE MALOT
RUE BISCORNET
RUE LACUÉE
AVENUE DAUMESNIL
La Promenade Plantée
RUE JULES CÉSAR
AVENUE DE LYON
RUE MICHEL
RUE PARROT
RUE CHASLES
R LEGRAVEREND
RUE ABEL
HECTOR
DIDEROT
RUE JEAN
GUILLAUMOT
R BOUTON
RUE ÉMILE GILBERT
RUE D'AUST-ERLITZ
RUE CRÉMIEUX
Gare de Lyon
Place Henri Frenay
RUE DE BERCY
RUE DE CHALON
COUR DE CHALON
BOULEVARD
R AUDUBON
COUR DIDEROT
Gare de Lyon
SQRE GEORGES LESAGE
AVENUE
RUE VAN GOGH
RUE DE BERCY
MAZAS
QUAI DE LA RAPÉE
La Seine
PONT CHARLES DE GAULLE
BLVD DE L'HÔPITAL
QUAI D'AUST-ERLITZ
Gare d'Austerlitz
0 50 M 0 50 YDS DISTANCE ACROSS MAP: 1.7 KM / 1.1 MI

SIGHTS

D2 **29** ★ Centre Pompidou, p. 17
D4 **40** Rue des Rosiers, p. 18
E2 **48** Hôtel de Ville, p. 18

RESTAURANTS

A3 **3** Chez Omar, p. 42
A4 **4** Café Pinson, p. 42
A4 **6** Taéko, p. 44
A5 **7** Le Mary Celeste, p. 44
B1 **8** Derrière, p. 43
B1 **9** Le 404, p. 43
B4 **15** Breizh Café, p. 42
C1 **17** L'Ambassade d'Auvergne, p. 42
C3 **21** Dôme du Marais, p. 43
D1 **27** Café Beaubourg, p. 42
D4 **36** Jaja, p. 43
D4 **38** L'Etoile Manquante, p. 43
D4 **39** L'As du Fallafel, p. 42
D5 **42** Le Loir dans la Théière, p. 44

NIGHTLIFE

A4 **5** Candelaria, p. 60
B1 **10** Andy Wahloo, p. 60
B2 **11** Le Duplex, p. 60
C4 **22** La Perle, p. 61
D3 **33** Mixer Bar, p. 61
D4 **37** La Belle Hortense, p. 60
D4 **41** Le 3W Kafé, p. 61
E1 **46** Dernier Bar Avant la Fin du Monde, p. 60

SHOPS

A3 **2** The Broken Arm, p. 80
B4 **13** Anna Rivka, p. 79
B4 **14** Surface to Air, p. 81
B6 **16** Merci, p. 81
C3 **20** Les Archives de La Presse, p. 79
C4 **23** Rue des Francs Bourgeois, p. 81
D2 **31** BHV, p. 80
D3 **32** Les Bains du Marais, p. 80
D3 **35** Mariage Frères, p. 81
D5 **43** Bensimon Autour du Monde, p. 80
D5 **44** Vert d'Absinthe, p. 81
D6 **45** Antik Batik, p. 79
E4 **50** Chez Izrael, p. 80
E5 **52** Village St-Paul, p. 81

ARTS AND LEISURE

A1 **1** Musée des Arts et Métiers, p. 94
C2 **18** Musée National d'Art Moderne – Centre Pompidou, p. 94
C2 **19** Musée d'Art et d'Histoire du Judaïsme, p. 93
C5 **24** Musée National Picasso, p. 94
C5 **25** Musée Cognacq-Jay, p. 93
C5 **26** Musée Carnavalet, p. 93
D2 **30** Café de la Gare, p. 99
E2 **47** Paris Rando Vélo, p. 105
E5 **51** Maison Européenne de la Photographie, p. 93
E6 **53** Musée de la Magie, p. 93
F5 **54** Paris Plages, p. 104

HOTELS

B4 **12** Hôtel du Petit Moulin, p. 119
D1 **28** Hôtel Saint Merry, p. 119
D3 **34** Hôtel Bourg Tibourg, p. 119
E4 **49** Hôtel Caron de Beaumarchais, p. 119

SIGHTS

- B5 **6** ★ La Basilique Sacré-Coeur de Montmartre, p. 20
- C4 **11** Place du Tertre, p. 21
- D1 **12** Cimetière de Montmartre, p. 21
- D4 **20** Place des Abbesses, p. 21

RESTAURANTS

- A4 **2** Chamarré Montmartre, p. 46
- C2 **9** Le Café Qui Parle, p. 46
- D3 **18** Le Chinon, p. 46
- D5 **22** Milk, p. 47
- F5 **36** Hôtel Amour, p. 47
- F6 **37** Rose Bakery, p. 47

NIGHTLIFE

- A3 **1** Les Taulières, p. 63
- A6 **3** Le Chope du Château Rouge, p. 62
- D6 **26** L'Elysée-Montmartre, p. 63
- E4 **28** Marlusse et Lapin, p. 63
- E5 **29** Le Divan du Monde, p. 62
- E5 **30** La Fourmi, p. 63
- F3 **33** Le Carmen, p. 62
- F4 **35** Chez Moune, p. 62

SHOPS

- B6 **7** A.P.C. Surplus, p. 83
- D3 **15** Generation 1962, p. 83
- D3 **17** Rose Bunker, p. 84
- D5 **21** Spree, p. 84
- D5 **23** BA&SH, p. 83
- D5 **24** L'Objet Qui Parle, p. 84
- D5 **25** Emmanuelle Zysman, p. 83
- F1 **32** Grand Herboristerie Médicale de La Place de Clichy, p. 83

ARTS AND LEISURE

- B3 **4** Au Lapin Agile, p. 101
- B4 **5** Musée de Montmartre, p. 95
- C4 **10** Espace Montmartre Dalí, p. 95
- D3 **14** Cinéma Studio 28, p. 100
- D4 **19** Les Abbesses, p. 100
- E2 **27** Bal du Moulin Rouge, p. 100
- E5 **31** La Cigale, p. 100
- F3 **34** Musée de la Vie Romantique, p. 95

HOTELS

- C2 **8** Hôtel Particulier Montmartre, p. 120
- D2 **13** Terrass Hôtel, p. 120
- D3 **16** Plug-Inn Hostel, p. 120
- F5 **36** Hôtel Amour, p. 120

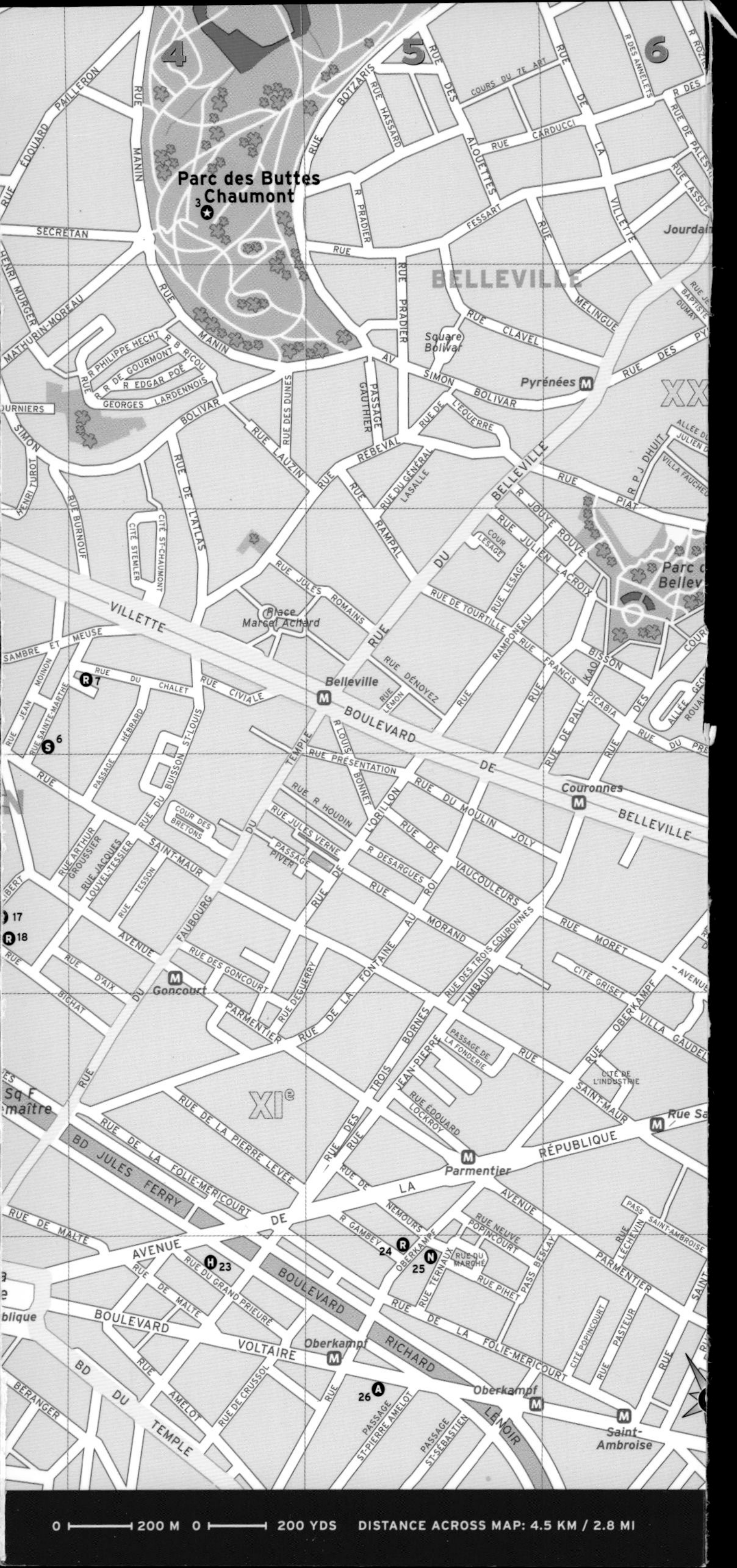

4
5
6
Parc des Buttes Chaumont
BELLEVILLE
XXe
XIe
Pyrénées
Belleville
Couronnes
Goncourt
Parmentier
Oberkampf
Saint-Ambroise
Rue Saint-Maur
Jourdain
Place Marcel Achard
Square Bolivar
Sq F Lemaître
Parc de Belleville
BOULEVARD DE BELLEVILLE
BOULEVARD DE LA VILLETTE
AVENUE DE LA RÉPUBLIQUE
BOULEVARD RICHARD LENOIR
BD JULES FERRY
BOULEVARD VOLTAIRE
BD DU TEMPLE
RUE DU FAUBOURG DU TEMPLE
RUE DE BELLEVILLE
AVENUE PARMENTIER
RUE OBERKAMPF
RUE JEAN-PIERRE TIMBAUD
RUE DE LA FONTAINE AU ROI
RUE DES TROIS BORNES
RUE SAINT-MAUR
AV SIMON BOLIVAR
RUE MANIN
RUE BOTZARIS
RUE DE LA VILLETTE
RUE DES PYRÉNÉES
RUE DE LA FOLIE-MÉRICOURT
RUE DE LA PIERRE LEVÉE
RUE DE MALTE
RUE DE CRUSSOL
RUE AMELOT
RUE SECRÉTAN
RUE DE MEAUX
0 200 M 0 200 YDS DISTANCE ACROSS MAP: 4.5 KM / 2.8 MI

SIGHTS

A4 **3** Parc des Buttes Chaumont, p. 22

RESTAURANTS

C3 **5** Youpi et Voilà, p. 49
C4 **7** Le Galopin, p. 47
D2 **9** Ten Belles, p. 49
D2 **10** Pink Flamingo Pizza, p. 48
D2 **14** La Verre Volé, p. 49
D3 **17** Le Petit Cambodge, p. 48
D3 **18** Helmut Newcake, p. 48
E2 **19** Bob's Juice Bar, p. 47
E2 **20** Du Pain et des Idées, p. 48
F5 **24** Restaurant Pierre Sang Boyer, p. 49

NIGHTLIFE

B2 **4** Point Éphémère, p. 64
D2 **8** Hôtel du Nord, p. 64
D3 **16** Le Comptoir Général, p. 64
E3 **21** Chez Prune, p. 64
F5 **25** Ave Maria, p. 64

SHOPS

C3 **6** La Tête Dans les Olives, p. 85
D2 **11** Carmen Ragosta, p. 85
D2 **13** Antoine et Lili, p. 84
D2 **15** Artazart, p. 84

ARTS AND LEISURE

A2 **1** Paris Plages, p. 104
A2 **2** Canauxrama, p. 105
F5 **26** Le Bataclan, p. 100

HOTELS

D2 **12** Hôtel le Citizen du Canal Paris, p. 120
F2 **22** Hôtel Taylor, p. 121
F4 **23** Hôtel 20 Prieure, p. 121

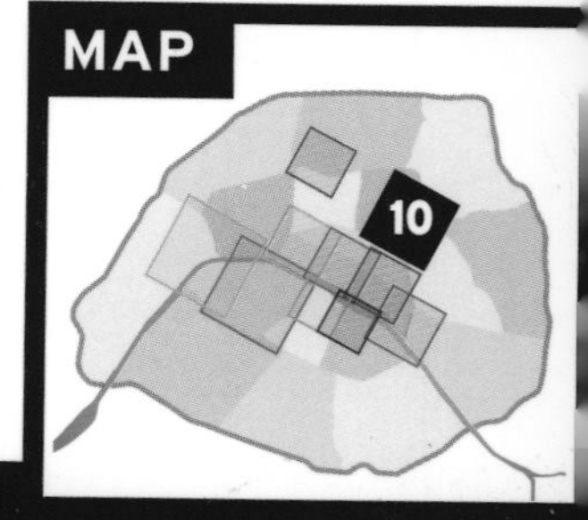

SIGHTS

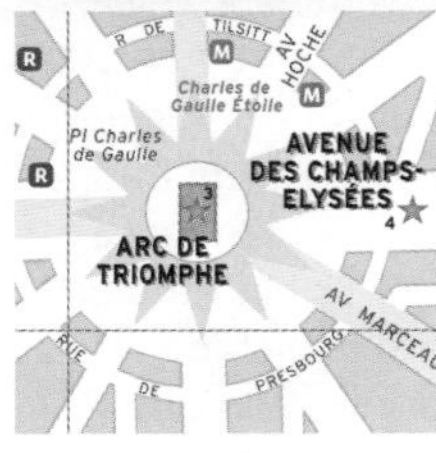

Best place to learn about medieval Paris: **MUSÉE NATIONAL DU MOYEN AGE – THERMES ET HÔTEL DE CLUNY,** p. 2

Most impressive facade: **NOTRE-DAME DE PARIS,** p. 2

Most beautiful stained glass: **SAINTE-CHAPELLE,** p. 3

Best place for couples to escape crowds: **JARDIN DU LUXEMBOURG,** p. 5

Best example of belle époque grandeur: **GRAND PALAIS/PETIT PALAIS,** p. 7

Best place for military history fans: **LES INVALIDES,** p. 8

Best museum if you only have time for one: **MUSÉE D'ORSAY,** p. 9

Best panoramic view of the city: **ARC DE TRIOMPHE/ CHAMPS-ELYSÉES,** p. 11

Coolest place to stamp your postcards: **TOUR EIFFEL,** p. 11

Best place to people-watch: **JARDIN DES TUILERIES,** p. 13

Most opulent monument: **OPÉRA GARNIER,** p. 14

Largest museum in the world: **MUSÉE DU LOUVRE,** p. 15

Strangest contemporary architecture: **CENTRE POMPIDOU,** p. 17

Best place to get your portrait painted: **LA BASILIQUE SACRÉ-COEUR DE MONTMARTRE,** p. 20

Best places for a canoe cruise: **BOIS DE BOULOGNE/BOIS DE VINCENNES,** p. 22

MUSÉE NATIONAL DU MOYEN AGE – THERMES ET HÔTEL DE CLUNY

Commonly known as the Musée de Cluny, this museum has one of Europe's finest collections of medieval artifacts, including the famous *Lady and the Unicorn* tapestries and 21 of the original statues from Notre-Dame's facade, knocked off by French revolutionaries and discovered during road construction. The museum has many other precious exhibits, including stained-glass panels from Saint-Denis and Sainte-Chapelle and illuminated books. In 1998 a new section was added, which portrays everyday life at the end of the Middle Ages. As at many museums in Paris, the setting alone – a remarkably well-preserved 15th-century abbey built right up against the remains of a Gallo-Roman-era bathhouse – is worth a visit. In 2000 a neo-medieval public garden was added, with 58 species of the flora depicted in the *Lady and the Unicorn,* including lily of the valley, hawthorn, giant daffodil, and daisy. There are also herbs such as mint, sage, absinthe, and thyme, prized in the Middle Ages for their medicinal qualities.

MAP 1 D2 19 6 PL. PAUL PAINLEVÉ, 5E 01-53-73-78-00
WWW.MUSEE-MOYENAGE.FR
HOURS: WED.-MON. 9:15 A.M.-5:45 P.M.
ADMISSION: €8

NOTRE-DAME DE PARIS

Architects, craftspeople, and artists labored for nearly two centuries (1163–1345) to build Notre-Dame, France's most famous cathedral. On the architectural side, its flying buttresses (best admired from the banks of the Seine in the Latin Quarter) and stained-glass windows attract the most attention. But Notre-Dame is really famous for its role in French history as one of the city's oldest cathedrals, built on the ruins of a Roman temple and witness to events such as Napoléon crowning himself emperor. Later generations of Parisians altered, plundered, and restored it, from Viollet-le-Duc's addition of the neo-Gothic spire and famous gargoyle statues in the late 1800s to the restoration and cleaning of the cathedral's facade in 2000. There's even a low-voltage shock system to keep pigeons off the gargoyles. Despite the constant traffic of camera-wielding visitors, Masses are still performed regularly, including

NOTRE-DAME DE PARIS

SAINTE-CHAPELLE

Sunday-afternoon recitals on one of the largest organs in France.

To avoid crowds, visit early in the morning. If you want the same view as the gargoyles, climb the 387 steps of the north bell tower, past the 13-ton Emmanuel bell, still hanging from its original supports, and up onto the fenced-in balcony. Underneath Notre-Dame, the Crypte Archéologique holds ancient building foundations and vestiges of Paris's history dating back to Roman times, with scenes of everyday life on the Île de la Cité from the 3rd through 18th century.

PL. DU PARVIS NOTRE-DAME, 4E 01-42-34-56-10
WWW.NOTREDAMEDEPARIS.FR
CATHEDRAL HOURS: MON.-FRI. 8 A.M.-6:45 P.M., SAT.-SUN. 9:15 A.M.-6:45 P.M.
TOWER HOURS: APR.-SEPT. DAILY 10 A.M.-6:30 P.M., LATER ON WEEKENDS, OCT.-MAR. DAILY 10 A.M.-5:30 P.M. ADMISSION: CATHEDRAL FREE; TOWER €8.50

SAINTE-CHAPELLE

Few sights, even in Paris, rival the royal chapel of Sainte-Chapelle. This tiny jewel of Gothic architecture, completed in the 13th century 100 years before Notre-Dame, has a series of 16 exquisite stained-glass windows constituting the sides and end of the sanctuary. The windows rise to the vaulted ceiling and are held in place by the frailest possible stonework. Louis IX (a.k.a. Saint-Louis) commissioned Sainte-Chapelle to house the religious relics he bought back from the Crusades, all of which are now in Notre-Dame. Created by anonymous master craftspeople, the windows are among the oldest in Paris. They depict the entire history of creation and redemption – to the medieval mind – in 1,134 different scenes, rendered in infinite shades of sapphire, ruby, emerald, and topaz. A great rose window, added in the 15th century, completes the collection. It contains 86 panes of glass and tells the story of the Apocalypse.

RUE MOUFFETARD

PANTHÉON

Though it looks fragile, the miraculous chapel is solid—no cracks have appeared in the delicate vaulting in seven centuries. Try to visit on a sunny day and bring binoculars. Take a wall seat and read the windows left to right, from bottom to top. There's also a regular schedule of classical music concerts in the chapel throughout the year.

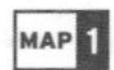 A1✪2

4 BD. DU PALAIS, 1ER 01-53-40-60-80
WWW.SAINTE-CHAPELLE.MONUMENTS-NATIONAUX.FR
HOURS: MAR.-OCT. DAILY 9:30 A.M.-6 P.M., NOV.-FEB. DAILY 9 A.M.-5 P.M.
ADMISSION: €8.50

LES ARÈNES DE LUTÈCE

A vestige of Paris's Roman past tucked into the Latin Quarter, the arena was rediscovered during construction in 1869. Once 15,000 people could watch gruesome spectacles here; now children come to play in ancient dust.

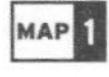 E6✪26

ACCESS VIA RUE MONGE AND RUE DE NAVARRE, 5E
HOURS: SPRING/SUMMER DAILY 9 A.M.-9:30 P.M., FALL/WINTER DAILY 8 A.M.-5:30 P.M.
ADMISSION: FREE

PANTHÉON

Louis XV's Greek-style church was transformed during the French Revolution into a temple dedicated to the greats of French history, such as Voltaire, Victor Hugo, and Pierre and Marie Curie. Currently undergoing a facelift slated for completion in 2022, it's open to visitors throughout the construction.

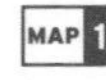 F3✪28

PL. DU PANTHÉON, 5E 01-44-32-18-00
WWW.PANTHEON.MONUMENTS-NATIONAUX.FR
HOURS: APR.-SEPT. DAILY 10 A.M.-6:30 P.M., OCT.-MAR. DAILY 10 A.M.-6 P.M.
ADMISSION: €7.50

RUE MOUFFETARD

One of the oldest market streets in Paris, Mouffetard is lined with cafés, cheap restaurants, clothing shops, gourmet-food boutiques, and market stalls every day but Monday. On Sundays at Place de la Contrescarpe, open-air waltzing with a live accordionist draws locals.

MAP 1 F5 31 RUE MOUFFETARD BTWN. PL. DE LA CONTRESCARPE AND RUE CENSIER, 5E

MAP 2 ST-GERMAIN-DES-PRÉS

JARDIN DU LUXEMBOURG

The wildly popular Jardin du Luxembourg (Luxembourg Garden) functions as a green oasis on the bustling Left Bank with 60 acres of formal gardens extending south from the Palais du Luxembourg. A favorite of visitors and residents alike, the gardens are embellished with 100 statues, leafy avenues, and an ornate octagonal pond on which generations of Parisian children have sailed toy boats. The splendid baroque Fontaine de Médicis pays homage to Marie de Médici, who had the Luxembourg palace and its expansive garden built after the assassination of her husband Henri II in 1612, to remind her of her native Florence. She never lived in the palace though, after being banished to the countryside for scheming against Richelieu, adviser to her son, King Louis XIII. Since 1804, it has housed the French Senate, except during World War II when the German Luftwaffe made it their headquarters. Next to the Senate, the Musée du Luxembourg hosts prestigious temporary art exhibits, while the garden gates have been used as a perfect outdoor gallery ever since Yann-Arthus Bertrand's majestic "The Earth Seen from the Sky" photos first awed passersby in 2000. Sit in the wrought-iron chairs and watch the

SIDE WALKS

Enjoy the literary side of St-Germain-des-Prés with a visit to **Café de Flore (p. 30)** or **Les Deux Magots (p. 31).** Both cafés previously hosted luminaries like Hemingway and Sartre, and they are still hangouts for some of today's writers, artists, and philosophers.

Visit the **Musée des Lettres et Manuscrits (p. 89)** for a French history lesson explained through the texts of La Belle France's most celebrated writers – Baudelaire, André Breton, and Victor Hugo among them.

Partake in a romantic local custom and affix a "love lock" inscribed with the initials of you and your sweetheart to the **Pont Des Arts (p. 6).** Tossing the key into the river afterward is optional.

Go for a luxurious dinner at **Le Restaurant (p. 32),** the chic hotel, bar, and restaurant (and former brothel) where Oscar Wilde spent his last years.

PONT DES ARTS

PONT NEUF

strollers, necking couples, old men playing *boules* (akin to lawn bowling), chess players, and daydreamers. There are also tennis courts, a marionette house, a bandstand, and an open-air café.

 MAP 2 F6 50

RUE DE VAUGIRARD AT RUE DE MÉDICIS, 6E 01-40-13-62-00 (MUSÉE DU LUXEMBOURG)
WWW.SENAT.FR/WWW.MUSEEDULUXEMBOURG.FR
GARDEN HOURS: APR.-OCT. DAILY 7:30 A.M.-9:30 P.M., NOV.-MAR. DAILY 8:15 A.M.-5 P.M.
MUSEUM HOURS: DAILY 10 A.M.-7:30 P.M., FRI. AND MON. TILL 10 P.M.
ADMISSION: GARDEN FREE; MUSEUM €11

ÉGLISE SAINT-GERMAIN-DES-PRÉS

This is the oldest church in Paris, and most of the surviving architecture dates from the 11th and 12th centuries. It's one of the few Parisian churches with a painted interior.

 MAP 2 D3 29

3 PL. ST-GERMAIN-DES-PRÉS, 6E 01-55-42-81-10
WWW.EGLISE-SGP.ORG
HOURS: DAILY 8:30 A.M.-7:30 P.M.
ADMISSION: FREE

ÉGLISE SAINT-SULPICE

The second largest church in Paris is best known for its free pipe-organ concerts, spectacular murals by Eugène Delacroix, and, more recently, as the location for the Rose Line from Dan Brown's *The Da Vinci Code*.

 MAP 2 E3 39

2 RUE PALATINE, PL. ST-SULPICE, 6E 01-42-34-59-98
WWW.PAROISSE-SAINT-SULPICE-PARIS.ORG
HOURS: DAILY 7:30 A.M.-7:30 P.M.
ADMISSION: FREE

PONT DES ARTS

Also known as the Passerelle des Arts, this bridge has the most romantic views of central Paris, and attracts couples from around the world who come to affix a "love lock" to its parapets. Warm weather also draws picnic-mad Parisians.

 MAP 2 A2 1

ENTER AT THE QUAI DE CONTI (6E) OR THE QUAI DE FRANÇOIS MITTERRAND (1ER)

LA SEINE

The river that runs through Paris, the Seine, is itself one of the city's most memorable and romantic sights. For more than 2,000 years, Parisians have built their most impressive monuments on or near its banks, which means you can see much of Paris by boat, embarking in one of the modest **Vedettes du Pont Neuf (p. 103)** or one of the enormous **Bateaux-Mouches (p. 103).** Daytime rides are more popular, but a night cruise offers a romantic glimpse of the City of Light. The many *ponts* (bridges) connecting the Right Bank and Left Bank add to the river's beauty. Among them, the **Pont des Arts (p. 6)** has the best views of central Paris, while the **Pont Neuf (p. 7)** offers stone benches, often sought out by couples intent on viewing a picturesque sunset.

PONT NEUF

Despite its name, Pont Neuf (New Bridge) is actually the oldest bridge. It's also the city's longest and widest, and is the only bridge in Paris that has never been rebuilt. Now it's conveniently outfitted with roomy stone benches.

A4 ✪3 ENTER AT QUAI DES GRANDS AUGUSTINS AND RUE DAUPHINE, 1ER

MAP 3 INVALIDES

GRAND PALAIS/PETIT PALAIS

The hulking Grand Palais, an elegant art nouveau structure built for the 1900 Exposition Universelle, has one of the most spectacular interiors in all of Paris. Imagine a 335-meter (1,100-foot) glass arcade with a glass-and-iron dome at its center, along with multiple layers of balconies, and sculpture so voluptuous it seems almost flesh-and-blood. The Grand Palais is put to many uses. The Galeries Nationales host blockbuster art exhibitions, while the wing on avenue Franklin D. Roosevelt houses the Palais de la Découverte, the world's first interactive museum, where demonstrations of scientific "experiments" take place several times a day. There is also a planetarium that travels back to the past and ahead to

LES INVALIDES

MUSÉE D'ORSAY

future solar and lunar eclipses – viewers can see the Paris night sky as it will look in 14,000 years.

Like its big brother, the Petit Palais was built for the 1900 Expo, but its more unified style is the work of a single architect. The facade of the not-so-petite building was influenced by the Louvre; the bas-relief shows the city of Paris protecting the arts. The "little palace" now houses the Musée des Beaux-Arts de la Ville de Paris, reopened in December 2005 after extensive renovations, which contains a strong collection of 19th-century artists.

MAP 3 A1 1 GRAND PALAIS: 3 AV. DU GÉNÉRAL EISENHOWER, 8E 01-44-13-17-17
WWW.GRANDPALAIS.FR
HOURS: FRI.-MON. AND WED. 10 A.M.-10 P.M., TUES. 10 A.M.-2 P.M., THURS. 10 A.M.-8 P.M.
ADMISSION: VARIES DEPENDING ON EVENT

MAP 3 A2 4 PETIT PALAIS: AV. WINSTON CHURCHILL, 8E 01-44-51-19-31
WWW.PETIT-PALAIS.PARIS.FR
HOURS: TUES.-SUN. 10 A.M.-6 P.M., CLOSED ON NATIONAL HOLIDAYS.
ADMISSION: FREE TO VISIT PERMANENT COLLECTION; SPECIAL EXHIBIT PRICES VARY

MAP 3 A1 3 PALAIS DE LA DÉCOUVERTE: AV. FRANKLIN ROOSEVELT, 8E 01-56-43-20-20 HOURS: TUES-SAT. 8 A.M.-6 P.M., SUN. 10 A.M.-7 P.M.
ADMISSION: €8

LES INVALIDES

In 1670, Louis XIV built this military hospital and retirement home for the soldiers who'd fought in his wars, many of whom lived in poverty. It includes the soldiers' church, Saint-Louis-des-Invalides, lined with the captured flags of France's military campaigns, and the royal chapel Église du Dôme, where Napoléon's exhumed remains rest under the gilded dome in no fewer than six coffins, all enveloped in an oversize sarcophagus of Finnish red granite. Part of the Invalides complex is still used as a residence for war veterans and victims of terrorism, but it also houses the Musée de l'Armée, one of the world's largest collections of military weapons

PARISIAN PASSAGES

The early-19th-century industrial revolution forever changed the Parisian landscape. With the modernizing movement came wide, pie-slice boulevards, functional canals, and the capital's first commercial shopping centers: the *passages couverts*. A couple dozen of these 200-year-old, iron-and-glass-topped arcades have stood the test of time, luring shoppers and *flâneurs* (strolling pedestrians) seeking respite from the elements. Passage Jouffroy (www.passagejouffroy.com) welcomes the world with its wax museum, art galleries, and a quaint hotel that first opened in 1849, the year the passage was built. Just down the street, chic **Galerie Vivienne (p. 78)** lures discerning *promeneurs* (walkers) to its sophisticated boutiques and restaurants. Farther north, Passage Brady (between rue Faubourg St-Denis and bd. de Strasbourg) has a flavor all its own, spiced with curry and incense. Indian restaurants line the tiled corridor, and the competition is on for the cheapest *plat du jour* (daily special).

and uniforms from the Stone Age to Hiroshima, rich in Napoleonic memorabilia, such as Ingres's famous portrait of him as emperor, his cocked hat and signature gray overcoat, and the fold-up bed on which he died in exile. Your ticket is also valid for entry into the Musée des Plans-Reliefs, which contains scale models of entire French cities inside illuminated glass cases. Created between the 17th and 18th centuries and astonishingly precise, these models of fortified cities were once classified as military secrets.

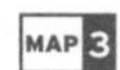

C2 28

PL. DES INVALIDES, 7E 01-44-42-38-77
WWW.INVALIDES.ORG
HOURS: OCT.-MAR. DAILY 10 A.M.-5 P.M., APR.-SEPT. DAILY 10 A.M.-6 P.M.
ADMISSION: €9.50

MUSÉE D'ORSAY

One of the world's great museums, the Musée d'Orsay unites many of the 19th century's most celebrated images – Manet's *Le Déjeuner sur l'Herbe,* Van Gogh's *L'Arlésienne,* Whistler's *Arrangement in Black and Gray (Portrait of the Artist's Mother),* Renoir's *Le Moulin de la Galette,* and Degas's ballet paintings. Opened in 1986, it focuses specifically on sculpture, painting, architecture, decorative arts, and photography created from 1848

PONT ALEXANDRE III

ARC DE TRIOMPHE

(the year of Marx's *Communist Manifesto*, populist revolutions, and the collapse of monarchies) up to 1914 (the beginning of the Great War). The collection is housed in the soaring spaces of the old Gare d'Orsay railway station, itself a turn-of-the-20th-century work inaugurated at the 1900 Exposition Universelle. The carved limestone facade, punctuated by large clock-face windows, extends 205 meters along the Seine. On the ground floor you'll find temporary exhibits and works from the mid- to late-19th century; the middle level has art nouveau and late-19th-century sculpture; and the top floor is devoted to Impressionism and post-Impressionism. With a multitude of pieces by Van Gogh, Cézanne, Monet, Manet, Renoir, and an array of Degas bronzes, the uppermost level is the most popular. Don't miss the romantic museum restaurant on the middle level, with parquet floors, marble columns, ceiling frescoes, and views over the Seine and Tuileries Garden.

1 RUE DE LA LEGION D'HONNEUR, 7E 01-40-49-48-14
WWW.MUSEE-ORSAY.FR
HOURS: TUES.-WED. AND FRI.-SUN. 9:30 A.M.-6 P.M., THURS. 9:30 A.M.-9:45 P.M.
ADMISSION: €9

PONT ALEXANDRE III

The gilded Pont Alexandre III was inaugurated at the 1900 Exposition Universelle in honor of the visiting czar of Russia. Newlyweds often have their nuptial portraits snapped amid the ornamental lampposts with the Tour Eiffel in the background.

 B2✪10 ENTER AT QUAI D'ORSAY AND AV. DU MARECHAL GALLIENI, 8E

ARC DE TRIOMPHE/CHAMPS-ELYSÉES

Built by Napoléon starting in 1806 to commemorate his military victories, the Arc de Triomphe was completed in 1836, after the emperor died. Elaborately decorated with statues and reliefs celebrating the battles of Austerlitz and Aboukir, the arch also protects the everlasting flame of the Tomb of the Unknown Soldier, lit on November 11, 1923. Surrounded by a swirling traffic circle called l'Étoile, the arch is accessed via an underground passage (from avenue des Champs-Elysées). Once inside, climb the 284 steps to the excellent viewing platform, which has some of the best vistas of Paris, including the Voie Triomphal (Triumphal Way) extending from the Grande Arche de La Défense to the Louvre.

Of the 12 roads radiating from the Arc, the busiest and best known is avenue des Champs-Elysées, which translates as Elysian Fields. The tree-lined thoroughfare is the backdrop for the annual Bastille Day Parade on July 14, as well as the finish of the Tour de France in late July. There is little of architectural interest except for the Grand Palais on the southeast end and the Elysée Palace (the president's official residence), which is set back from the street. Instead, you'll find auto dealers, cinemas showing Hollywood blockbusters, multinational names like McDonald's and Nike, and cafés competing to serve the world's most expensive Coke.

A2 3 ARC DE TRIOMPHE: PL. CHARLES DE GAULLE, 8E 01-55-37-73-77
WWW.ARC-DE-TRIOMPHE.MONUMENTS-NATIONAUX.FR
HOURS: APR.-SEPT. DAILY 10 A.M.-11 P.M., OCT.-MAR. DAILY 10 A.M.-10:30 P.M.
ADMISSION: €9.50

A2 4 CHAMPS-ELYSÉES: AV. DES CHAMPS-ELYSÉES
WWW.CHAMPSELYSEES.ORG

TOUR EIFFEL

The symbol of Paris and arguably the world's most famous landmark, the Tour Eiffel (Eiffel Tower) was constructed for the Paris Exhibition in 1889 by Alexandre-Gustave Eiffel, the same engineer who created the steel skeleton for the Statue of Liberty. Not always the source of local adoration, the tower faced opposition from writers Alexandre Dumas and Guy de Maupassant, along with many other irate artists who tried to prevent its construction, protesting against "this useless and monstrous tower...dominating Paris like a black factory

TOUR EIFFEL

JARDIN DES TUILERIES

chimney." It was never intended to be a permanent feature of the Paris skyline, but escaped being torn down in 1909 with its new role as a military radio transmitter and navigational aid for aircraft. The Tour Eiffel was the tallest building in the world until New York's Chrysler Building surpassed it in 1930. Visitors can climb the stairs to the first or second level; take the elevator to the first, second, or top level; or make reservations well in advance at one of the two restaurants to bypass the lines. From the top on a clear day, you can see the spire of Chartres cathedral, 89 kilometers (55 miles) away. Besides being one of the most-visited monuments in France, the tower also serves as the focal point for the elaborate pyrotechnics of the annual Bastille Day (July 14) fireworks show.

MAP 4 E4 37
BTWN. QUAI BRANLY AND PARC DU CHAMP DE MARS, 7E
01-44-11-23-23
WWW.TOUR-EIFFEL.FR
HOURS: JUNE 15-SEPT. DAILY 9 A.M.-12:45 A.M., OCT.-JUNE 14 DAILY 9:30 A.M.-11:45 P.M.
ADMISSION: €5 TO ACCESS THE FIRST AND SECOND FLOORS VIA STAIRCASE, €8.50 FOR THE SECOND FLOOR ELEVATOR, €14.50 FOR ACCESS TO ALL THREE FLOORS VIA ELEVATOR

LES ÉGOUTS DE PARIS

A wacky and very urban tour option is a descent into the belly of one of the Second Empire's greatest inventions – a complex sewer system. Literary hero Jean Valjean (of *Les Misérables*) found an escape route here.

MAP 4 D5 29
ENTRANCE OPPOSITE 93 QUAI D'ORSAY, 7E 01-53-68-27-81
WWW.PARIS.FR
HOURS: OCT.-APR. 11 A.M.-4 P.M., MAY-SEPT. 11 A.M.-5 P.M.
ADMISSION: €4.30

PALAIS DE CHAILLOT

The neoclassical Palais de Chaillot was built for the 1937 Paris World Exhibition. In addition to housing a theater and several museums, the palace offers some of the city's best views of the Tour Eiffel.

 E2 33 17 PL. DU TROCADÉRO, 16E 01-44-05-72-72
HOURS: 11 A.M.-7 P.M.; CLOSED TUES.
ADMISSION: GROUNDS FREE; MUSEUM FEES VARY

TROCADÉRO

The location of the Palais de Chaillot, the hilltop Place du Trocadéro takes its name from a Spanish city captured by the French in 1823 and is the hub for six avenues that radiate out from it.

 E2 32 PL. DU TROCADÉRO, 16E

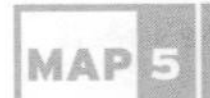

GRANDS BOULEVARDS

JARDIN DES TUILERIES

The Tuileries Garden stretches from the Arc du Carrousel at the Louvre to the Place de la Concorde. It is named for the royal palace set on fire and destroyed during the suppression of the 1871 Paris Commune government, which used to connect the Louvre's two western wings. The 63 acres of formal French gardens were originally created by André Le Nôtre, the landscape architect of Versailles, and feature his signature horseshoe-shaped staircase at the western end, flanked today by replicas of the *Chevaux de Marly* horse sculptures. (All of the garden's original statues are housed at the Louvre, protected from the elements.)

Restored in the late 1990s, the gardens offer a mix of classical fountains, sculptures, and temporary art installations beneath their tree-lined alleys. In mild weather this is one of the best places for people-watching, either on a reclined park chair next to the main water fountain or at one of the open-air cafés. The garden hosts two historic buildings: the Musée de l'Orangerie, home to Claude Monet's famous *Nymphéas* (Water Lilies) paintings, and the Jeu de Paume, an exhibition center dedicated to photography and the visual arts.

 E3 51 ACCESS VIA RUE DE RIVOLI AND PL. DE LA CONCORDE, 1ER
01-40-20-90-43
WWW.LOUVRE.FR/EN/DEPARTEMENTS
HOURS: SUNRISE-SUNSET
ADMISSION: FREE

PALAIS ROYAL

CENTRE POMPIDOU

16th century and transformed after the Revolution into a public museum in 1793. After extensive "Grand Louvre" renovations in the late 1980s and early 1990s, including the addition of I. M. Pei's 20-meter (67-foot) glass pyramid entrance and the opening of the Carrousel commercial center, the Louvre is considered the greatest museum in the world in terms of size and prestige of its collections. Well-known treasures such as the *Mona Lisa, Venus de Milo,* and *Winged Victory* attract the most attention, but the secret to enjoying such an overwhelming place is to pursue your own personal list of highlights. On each floor the galleries are arranged chronologically and geographically, from the Far East, ancient Egypt, Rome and Greece, Islamic arts, and European paintings from the Dutch masters to the Italian Renaissance.

The free map from the information desk below the inverted pyramid at the main entrance is essential for getting around. Some lesser-visited sections of the museum are closed on a rotating basis due to lack of staff, so be sure to check the online schedule or at the information desk if you have your heart set on a particular collection.

COUR NAPOLÉON, 34 QUAI DU LOUVRE, 1ER 01-40-20-50-50
WWW.LOUVRE.FR
HOURS: THURS. AND SAT.-MON. 9 A.M.-6 P.M., WED. AND FRI. 9 A.M.-9:45 P.M.
ADMISSION: €11

PALAIS ROYAL

This 17th-century childhood home of Louis XIV features a peaceful garden retreat surrounded by exclusive boutiques and restaurants. Nearby are the historic Comédie Française Theater and the bizarre striped columns of installation artist Daniel Buren.

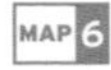

PL. DU PALAIS ROYAL, 1ER 01-47-03-92-16
WWW.PALAIS-ROYAL.MONUMENTS-NATIONAUX.FR
HOURS: OCT.-MAR. DAILY 7 A.M.-8:30 P.M., APR.-MAY DAILY 7 A.M.-10:15 P.M., JUNE-AUG. DAILY 7 A.M.-11 P.M., AND SEPT. DAILY 7 A.M.-9:30 P.M.
ADMISSION: FREE

TOUR DE JEAN SANS PEUR

This 15th-century Gothic turret belonged to the Duke of Burgundy, "Fearless Jean," whose assassination of the king's cousin, Louis d'Orléans, started the Hundred Years' War.

 B5 ✪12

20 RUE ETIENNE MARCEL, 2E 01-40-26-20-28
WWW.TOURJEANSANSPEUR.COM
HOURS: MID-NOV.-MID-APR. WED., SAT., SUN. 1:30-6 P.M.; MID-APR.-MID-NOV. WED.-SUN. 1:30-6 P.M.
ADMISSION: €5

MAP 7 MARAIS

CENTRE POMPIDOU

The biggest modern-art attraction in Europe, the Centre Pompidou (or "Beaubourg" to the locals) is known for its controversial "inside-out" architecture designed by the British-Italian architects Richard Rogers and Renzo Piano. The immense exposed pipes are actually color-coded: blue for air-conditioning ducts, green for water, and yellow for electricity lines. Opened in 1970 and heavily renovated and reorganized in 2000, the building receives more than eight million visitors per year. The top three floors house the Musée National d'Art Moderne, whose grand galleries expose artworks spanning 1905 to 1960, including masterpieces by Cézanne, Picasso, Ernst, Giacometti, and Kandinsky.

The Pompidou also houses four theaters for dance, music, cinema, and plays; the Public Information Library; the Industrial Design Center; and the Institute for Acoustic and Musical Research. The cavernous lobby is flanked

SIDE WALKS

When making a trip to Centre Pompidou, be sure to save time to explore the neighborhoods nearby. On pedestrian promenade rue Montorgueil, just north and west of the museum, Paris's oldest *boulangerie*, **Stohrer, (p. 79),** beckons with buttery aromas in a sea of gourmet food shops and sidewalk cafés.

In the Marais, Paris's gay and lesbian district and historic Jewish center, stroll down **rue des Rosiers (p. 18),** where trendy fashion boutiques cohabitate with kosher bakeries and hyperkinetic falafel shops.

Stop by **La Belle Hortense (p. 60)** on rue Vieille du Temple for a glass of wine and a plate of charcuterie (deli meats). It also has a well-stocked book section popular with Parisian literati.

Browse the quaint shops on **rue des Francs-Bourgeois (p. 81),** a local favorite shopping area, then pop into the courtyard at #35, which leads to a secret public garden, for a quiet respite in the sun.

HÔTEL DE VILLE

RUE DES ROSIERS

by two mezzanines, one containing a mini design store run by Le Printemps. Georges, the rooftop restaurant accessible from the red elevator to the left of the main entrance, has stunning nighttime views of the city. The Brancusi Atelier, a small building adjacent to the center, houses the contents of the sculptor's original studio, including tools and sculptures. Not all of the Pompidou's attractions lie within its postmodern walls – the square outside is a never-ending street party with buskers, artists, and political orators.

 D2 29

PL. GEORGES POMPIDOU, 4E 01-44-78-12-33
WWW.CNAC-GP.FR
HOURS: WED.-MON. 11 A.M.-10 P.M. (MUSEUM UNTIL 9 P.M.; BRANCUSI ATELIER DAILY 2-6 P.M.)
ADMISSION: €11

HÔTEL DE VILLE

This majestic City Hall, built to replace an older one destroyed by the 1871 Commune, is mostly closed to the public except for the Salon d'Accueil, which hosts free historical expositions ranging from photography to fashion.

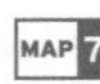 E2 48

29 RUE DE RIVOLI, 4E 01-42-76-43-43
WWW.PARIS.FR
HOURS: MON.-WED. AND FRI. 8:30 A.M.-5 P.M., THURS. 8:30 A.M.-7:30 P.M., SAT. 9 A.M.-12:30 P.M.
ADMISSION: FREE

RUE DES ROSIERS

Smack in the center of Paris's oldest Jewish neighborhood, this kinetic street hums with energy 365 days a year. Besides the Old World ambience, visitors come to experience its many falafel stands, kosher delis, and trendy boutiques.

 D4 40

RUE DES ROSIERS BTWN. RUE MALHER AND RUE VIEILLE DU TEMPLE, 4E

JARDIN DES PLANTES PLACE DES VOSGES

MAP 8 BASTILLE

JARDIN DES PLANTES

This immense garden surrounds the Muséum National d'Histoire Naturelle and gorgeous greenhouses. Beloved of Parisians, it showcases many tree and plant varieties, as well as a very popular labyrinth.

MAP 8 F2 31

57 RUE CUVIER, 5E 01-40-79-30-00
WWW.JARDINDESPLANTES.NET
HOURS: SUMMER DAILY 7:30 A.M.-8 P.M., WINTER DAILY 8 A.M.-5:30 P.M.
ADMISSION: FREE

MARCHE D'ALIGRE

This colorful fruit-and-vegetable market has served the neighborhood since 1650. Stroll through the rows of picture-perfect produce, then hit the small flea market on the square for bargains. The people-watching alone is worth the visit.

MAP 8 B5 23

PLACE D'ALIGRE, 12E
HTTP://MARCHEDALIGRE.FREE.FR
HOURS: TUES.-SUN. 9 A.M.-1 P.M.

PLACE DES VOSGES

Built in 1605, the oldest square in Paris is considered a near-perfect expression of French Renaissance architecture. It's a popular place to lounge in the grass listening to musicians perform under the stone arcades.

MAP 8 A1 2

RUE DES FRANCS BOURGEOIS BTWN. RUE DE TURENNE AND RUE DES TOURNELLES, 4E

LA BASILIQUE SACRÉ-COEUR DE MONTMARTRE

Crowning the hill of Montmartre like a giant wedding cake, the great white Basilique Sacré-Coeur de Montmartre is one of the city's most visible monuments. Relatively "new" on the Parisian landscape, the church was built as an "act of penance" after the catastrophic Franco-Prussian war of 1870. Work proceeded slowly, and the church wasn't finished until 1914. World War I intervened, and Sacré-Coeur was not consecrated until 1919. Unlike most other Paris monuments, the basilica isn't a beloved architectural masterpiece, and aesthetes decry its popularity as a postcard shot. Its extravagant mock Romanesque-Byzantine style was loosely inspired by the real Romano-Byzantine church of Saint-Front in Périgueux. Left-wing Paris has always hated the symbolism of the church, seen as a slight to the memory of the Communards, working-class radicals who seized power in Montmartre in 1871 after the Prussian siege of Paris. Protesters have invaded the church several times, and there was once an attempt to blow up one of the towers. Its location on the highest point in the city means that you'll have to climb several stairs or take the funicular to reach it. Its bell tower, 80 meters (262 feet) high, supports one of the world's heaviest bells, weighing 18.5 tons – plus

SIDE WALKS

As one of the most popular tourist destinations in Paris, Montmartre can sometimes feel like an overcrowded victim of its own success. For a change of pace, step away from the tourist-mobbed Place du Tertre to explore the many sights along the quiet side streets.

Walk to Sacré-Coeur via rue La Vieuville; the various boutiques, including **Spree (p. 84),** are sure to charm with their unconventional bohemian wares.

On the other side of Sacré-Coeur, the **Musée de Montmartre (p. 95)** was once a studio for such artists as Renoir and Utrillo. Today the 17th-century building houses a collection of paintings and memorabilia recalling the illustrious heyday of old Montmartre.

Take a sightseeing break at the lively café **Le Chinon (p. 46).** Have lunch on an outside table for excellent people-watching.

The pink and green cottage on rue St-Vincent is called **Au Lapin Agile (p. 101),** a historic bar where Picasso and his friends used to drink. It's one of the last authentic Parisian cabarets, and it hosts nightly shows.

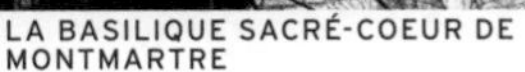
LA BASILIQUE SACRÉ-COEUR DE MONTMARTRE

CIMETIÈRE DE MONTMARTRE

another 2,000 pounds for the clapper. The statue-filled interior is decorated in colorful neo-Byzantine mosaics.

 B5 6

35 RUE DU CHEVALIER DE LA BARRE, 8E 01-53-41-89-00
WWW.SACRE-COEUR-MONTMARTRE.COM
HOURS: DAILY 6 A.M.-10:30 P.M.
ADMISSION: FREE

CIMETIÈRE DE MONTMARTRE

Take a peaceful stroll through the tranquil resting place of luminaries like Berlioz, Fragonard, Degas, and Offenbach, and the first great cancan star immortalized by Toulouse-Lautrec, La Goulue.

 D1 12

20 AV. RACHEL, 18E 01-53-42-36-30
HOURS: DAILY 8:30 A.M.-5:30 P.M.

PLACE DES ABBESSES

Abbesses, as locals call it, reverberates with an authentic Parisian neighborhood vibe. Alighting from the Metro station, you're greeted by an impressive Art Nouveau church, flashy carousel, and crêpe stands. Charming boutiques, cozy cafés, and homey wine bars stretch in either direction.

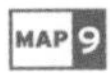 D4 20 PLACE DES ABBESSES, 18E

PLACE DU TERTRE

Strolling the atmospheric Place du Tertre, one of Paris's most vibrant squares, is a must for first-time visitors, but don't say we didn't warn you about the enthusiastic artists, mobs of tourists, and overpriced restaurants.

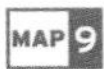 C4 11 PLACE DU TERTRE, 18E

MAP 10 CANAL ST-MARTIN

PARC DES BUTTES CHAUMONT

Inaugurated at the Exposition Universelle in 1867 by Napoléon III, this beautiful green space has stood the test of time. Come for an urban nature fix, then relax over a *pinte* at Rosa Bonheur, the park's highly rated café.

RUE MANIN, 19E
HOURS: WINTER DAILY 7:30 A.M.-9 P.M., SUMMER DAILY 7:30 A.M.- 11 P.M.

OVERVIEW MAP

BOIS DE BOULOGNE/BOIS DE VINCENNES

Known as the "Lungs of Paris," the forests at the far eastern and western borders of the city were created in the mid-1800s under Emperor Napoléon III. Inspired by the parks of London, he hired an engineer to create ornamental lakes, grottoes, waterfalls, and gardens. The Bois de Boulogne has two horse-racing tracks, lakes for rowing, bike and horse paths, and the Jardin d'Acclimatation, a children's amusement park with puppet shows, a circus, a mini farm, a children's zoo, bumper cars, and trampolines. Within the *bois* (woods) are two gardens: Jardin de Bagatelle, Paris's finest rose garden, and the Pré Catalan, home to a Shakespeare garden that doubles as an open-air theater.

The Bois de Vincennes to the east is Paris's largest forest, with 97 kilometers (60 miles) of paths and trails, a romantic grotto on Lac Daumesnil, and Paris's "trotting" racetrack, the Hippodrôme de Vincennes. The two most popular attractions are the Château de Vincennes, restored in 2004 and notable for its 14th-century dungeon and flamboyant Gothic royal chapel, and the vast Parc Floral, a botanical garden that hosts free open-air jazz and classical music concerts summer-fall. Walking after sunset should be avoided in both *bois*.

OVERVIEW MAP C1

BOIS DE BOULOGNE: ACCESS VIA PL. DU MARÉCHAL DE LATTRE DE TASSIGNY, 16E
HOURS: DAILY SUNRISE-SUNSET

CHÂTEAU DE VERSAILLES

The Château de Versailles (Place d'Armes, 78000, Versailles, 01-30-83-78-00, www.chateauversailles.fr, daily 9 A.M.-6:30 P.M.) was the residence of French kings Louis XIV, Louis XV, and Louis XVI. Construction on the then-modest royal hunting lodge began in the time of Louis XIII, but it was his son, Louis XIV, "the Sun King," who had the vision to expand the old edifice and install his court in 1682. Additions continued to be made to the building by each succeeding king, making it the magnificent royal palace it is today.

Since its opening to the public in 1837, visitors have marveled at the Hall of Mirrors, the king's apartments, apartments of the dauphin and the dauphine, the Trianon Palace, Marie-Antoinette's hamlet, and many more breathtaking works of art and architecture.

To visit the Château de Versailles, take the regional train RER C (€6.70 round-trip) from central Paris and stop at the Versailles Rive Gauche station. From here, it's a 10-minute walk to the château entrance, though you may be enticed by the guided-tour possibilities you pass along the way, including **Fat Tire Bike Tours (p. 106)** and Guidatours (10 Avenue du General de Gaulle, Versailles, 01-39-02-05-18, www.guidatours.com). Explore the manicured grounds (free) on your own, or purchase your entry ticket (€18) at the gates, though reserving online in advance is recommended to beat long lines. A variety of on-site dining possibilities exist, from pizza and hot dogs to multi-course meals at a Michelin-starred celebrity restaurant (Gordon Ramsey au Trianon, 1 Boulevard de la Reine, Versailles, 01-30-84-50-00, www.trianon-palace.com/gordon-ramsay), where diners are treated like visiting royalty.

OVERVIEW MAP **E6** BOIS DE VINCENNES: ACCESS TO CHÂTEAU VIA AV. DES MINIMES, 12E 01-48-08-31-20
HOURS: DAILY SUNRISE-SUNSET

BASILIQUE CATHÉDRALE DE SAINT-DENIS

This is the resting place for the kings and queens of France, including Marie-Antoinette and Louis XVI.

PARC DES BUTTES CHAUMONT

BOIS DE VINCENNES

Construction on this now Gothic-style basilica began in A.D. 475.

OVERVIEW MAP A4 1 RUE DE LA LÉGION D'HONNEUR, 93200, ST-DENIS
01-48-09-83-54
WWW.SAINT-DENIS.MONUMENTS-NATIONAUX.FR
HOURS: APR.-SEPT. MON.-SAT. 10 A.M.-6:15 P.M., SUN. NOON-6:15 P.M.; OCT.-MAR. MON.-SAT. 10 A.M.-5 P.M., SUN. NOON-5:15 P.M.
ADMISSION: €7.50

BIBLIOTHÈQUE NATIONALE MITTERRAND

Named after former president François Mitterrand in 1998, the new national library (as opposed to the 1537 Bibliothèque Richelieu) is a striking modernist monument open to visitors, with frequent exhibits and events.

OVERVIEW MAP E5 11 QUAI FRANÇOIS MAURIAC, 13E 01-53-79-59-59
WWW.BNF.FR
HOURS: TUES.-SAT. 9 A.M.-7 P.M., MON. 2-7 P.M., SUN. 1-7 P.M.
ADMISSION: €3.50

LES CATACOMBES

In the late 18th century the bones of more than six million Parisians were removed from the city's overflowing cemeteries and displayed in the quarry tunnels beneath the Left Bank. Bring a sweater. Claustrophobics might want to pass.

OVERVIEW MAP E3 1 PL. DENFERT-ROCHEREAU, 14E 01-43-22-47-63
WWW.CATACOMBES.PARIS.FR
HOURS: TUES.-SUN. 10 A.M.-5 P.M.
ADMISSION: €8

CIMETIÈRE DU MONTPARNASSE

This tiny cemetery is the eternal resting place for literary figures such as Baudelaire and the existentialist lovers Simone de Beauvoir and Jean-Paul Sartre. Cigarettes adorn the grave of the French bad boy of rock, Serge Gainsbourg.

OVERVIEW MAP E3 3 BD. EDGAR QUINET, 14E 01-44-10-86-50
HOURS: WINTER DAILY 9 A.M.-5:30 P.M., SUMMER DAILY 9 A.M.-6 P.M.

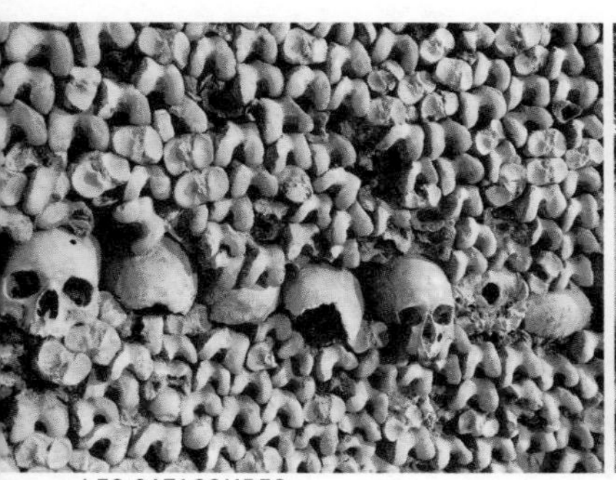

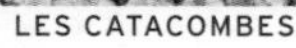
LES CATACOMBES

CIMETIÈRE DU PÈRE LACHAISE

CIMETIÈRE DU PÈRE LACHAISE

More than 200 years old, this enormous cemetery is as famous for its sculpted statues and sarcophagi as for its illustrious residents, including Chopin, Oscar Wilde, Edith Piaf, and Jim Morrison. Be sure to get a map at the entrance.

OVERVIEW **MAP C6** 6 RUE DE REPOS, 20E 01-55-25-82-10
WWW.PERE-LACHAISE.COM
HOURS: WINTER DAILY 9 A.M.-5:30 P.M., SUMMER DAILY 9 A.M.-6 P.M.

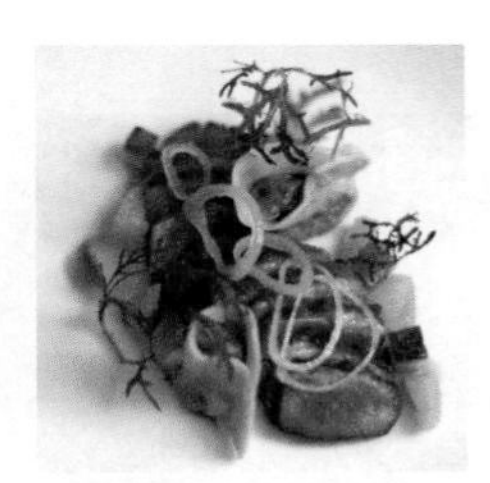

RESTAURANTS

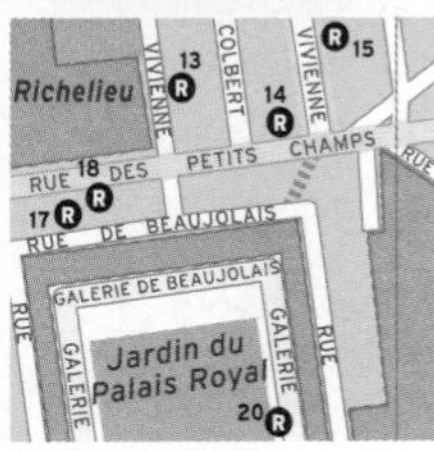

Best terrace: **CHEZ LENA ET MIMILE,** p. 28

Best café: **CAFÉ DE FLORE,** p. 30

Most exotic: **FOGÓN,** p. 31

Most romantic: **LAPÉROUSE,** p. 31

Most quintessentially Parisian: **LE BISTROT DE PARIS,** p. 33

Best splurge: **LE VOLTAIRE,** p. 35

Hottest restaurant of the moment: **VERJUS,** p. 38

Most traditional: **CHEZ GEORGES,** p. 39

Most historic: **LE GRAND VÉFOUR,** p. 40

Best vegetarian options: **CAFÉ PINSON,** p. 42

Most fun: **DERRIÈRE,** p. 43

Hippest space for small plates: **LE MARY CELESTE,** p. 44

Best fast food: **TAÉKO,** p. 44

Best place to sip wine with your oysters:
LE BARON ROUGE, p. 44

PRICE KEY

$ ENTRÉES UNDER $20

$$ ENTRÉES $20-30

$$$ ENTRÉES OVER $30

ATELIER MAITRE ALBERT
AFTER HOURS • CONTEMPORARY FRENCH $$
The best dish at this chic Guy Savoy-managed rotisserie is the signature roast chicken, which is tender, meticulously cut, and served with a side of creamy mashed potatoes. Fish dishes are also consistently top-notch. The front room tends to be a little quieter.

MAP 1 C4 R 12 1 RUE MAITRE ALBERT, 5E
01-56-81-30-01 WWW.ATELIERMAITREALBERT.COM

BRASSERIE BALZAR *HOT SPOT • FRENCH $$*
With its classic brasserie decor and well-groomed clientele, Brasserie Balzar was the original inspiration for the fashionable restaurant Balthazar in New York City. The excellent *poulet frites* (roast chicken with fries) is a favorite on the traditional French menu.

MAP 1 D2 R 21 49 RUE DES ÉCOLES 5E
01-43-54-13-67 WWW.BRASSERIEBALZAR.COM

BRASSERIE DE L'ISLE ST-LOUIS *AFTER HOURS • FRENCH $*
This old-fashioned brasserie crams its wooden tables with diners, and its dark-wood walls reverberate with conversation. The rural atmosphere calls for rural food, in ample portions: sausages, game, pork knuckle with lentils. Finish with the house-made crème caramel.

MAP 1 A4 R 4 55 QUAI DE BOURBON, 4E
01-43-54-02-59 WWW.LABRASSERIE-ISL.FR

CAFÉ DELMAS *QUICK BITES • AMERICAN $*
Previously La Chope, this café is as popular now as when Hemingway, who lived nearby, was a regular. Literary groupies and local shoppers pack the sidewalk tables, mostly drinking coffee and talking, or indulging in the dishes of the day: salads, steaks, and burgers.

MAP 1 F5 R 30 2 PL. DE LA CONTRESCARPE, 5E
01-43-26-51-26

CHEZ LENA ET MIMILE *QUICK BITES • FRENCH $$$*
A real secret even among Parisians, Chez Lena et Mimile has one of the best raised terraces in the city. With flowering greenery overlooking a picturesque fountain, and dishes like the deceptively simple mushroom velouté soup, this is the perfect location to pretend you're enjoying a quiet country brunch.

MAP 1 F5 R 33 32 RUE TOURNEFORT, 5E
01-47-07-72-47 WWW.CHEZLENAETMIMILE.FR

MOISSONIER *CAFÉ • COUNTRY FRENCH $$$*
Rustic, stick-to-your-ribs Lyonnaise cuisine served in a cozy dining room is the perfect antidote to a gray Paris day. Tuck into tasty rabbit terrine, fish soufflé, or chicken and mushrooms, and save room for the chocolate mousse.

MAP 1 C6 R 17 28 RUE DES FOSSÉS ST-BERNARD, 5E
01-43-29-87-65

GLUTEN-FREE Á LA MODE

Paris is in the throes of an unexpected food trend: gluten-free dining. Restaurants, bakeries, and entire aisles at the supermarket are geared toward those who want to have their cake and eat it, too, without a vacation-busting allergic reaction.

At **Helmut Newcake (p. 48),** éclairs, cakes, and savory tarts are weekday possibilities, as is a pancake-and-eggs Sunday brunch. At **Café Pinson (p. 42),** only non-gluten flours are used to create savory and sweet madeleines and crunchy house-made granola.

At chic and cheerful NoGlu (16 Passage des Panoramas, 2E, 01-40-26-41-24), carrot cake and warm banana bread are yours for dessert, if you have room after your hefty steak-and-potatoes lunch. Save your last wheat-free adventure for Soya (20 rue de la Pierre Levée, 10E, 01-48-05-13-00), a cozy vegetarian spot with a resident cat and a wholesome menu based on fresh vegetables, grains, and legumes.

MON VIEIL AMI *HOT SPOT • FRENCH $$$*

The celebrated Antoine Westermann has brought his zesty Alsatian touch to hearty and classic French cooking. Vegetables are the main attraction here, inspiring dishes like the sublime *mignon de porc* (pork filet paired with a zucchini puree and slightly caramelized apricots.

MAP 1 A5 R 5 69 RUE ST-LOUIS-EN-L'ÎLE, 4E
01-40-46-01-35 WWW.MON-VIEIL-AMI.COM

RESTAURANT ITINERAIRES

HOT SPOT • CONTEMPORARY FRENCH $$

A friendly husband-wife team runs this relaxed, modern bistro where local, organic ingredients are the main attraction. Try the cod steamed in a fig-laurel bouillon or the house-made chèvre ravioli, and polish off your stellar meal with glass of Burgundy bearing the sought-after Ecocert seal.

MAP 1 C5 R 15 5 RUE DE POINTOISE, 5E
01-46-33-60-11 WWW.RESTAURANT-ITINERAIRES.COM

LA TOUR D'ARGENT *ROMANTIC • FRENCH $$$*

The spectacular dining room of La Tour d'Argent, with views across the Seine to Notre-Dame, drips opulence, as do some of its guests. A more affordable lunchtime menu brings classics like duck à l'orange and crêpes belle époque within reach of slimmer pocketbooks.

B5 R 10 15-17 QUAI DE LA TOURNELLE, 5E
01-43-54-23-31 WWW.LATOURDARGENT.COM

LA TRUFFIÈRE *ROMANTIC • SOUTHWESTERN FRENCH $$$*
Residing in a 17th-century building near the Panthéon, La Truffière focuses its attention on southwestern French cooking, with truffles (naturally), goose, and duck on the menu. In winter, the roaring fire is a great asset.

MAP 1 F5 R 32 4 RUE BLAINVILLE, 5E
01-46-33-29-82 WWW.LA-TRUFFIERE.FR

MAP 2 ST-GERMAIN-DES-PRÉS

BRASSERIE LIPP *BUSINESS • FRENCH $$*
Famous politicians sit shoulder to shoulder with writers and fashion types. Classic brasserie dishes like steak tartare and Alsatian choucroute (sauerkraut), known here as the Choucroute Lipp, are staples on the traditional menu, which hasn't changed in 50 years. Don't be offended if you, like most foreigners, are seated on the second floor.

MAP 2 D2 R 28 151 BD. ST-GERMAIN, 6E
01-45-48-53-91 WWW.GROUPE-BERTRAND.COM

CAFÉ DE FLORE *CAFÉ • FRENCH $$*
Hemingway, Dalí, Picasso, Sartre, de Beauvoir – the list of the café's visitors could hardly be more impressive, and the café is still a treasured haunt of contemporary artists and philosophers, not to mention curious tourists. Enjoy traditional French onion soup or a *croque-monsieur* (grilled ham and cheese sandwich) and bask in the sun on the street-side terrace.

MAP 2 D2 R 26 172 BD. ST-GERMAIN, 6E
01-45-48-55-26 WWW.CAFEDEFLORE.FR

LE COMPTOIR DU RELAIS *HOT SPOT • FRENCH $$$*
Chef Yves Camdebourde is at the forefront of *bistronomie*, the bistro gastronomy trend that's now part of Paris's culinary culture. Roasted scallops and pot-au-feu (a traditional dish of boiled meats and vegetables) of foie gras have made him a star. Reserve a table at least three months in advance, or stop by l'Avant Comptoir (next door) instead.

MAP 2 D5 R 32 9 CARREFOUR DE L'ODÉON, 6E
01-43-29-12-05
WWW.HOTEL-PARIS-RELAIS-SAINT-GERMAIN.COM

COSI *QUICK BITES • INTERNATIONAL $*
The secret to its lasting success? Cosi bakes its own bread creations in a slow-burning brick oven, specially built on the premises. Fresh, high-quality ingredients make sandwiches like the Salmo, with smoked salmon and walnut ricotta cheese, perennial favorites with those looking for superior fast food.

MAP 2 C3 R 17 54 RUE DE SEINE, 6E
01-46-33-35-36

LA CUISINE DE BAR *QUICK BITES • CONTEMPORARY FRENCH $*
Dig into delicious home-style *tartines* – open-faced sandwiches with mouthwatering toppings like smoked salmon, foie gras, and

LA TRUFFIÈRE

FOGÓN

thinly sliced deli meats, baked onto crusty sourdough bread from the famous Poilâne bakery. There is usually a queue, but the service here is quick and cheerful.

MAP 2 F2 R 45 8 RUE DU CHERCHE-MIDI, 6E
01-45-48-45-69 WWW.CUISINEDEBAR.FR

LES DEUX MAGOTS *CAFÉ • FRENCH $$*
A perfectly situated St-Germain café, Les Deux Magots has hosted such luminaries as Wilde, Rimbaud, Verlaine, and of course Hemingway. You can savor a coffee, take a glass of wine, or sample the café fare, from simple steaks to indulgent caviar. It's overpriced but historic.

MAP 2 D2 R 27 6 PL. ST-GERMAIN-DES-PRÉS, 6E
01-45-48-55-25 WWW.LESDEUXMAGOTS.FR

FOGÓN *HOT SPOT • SPANISH $$$*
This Spanish bistro from chef Alberto Herráiz has had foodie tongues wagging since its opening. The house specialty is the *arroz,* a rice dish, here delectably paired with langoustines and thin strips of Spanish ham. The charcuteries (deli meats) are also renowned.

MAP 2 B5 R 7 45 QUAI DES GRANDS-AUGUSTINS, 6E
01-43-54-31-33 WWW.FOGON.FR

KGB *HOT SPOT • CONTEMPORARY FRENCH $$*
The little sister to chef William Ledeuil's über-successful Ze Kitchen Galerie, KGB continues to earn new fans with each passing year. His "zor d'oeuvres" starters are surprising combinations in tiny portions, meant to be shared. Culinary inspirations from Asia abound, like his chestnut cappuccino with black sesame ice cream.

MAP 2 C5 R 21 25 RUE DES GRANDS AUGUSTINS, 6E
01-46-33-00-85 WWW.KITCHENGALERIEBIS.COM

LAPÉROUSE *ROMANTIC • FRENCH $$$*
Try to book one of the private salons in this centuries-old restaurant, where Victor Hugo and Émile Zola used to dine. Expect classic French cuisine, such as *quenelles* (poached pike dumplings), and tuna with coriander, tomatoes, and eggplant. The Lapérouse soufflé is divine.

MAP 2 B5 R 6 51 QUAI DES GRANDS AUGUSTINS, 6E
01-43-26-68-04 WWW.LAPEROUSE.FR

PIZZA CHIC *BUSINESS • ITALIAN* *$$*
In the shadow of Montparnasse sits this smart, sophisticated eatery where rustic pizzas (try the artichoke and Parmesan) are transformed into refined, edible art. An attractive wine list and attentive staff add sparkle to the dining experience.

MAP 2 F2 R 47 13 RUE MÉZIÈRES, 6E
01-45-48-30-38 WWW.PIZZACHIC.FR

LE RELAIS DE L'ENTRECÔTE *QUICK BITES • FRENCH* *$*
This classic French steakhouse opened in 1959 with only one choice on its main course menu: steak, fries, and salad, accompanied by an addictive special sauce with a secret recipe. No reservations are taken, as the service is incredibly swift. A real Parisian experience awaits.

MAP 2 D2 R 23 20 RUE ST-BENOÎT, 6E
01-45-49-16-00 WWW.RELAISENTRECOTE.FR

LE RELAIS LOUIS XIII *BUSINESS • FRENCH* *$$$*
Once a monastery, the medieval-looking Relais makes for a sophisticated evening out and attracts well-heeled locals and visitors. Chef Manuel Martinez is celebrated for his subtle use of sauces and flavors: The lobster ravioli with foie gras and mushroom sauce is a notable example.

MAP 2 B5 R 8 8 RUE DES GRANDS AUGUSTINS, 6E
01-43-26-75-96 WWW.RELAISLOUIS13.COM

LE RESTAURANT *ROMANTIC • FRENCH* *$$$*
If you can't afford to stay at L'Hôtel, the quirky, luxurious hostelry where Oscar Wilde famously died, give its posh restaurant a go. Order the sea bass with olive puree and sesame in a neo-baroque setting designed by Jacques Garcia.

MAP 2 B2 R 4 L'HÔTEL, 13 RUE DES BEAUX ARTS, 6E
01-44-41-99-00 WWW.L-HOTEL.COM

MAP 3 INVALIDES

L'AFFRIOLÉ *ROMANTIC • FRENCH* *$$*
Here's a pleasant modern bistro in a quiet neighborhood that draws applause for its modern French *cuisine du marché*. That means using the freshest ingredients to turn out such dishes as spinach-and-mushroom cannelloni with ginger, and monkfish en brochette with eggplant and lavender.

MAP 3 C1 R 23 17 RUE MALAR, 7E
01-44-18-31-33

AIDA *BUSINESS • FUSION* *$$$*
Japanese chef Koji Aida has created an exquisite micro-universe of Franco-Japanese cuisine, which he cooks in front of lucky diners. The *omakase* (chef's choice) menu has over 12 services, with

LE RESTAURANT

L'ARPÈGE

subtle combinations like *tartare de veau* (veal tartare) and chateaubriand with sesame sauce.

MAP 3 E5 R 48 1 RUE PIERRE LEROUX, 7E
01-43-06-14-18

L'ARPÈGE *BUSINESS • FRENCH $$$*

Chef Alain Passard is revered for his innovative food, served in elegant contemporary surroundings of smooth wood and Lalique glassware. Go for the menu surprise if you're adventurous enough to order blindly – a *bavarois* (pudding) of avocado with pistachio oil and caviar, perhaps?

MAP 3 D4 R 39 84 RUE DE VARENNE, 7E
01-45-51-47-33 WWW.ALAIN-PASSARD.COM

L'ATELIER DE JOEL ROBUCHON
HOT SPOT • CONTEMPORARY FRENCH $$$

Reservations are finally accepted at celebrity chef Joel Robuchon's sleek Rive Gauche diner, designed by Pierre-Yves Rochon, and it's worth the wait. Mains include tournedos of beef with black pepper and foie gras with poached apples in hibiscus reduction.

MAP 3 B5 R 14 7 RUE MONTALEMBERT, 7E
01-42-22-56-56 WWW.JOEL-ROBUCHON.COM

LE BISTROT DE PARIS *ROMANTIC • FRENCH $$*

Neighboring antique dealers from the Carré Rive Gauche take long lunches at the Bistrot de Paris, while the evening is always teeming with groups of well-heeled, affluent locals. Expect crisp white tablecloths, impeccable service, and a traditional French bistro menu.

MAP 3 B5 R 13 33 RUE DE LILLE, 7E
01-42-61-16-83

CHEZ L'AMI JEAN *BUSINESS • BASQUE $$$*

With a homey tavernlike feel, this place offers a welcome break in what sometimes feels like an impersonal (if elegant) neighborhood. Step into "your friend Jean's place" and discover the warmth of the Basque country – tuna steak, duck confit, and a healthy dose of tomatoes.

C1 R 24 27 RUE MALAR, 7E
01-47-05-86-89 WWW.AMIJEAN.EU

GASTRONOMIE TO GO

Foodies in the French capital have American Kristin Frederick to thank for the food-cart craze sweeping the city. In late 2011, she launched Le Camion Qui Fume ("The Truck That Smokes," www.lecamionquifume.com), slinging messy burgers to lunch crowds near Place de la Madeleine.

Now, the competition is on. At Marché Raspail, Cantine California (www.cantinecalifornia.com) serves south-of-the-border fusion food – think tacos and milk shakes – to hungry hordes. Newbie Le Réfectoire's (www.le-refectoire.com) shiny black truck haunts the northern Paris markets, dishing burger-based brunch on Sundays with *pain perdu* (French toast) for dessert.

Glaces Glazed (www.glaces-glazed.com) breaks the mobile mold with artisanal ice creams bearing quirky names like My Bloody Clementine and Marron 5, which hit the spot on a hot summer's day.

COUTUME CAFÉ *BREAKFAST AND BRUNCH • FRENCH* $

The French-Australian duo that heads up this bright and inviting café knows a thing or two about coffee. Come in for a cup of their potent brew, and dig into a plate of perfect pancakes or colorful garden salad to calm the buzz.

 E4 R 47 47 RUE BABYLONE, 7E
01-45-51-50-47 WWW.COUTUMECAFE.COM

LE DIVELLEC *BUSINESS • SEAFOOD* $$$

One of the city's best seafood restaurants, Le Divellec attracts local business bigwigs and media folk to its large and well-lit dining room. Sample divine fish dishes, such as mussels with shallots and cod with caviar. Don't miss the old-fashioned dessert trolley.

 C2 R 26 107 RUE DE L'UNIVERSITÉ, 7E
01-45-51-91-96 WWW.LE-DIVELLEC.COM

L'EPI DUPIN *ROMANTIC • FRENCH* $$

Innovative food and a bustling atmosphere make this small restaurant a true find. Cod with saffron leeks tastes as good as it sounds, and the desserts, such as the apple tart, are renowned. It's too bad it's closed on weekends.

 D6 R 44 11 RUE DUPIN, 6E
01-42-22-64-56 WWW.EPIDUPIN.COM

HÉLÈNE DARROZE *HOT SPOT • SOUTHWESTERN FRENCH* $$$

Hélène Darroze is one of the very few one-star female chefs in Paris, and her pricey, eponymous Left Bank restaurant has earned a passionate following for its southwestern French specialties. If you're not up for delicious but more solemn fare upstairs, try her Salon d'Hélène downstairs, with exquisite tapas-size dishes.

MAP 3 D6 R 43 4 RUE D'ASSAS, 6E
01-42-22-00-11 WWW.HELENEDARROZE.COM

IL VINO *BUSINESS • CONTEMPORARY FRENCH $$$*
The wine comes first in this plush establishment, which has customers choosing their dishes by appellation and vintage first. Visit often enough and you'll see stars – literally; Angelina Jolie and Brad Pitt are among the elite clientele.

MAP 3 C2 R 27 13 BD. DE LA TOUR-MAUBOURG, 7E
01-44-11-72-00 WWW.ILVINOBYENRICOBERNARDO.COM

LEDOYEN *BUSINESS • FRENCH $$$*
The Napoléon III dining room perfectly suits the grand cooking of Christian Le Squer, who generally presents whatever is seasonal in two or more combinations. Sole with cucumber and ginger mayonnaise sauce is one mouthwatering option. The bar offers a simpler menu.

MAP 3 A2 R 5 1 AV. DUTUIT, 8E
01-53-05-10-00 WWW.LEDOYEN.COM

LE VOLTAIRE *BUSINESS • FRENCH $$$*
Le Voltaire is a classic of French cuisine, attracting the Paris elite with typically French dishes like steak tartare and *pigeon rôti* (roast pigeon). Perched between the Louvre and the Musée d'Orsay, it's a convenient lunch spot for hungry museum-goers.

MAP 3 A5 R 9 27 QUAI VOLTAIRE, 7E
01-42-61-17-49

MAP 4 TOUR EIFFEL/ARC DE TRIOMPHE/TROCADÉRO

ALAIN DUCASSE AU PLAZA ATHÉNÉE
BUSINESS • CONTEMPORARY FRENCH $$$
The name Alain Ducasse has become synonymous with haute cuisine, and nowhere else can you experience the magical culinary synthesis of both than at this super-exclusive restaurant. From the langoustines with caviar to the *baba au rhum* (rum cake), each plate dazzles, visually and otherwise.

MAP 4 B5 R 18 HÔTEL PLAZA ATHÉNÉE, 25 AV. MONTAIGNE, 8E
01-53-67-65-00 WWW.ALAIN-DUCASSE.COM

CHIBERTA *BUSINESS • FRENCH $$$*
Did somebody say power lunch? Guy Savoy and Stéphane Laruelle pull out all the stops with their imaginative menus, including the prix-fixe ode to black truffles. Request a seat in their wine cellar dining room, which is adorned with rare vintages.

MAP 4 A2 R 2 3 RUE ARSENE HOUSSAYE, 8E
01-53-53-42-00 WWW.LECHIBERTA.COM

58 TOUR EIFFEL *ROMANTIC • FRENCH $$*
With a view second only to that of Le Jules Vernes (one level up), 58 Tour Eiffel dishes up fine French regional cooking, at more

ANGELINA

BREAD AND ROSES

reasonable prices than its haute cuisine brother. The dining room has a cool, metallic, modern look reflecting the sleek Eiffel Tower location.

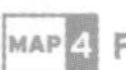

TOUR EIFFEL, FIRST LEVEL, CHAMP DE MARS, 7E
08-25-56-66-62 WWW.RESTAURANTS-TOUREIFFEL.COM

LA FONTAINE DE MARS *ROMANTIC • SOUTHWESTERN FRENCH $$*

Red-checked tablecloths and candlelit tables rest alongside the real Fontaine de Mars, a romantic sight that glows at nighttime, originally built in 1806. Barack Obama enjoyed the traditional southwestern French cuisine here during his European tour leading up to his first presidential campaign.

129 RUE ST-DOMINIQUE, 7E
01-47-05-46-44 WWW.FONTAINEDEMARS.COM

JAMIN *BUSINESS • FRENCH $$$*

Celebrity chef Joël Robuchon might have moved on from this refined eatery, but since late 2012, young chef de cuisine Jean-Christophe Guiony has kept diners intrigued with inventive dishes like squid Provençal and seared *noix de St. Jacques* (scallops) in a rich butter sauce.

32 RUE DE LONGCHAMP, 16E
01-45-53-00-07 WWW.RESTAURANT-JAMIN.COM

LE JULES VERNE *ROMANTIC • FRENCH $$$*

This quintessential haute cuisine restaurant was losing prestige until three-star chef Alain Ducasse took it over in 2008. Huge bay windows provide glimmering views of Paris, while the cuisine takes noble ingredients like lobster, truffles, and foie gras to another level.

TOUR EIFFEL, SECOND LEVEL, CHAMP DE MARS, 7E
01-45-55-61-44 WWW.LEJULESVERNE-PARIS.COM

MARKET *HOT SPOT • FUSION $$*

Mix New York-based superchef Jean-Georges Vongerichten with director Luc Besson, decorate with the earthy tones of a top designer, and serve up Asian-inspired traditional dishes, like steamed cod with eucalyptus emulsion and broccoli, and you've got Market.

15 AV. MATIGNON, 8E
01-42-63-48-18 WWW.JEAN-GEORGES.COM

PIERRE GAGNAIRE *HOT SPOT • CONTEMPORARY FRENCH $$$*
Some find the minimalist surroundings too stark, others find them totally relaxing, but no one argues over the food. Gagnaire is a culinary genius, offering such creative dishes as tender white tuna in a spider-crab broth, served with baby asparagus and caviar.

MAP 4 A3 R 6 6 RUE BALZAC, 8E
01-58-36-12-50 WWW.PIERRE-GAGNAIRE.COM

LA TABLE DU LANCASTER
BUSINESS • CONTEMPORARY FRENCH $$$
Chef Julien Roucheteau's dreamy menu takes its inspiration from the changing seasons, and each plate exits the kitchen with a freshness and vibrancy to match. Desserts lean toward the sublime; try the fluffy soufflé with pistachio ice cream for a little taste of heaven.

MAP 4 A4 R 10 HÔTEL LANCASTER, 7 RUE DE BERRI, 8E
01-40-76-40-76 WWW.HOTEL-LANCASTER.FR

LES AMBASSADEURS *BUSINESS • FRENCH $$$*
Gastronomes will have to wait to experience an opulent multi-course meal at Les Ambassadeurs. When the celebrated restaurant reopens in 2015, politicians and movie moguls will relish once again the impeccable service and exemplary dishes, such as glazed sole with St. Maur cheese and pine-nut stuffing.

MAP 5 E1 R 44 HÔTEL DE CRILLON, 10 PL. DE LA CONCORDE, 8E
01-44-71-16-16 WWW.CRILLON.COM

ANGELINA *CAFÉ • TEA $*
This popular tearoom has been in business since 1903, and many of its customers have been coming here for decades. The select teas come served in bone china, but the hot chocolate, made with top-quality molten *chocolat,* is the specialty.

MAP 5 E3 R 49 226 RUE DE RIVOLI, 1ER
01-42-60-82-00 WWW.ANGELINA-PARIS.FR

LES BACCHANTES *AFTER HOURS • WINE BAR $*
As the name's reference to the Greek god of wine suggests, wine is the only beverage on the menu here. It's not hard to imagine the boisterous mood in this temple to good living, where the food ranges from basic salads and charcuterie to escargots.

MAP 5 B2 R 4 21 RUE DE CAUMARTIN, 9E
01-42-65-25-35 WWW.LESBACCHANTES.FR

BREAD AND ROSES
BREAKFAST AND BRUNCH • CONTEMPORARY FRENCH $
The poetically named Bread and Roses has become a favored lunch spot with French celebrities and local fashion folk. Already famous for organic breads and freshly pressed juices, it has added a chic lunch and dinner service to this, its second location. Look for the original eatery on the Left Bank (62 Rue Madame, 6E).

D1 R 31 25 RUE BOISSY D'ANGLAS, 8E
01-47-42-40-00 WWW.BREADANDROSES.FR

LE CARRÉ DES FEUILLANTS *BUSINESS • FRENCH $$$*
The business-suit set comes here to impress and be impressed. Chef Alain Dutournier demonstrates his mastery of haute cuisine without losing his southwest France origins in such simple-sounding yet sublime dishes as wild hare with truffles and roast chicken with mushrooms.

MAP 5 D3 R 37 14 RUE DE CASTIGLIONE, 1ER
01-42-86-82-82 WWW.CARREDESFEUILLANTS.FR

DROUANT *BUSINESS • FRENCH $$$*
The jury of France's premier literary prize, the Prix Goncourt, meets upstairs at Drouant. The restaurant, too, could win prizes for cooking, with dishes like ravioli in truffle sauce and scallops on the half shell with salted butter.

MAP 5 B4 R 9 18 RUE GAILLON, 2E
01-42-65-15-16 WWW.DROUANT.COM

KUNITORAYA *HOT SPOT • JAPANESE $*
Hand-pulled noodles are the big draw at this authentic eatery in the heart of Japantown. Try your udon with curry, tempura vegetables, or fermented soybeans called *natto,* and wash it all down with a frosty class of Japanese beer.

MAP 5 C6 R 29 5 RUE VILLEDO, 1ER WWW.KUNITORAYA.COM

RESTAURANT LE MEURICE *BUSINESS • FRENCH $$$*
The glamorous dining room at Hôtel Le Meurice, designed by Philippe Starck, was inspired by the royal apartments at Versailles. Dishes such as truffled langoustine cassolette and decadent desserts add up to an unforgettable meal.

MAP 5 E3 R 48 HÔTEL LE MEURICE, 228 RUE DE RIVOLI, 1ER
01-44-58-10-10 WWW.LEMEURICE.COM

SENDERENS *BUSINESS • FRENCH $$$*
Former three-star chef Alain Senderens created a stir in the French food world when he declined his stars, closed the venerated house of Lucas Carton, and reopened as Senderens. The food is now significantly less stuffy, and the *gastronomique* bar on the second floor is a real treat.

MAP 5 C1 R 18 9 PL. DE LA MADELEINE, 8E
01-42-65-22-90 WWW.SENDERENS.FR

VERJUS *HOT SPOT • CONTEMPORARY FRENCH $$*
Americans Braden Perkins and Laura Adrian opened their combination fine-dining restaurant and casual wine bar after honing their skills at underground restaurant Hidden Kitchen. Inventive menus (cured trout and smoked potatoes, cherrystone clams with thyme oil and fresh, local ingredients mean everything tastes lip-smacking good. Verjus accommodates special diets and makes all who enter feel welcome.

MAP 5 C6 R 28 52 RUE DE RICHELIEU, 1ER
01-42-97-54-40 WWW.VERJUSPARIS.COM

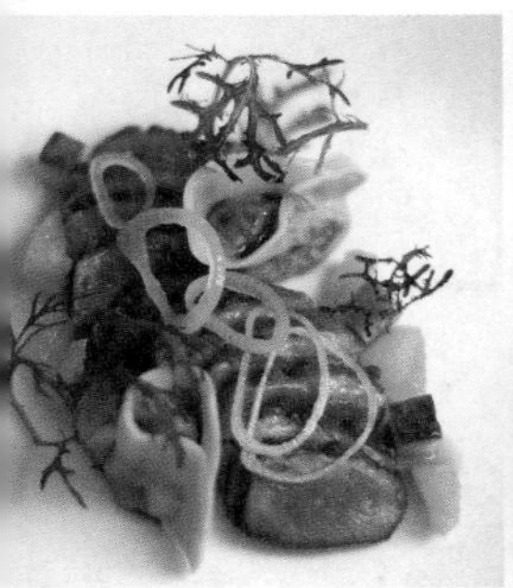
VERJUS

DROUANT

MAP 6 LOUVRE/LES HALLES

BISTROT VIVIENNE *ROMANTIC • FRENCH $$*
This bistro is an all-around pleasure – neither small, nor cavernous; comfortable but stylish; and with two terraces, one facing south onto the street, one onto the elegant Galerie Vivienne. Their dark chocolate mousse with salted-butter caramel brings tears to a chocolate lover's eyes.

MAP 6 C1 R 14 4 RUE DES PETITS CHAMPS, 2E
01-49-27-00-50 WWW.BISTROTVIVIENNE.COM

CHEZ GEORGES *BUSINESS • FRENCH $$*
Why does this tiny bistro hold such monumental standing with the food critics of Paris? Fans of *terroir* (local products) will tell you the answer can be found in a plate of andouillette sausage. At Chez Georges traditions prevail; even the menu is still written by hand.

MAP 6 B2 R 6 1 RUE DU MAIL, 2E
01-42-60-07-11

L'ESCARGOT MONTORGUEIL *BUSINESS • FRENCH $$*
What could be more French than a restaurant specializing in snails? Have them in mint, curried, with walnuts, or in a casserole. Charlie Chaplin and Salvador Dalí dined in this historic bistro, which is decked with huge mirrors, crystal chandeliers, and a giant golden snail above the entrance.

MAP 6 B4 R 11 38 RUE MONTORGUEIL, 2E
01-42-36-83-51

FRENCHIE *HOT SPOT • CONTEMPORARY FRENCH $$*
After a stint in London and New York, chef Grégory Marchand has returned to Paris to share an energetic appreciation for good products and creative dining. The menu is seasonal and changes daily. Book far in advance or try Frenchie Bar à Vins across from the restaurant for small plates.

MAP 6 A4 R 3 5-6 RUE DE NIL, 2E
01-40-39-96-19 WWW.FRENCHIE-RESTAURANT.COM

A PRIORI THÉ

WILLI'S WINE BAR

LE GRAND COLBERT *ROMANTIC • FRENCH* *$$*

Since its star turn in the movie *Something's Gotta Give,* this gorgeous belle époque brasserie has seen no shortage of Yankees, but happily its French flavor survives intact. Stick with time-honored classics like Lyonnaise lentil salad, roast chicken with fries, and French onion soup gratiné.

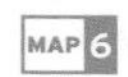 C1 R 13
2-4 RUE VIVIENNE, 2E
01-42-86-87-88 WWW.LEGRANDCOLBERT.FR

LE GRAND VÉFOUR *ROMANTIC • FRENCH* *$$$*

With painted glass ceilings, mirrored walls, and 18th-century moldings, the dining room at chef Guy Martin's haute-cuisine establishment ranks among Paris's finest. The well-heeled clientele comes for the modern cuisine – ravioli stuffed with foie gras in truffle sauce, for example – and spectacular decor.

 C1 R 17
17 RUE DE BEAUJOLAIS, 1ER
01-42-96-56-27 WWW.GRAND-VEFOUR.COM

AU PIED DE COCHON *AFTER HOURS • FRENCH* *$*

Waiters in black tie attend to your every need at this longtime, 24-hour Les Halles favorite. Take a seat beneath the red awning and allow them to serve you the pig's feet – or that less daring perennial comfort food, onion soup.

 C3 R 24
6 RUE COQUILLIÈRE, 1ER
01-40-13-77-00 WWW.PIEDDECOCHON.COM

LE POULE AU POT *AFTER HOURS • FRENCH* *$$*

If supping on filling traditional fare in the wee hours of the morning is your cup of tea, you'll find comfort at this art deco-era bistro. French onion soup, hearty salads, and steak tartare are yours to devour until 5 A.M.

 D4 R 33
9 RUE VAUVILLIERES, 1ER
01-42-36-32-96 WWW.LAPOULEAUPOT.COM

A PRIORI THÉ *BREAKFAST AND BRUNCH • FUSION* *$$*

Tucked inside a belle époque shopping arcade, this homey café serves delectable lunch and afternoon tea in a visually rich setting. Sip a soothing cup of Earl Grey and just try to resist the call of homemade cheesecakes, scones, and crumbles.

35 GALERIE VIVIENNE, 2E
01-42-97-48-75 WWW.APRIORITHE.COM

LE RESTAURANT DU PALAIS ROYAL *ROMANTIC • FRENCH $$*
What could be better than strolling the historic arcades of the Palais Royal? Why, dining underneath them, of course. That proposition is made all the more appealing when the menu includes the likes of truffled risotto with porcini, and endive with Stilton, walnuts, and pear.

MAP 6 C1 R 20 110 GALERIE DE VALOIS, 1ER
01-40-20-00-27 WWW.RESTAURANTDUPALAISROYAL.COM

SATURNE *BUSINESS • CONTEMPORARY FRENCH $$*
Talented young chef Sven Chartier deserves all the praise showered on him of late; his daring takes on traditional French cuisine and turns the staid into the sublime. Expect fixed menus bursting with color, flavor, and texture, presented in a contemporary dining space.

MAP 6 A2 R 2 17 RUE NOTRE DAME DES VICTOIRES, 2E
01-42-60-31-90 WWW.SATURNE-PARIS.FR

SPRING *HOT SPOT • CONTEMPORARY FRENCH $$*
When American chef Daniel Rose opened Spring back in 2006, the media dubbed him a "one man *chaud.*" Several years and countless accolades later, he continues to wow diners with his fresh approach to French cuisine. Book your table far, far in advance to see what all the fuss is about.

MAP 6 E3 R 39 6 RUE BAILLEUL, 1ER
01-45-96-05-72 WWW.SPRINGPARIS.FR

WILLI'S WINE BAR *BUSINESS • WINE BAR $*
Englishman Mark Williamson's seminal wine bar has been a revered neighborhood fixture since 1980. The kitchen has perfected a cuisine that is simple and discreet, allowing wine enthusiasts and neophytes alike to enjoy their selection of over 250 vintages.

MAP 6 C1 R 18 13 RUE DES PETITS-CHAMPS, 1ER
01-42-61-05-09 WWW.WILLISWINEBAR.COM

YAM'TCHA *HOT SPOT • FUSION $$$*
After a stint in Asia, chef Adeline Grattard returned to Paris with a heart full of both cultures. Since she opened Yam'Tcha, the awards have followed for her inspired dishes, like sautéed squid with sweet potato noodles and roast duck with Sichuan-style eggplant. Make reservations at least two months in advance.

MAP 6 D3 R 33 4 RUE SAUVAL, 1ER
01-40-26-08-07 WWW.YAMTCHA.COM

LE ZIMMER *CAFÉ • FRENCH $$*
This 1896 café, given a plush makeover by designer Jacques Garcia, can always be counted on for quality and copious portions served by friendly staff. The menu veers from bacon cheeseburgers to roast veal, and each plate seems to taste better when enjoyed on the sunny sidewalk terrace.

MAP 6 F6 R 47 1 PL. DU CHÂTELET, 1ER
01-42-36-74-03 WWW.LEZIMMER.COM

MAP 7 MARAIS

L'AMBASSADE D'AUVERGNE *HOT SPOT • FRENCH $$*
This family eatery feels more like the owner's two-story farmhouse than a restaurant. Hearty dishes of pork, beef, and cabbage fill the menu. Be sure to indulge in a side order of *aligot,* a typical Auvergne-region dish made from gooey mashed potatoes mixed with mild Cantal cheese and garlic.

MAP 7 C1 R 17 22 RUE DU GRENIER ST-LAZARE, 3E
01-42-72-31-32 WWW.AMBASSADE-AUVERGNE.COM

L'AS DU FALLAFEL *QUICK BITES • INTERNATIONAL $*
Don't let the long line at this Marais institution deter you; you'll be inside eating the world-famous falafel in less than 10 minutes. Warning: The garlicky house-made harissa is addictive, and the jars for sale at the counter encourage impulse buying.

MAP 7 D4 R 39 34 RUE DES ROSIERS, 4E
01-48-87-63-60

BREIZH CAFÉ *CAFÉ • COUNTRY FRENCH $*
There's an art to crêpe-making – just ask any Breton. True to tradition, the galettes at this corner *crêperie* are made with *sarrasin* (buckwheat) flour and are cooked with either sweet or savory ingredients. Next door, the new Breizh *épicerie* (food shop) sells treats from Brittany, including chewy salted butter caramels.

MAP 7 B4 R 15 109 RUE VIEILLE-DU-TEMPLE, 4E
01-42-72-13-77 WWW.BREIZHCAFE.COM

CAFÉ BEAUBOURG *BREAKFAST AND BRUNCH • FRENCH $$*
An excellent spot for breakfast or a late-night drink, the Beaubourg's terrace offers fantastic views of Centre Pompidou, while its interior is equally attractive. Have tea, coffee, or a glass of wine, or sample the menu of steaks, sandwiches, and pastries.

MAP 7 D1 R 27 43 RUE ST-MERRI, 4E
01-48-87-63-96 WWW.BEAUMARLY.COM/CAFE-BEAUBOURG/ACCUEIL

CAFÉ PINSON *BREAKFAST AND BRUNCH • VEGETARIAN $$*
When they opened Café Pinson in 2013, Agathe Audouze and Damien Richardot aimed to offer beautiful food that's healthy and satisfying. The line at the door is a testament to their success. Gluten-free and organic lunches, brunches, and light meals are served in their bright, cozy-modern dining room by an attentive, professional, bilingual staff.

MAP 7 A4 R 4 6 RUE DU FOREZ, 3E
09-83-82-53-53 WWW.CAFEPINSON.COM

CHEZ OMAR *HOT SPOT • MOROCCAN $*
Omar has seen supermodels and movie stars pass his door, but each new person is still greeted like a long lost friend. Known for its exquisite Couscous Royale, this Moroccan restaurant is always packed to the brim, while maintaining a lively and convivial atmosphere.

MAP 7 A3 R 3 47 RUE DE BRETAGNE, 3E
01-42-72-36-26

CAFÉ PINSON

JAJA

DERRIÈRE *HOT SPOT • FRENCH* $$
What lies *derrière* (behind) this quirky restaurant from the owners of Le 404, are the beautiful people of Paris, who can't get enough of the cozy apartment-style decor. Secret doors reveal hidden rooms and even a Ping-Pong table. Great for large groups.

MAP 7 B1 R 8 69 RUE DES GRAVILLIERS, 3E
01-44-61-91-95 WWW.DERRIERE-RESTO.COM

DÔME DU MARAIS *ROMANTIC • CONTEMPORARY FRENCH* $$
This former chapel, hidden from the street, now extends more earthly offerings, like risotto with asparagus and foie gras and truffled pizzas. The combination of setting and savor win many a diner over at this dramatic, domed temple.

MAP 7 C3 R 21 53-BIS RUE DES FRANCS-BOURGEOIS, 3E
01-42-74-54-17 WWW.LEDOMEDUMARAIS.FR

L'ETOILE MANQUANTE *CAFÉ • FRENCH* $
The perfect café for a typical Marais pastime: people-watching and passing the time over a *noisette* (a typical French coffee). It's open until 2 A.M. daily. Meet friends here or enjoy a solitary moment.

MAP 7 D4 R 38 34 RUE VIELLE DU TEMPLE, 4E
01-42-72-48-34

LE 404 *HOT SPOT • MOROCCAN* $$
The French capital abounds in delicious North African restaurants, and the stylish and ever-popular "family-style Moroccan" 404, owned by the actor Momo, is one of the best. Friendly waiters navigate the tiny, packed tables and noisy crowds with couscous, *tagines* (stews), and mint tea in tow.

MAP 7 B1 R 9 69 RUE DES GRAVILLIERS, 3E
01-42-74-57-81 WWW.404-RESTO.COM

JAJA *BUSINESS • CONTEMPORARY FRENCH* $$$
Nestled in a pretty courtyard in the thick of the Marais, this discreet lunch and dinner spot serves modern takes on global classics, from burgers to bouillabaisse. The well-rounded wine list alone is enough to reel in faithful clients, including investor Marion Cotillard.

MAP 7 D4 R 36 3 RUE STE-CROIX DE LA BRETONNERIE, 4E
01-42-74-71-52 WWW.JAJA-RESTO.COM

LE MARY CELESTE

LE BARON ROUGE

LE LOIR DANS LA THÉIÈRE *BREAKFAST AND BRUNCH • FRENCH* $
This well-worn café is renowned for its desserts (the mile-high meringue is hard to miss) and makes a pleasant respite while sightseeing. Savory tarts, generous salads, and weekend brunch draw crowds, but arrive early to avoid a wait and ensure a varied selection.

MAP 7 D5 R 42 3 RUE DES ROSIERS, 4E
01-42-72-90-61

LE MARY CELESTE *HOT SPOT • FUSION* $$
Oysters from the Normandy coast, small plates representing Asia and Latin America, and killer cocktails form the backbone of this buzzworthy bar/restaurant in the trendy North Marais. Try the house kimchi and wash it down with the beer-of-the-moment, Brooklyn Lager.

MAP 7 A5 R 7 1 RUE COMMINES, 3E WWW.LEMARYCELESTE.COM

TAÉKO *QUICK BITES • JAPANESE* $
In the heart of the Marché des Enfants Rouge, an exceptional market in its own right, lies Taéko. It's not more than a small kiosk, so legions of trendy Parisians take over the covered bench area to enjoy their bento, yakitori, and *donburi* (rice bowl) delights.

MAP 7 A4 R 6 MARCHÉ DES ENFANTS ROUGE, 39 RUE DE BRETAGNE, 3E
01-48-04-34-59

MAP 8 BASTILLE

ASSAPORARE *BUSINESS • ITALIAN* $$
Expect a convivial welcome from Giuseppe, the Naples-born proprietor of this relaxed lunch and dinner spot serving classic Italian fare. Fresh pastas and bright salads burst with flavor, and desserts are heaven on a plate.

MAP 8 B4 R 18 7 RUE ST-NICOLAS, 12E
01-44-67-75-77

LE BARON ROUGE *QUICK BITES • WINE BAR* $
During the week, locals crowd in for cheese and charcuterie plates, interesting and dirt-cheap wines, and the homey welcome. On week-

ends, the diminutive drinking and dining spot morphs into a standing-room-only party with the added allure of briny Breton oysters.

MAP 8 B5 R 22 1 RUE THÉOPHILE ROUSSEL, 12E
01-43-43-41-32

BLÉ SUCRÉ *QUICK BITES • FRENCH $*

Each buttery croissant, light-as-air madeleine, and chewy baguette tastes (and looks) like an edible work of art. Grab a terrace table and enjoy the tranquility with *un café* (coffee) and a slice of caramel-y tarte tatin.

MAP 8 B5 R 20 7 RUE ANTOINE VOLLON, 12E
01-43-40-77-73 WWW.BLESUCRE.FR

BOFINGER *ROMANTIC • ALSATIAN $$*

This is one of the city's most appealing old-world brasseries, with lovely art nouveau decor and heart-stopping piles of oysters in winter. Its late-night service is a hit with opera-goers, who only have to cross the Place de la Bastille to be rewarded with an Alsatian *choucroute de la mer*, a French specialty of earthy sauerkraut and fresh seafood.

MAP 8 B2 R 11 5 RUE DE LA BASTILLE, 4E
01-42-72-87-82 WWW.BOFINGERPARIS.COM

CAFÉ DE L'INDUSTRIE *CAFÉ • FRENCH $$*

Abuzz with Bastille students and wannabe bohemians, l'Industrie's arty style lies somewhere between junk shop, bistro, and French Colonial. The food is classic French: *boudin noir* (blood sausage ,
steak tartare, and fruit tarts for dessert.

MAP 8 A3 R 3 16 RUE ST-SABIN, 11E
01-47-00-13-53

LE CAFÉ DU PASSAGE *QUICK BITES • WINE BAR $*

You could catch a quick bite in this cross between wine bar and café, but the plush interior (or the secret courtyard) might tempt you to linger. Try the andouillette sausage with a glass of wine for something authentic and robust.

MAP 8 B4 R 14 12 RUE DE CHARONNE, 11E
01-49-29-97-64

LA GAZZETTA *HOT SPOT • CONTEMPORARY FRENCH $$*

The unofficial headquarters for the Bo-Bo (*"bourgeois-bohème"*) foodies of Paris. Eating from the set menu, which changes daily, means putting yourself at the mercy of chef Petter Nilsson, but he has kept customers coming back for more. Always full of surprises.

MAP 8 B5 R 21 29 RUE DE COTTE, 12E
01-43-47-47-05 WWW.LAGAZZETTA.FR

RINO *HOT SPOT • ITALIAN $$*

Four- and six-course tasting menus give diners the chance to explore all the revamped flavors of Italy dreamed up by chef Giovanni Passerini. Dishes like barley risotto with onion and calamari or grilled mackerel with mustard leaves and Chinese cabbage keep the crowds sated and happy.

MAP 8 A5 R 6 46 RUE TROUSSEAU, 11E
01-48-06-95-85 WWW.RINO-RESTAURANT.COM

SARDEGNA A TAVOLA *HOT SPOT • ITALIAN $$*
Stylish Parisians have adopted this trattoria dedicated to Sardinian specialties. With homemade pasta and a healthy selection of delectable charcuteries, this could be one of the best Italian restaurants in Paris. Seafood combinations like the *tagliatelle langoustine à l'orange* (fettuccine with lobster in an orange sauce) certainly set the mark.

MAP 8 C5 R 27 1 RUE DE COTTE, 12E
01-44-75-03-28

LE SIFFLEUR DE BALLONS *QUICK BITES • WINE BAR $*
At this frontrunner in the food-and-wine bar trend still sweeping Paris you'll find small plates – cheeses, charcuterie, terrines – that pair perfectly with every glass of red, white, and rosé in the house.

MAP 8 B6 R 24 34 RUE DE CITEAUX, 12E
01-58-51-14-04 WWW.LESIFFLEUR.BLOGSPOT.FR

LE TRAIN BLEU *ROMANTIC • FRENCH $$$*
In 1900, "Le Grand Buffet de la Gare de Lyon" was inaugurated to coincide with the Universal Exhibition. Renamed Le Train Bleu in 1963, this grand restaurant has kept its belle époque decoration untouched, much to the delight of history buffs and gastronomes alike.

MAP 8 D5 R 29 20 BD. DIDEROT, 12E
01-43-43-09-06 WWW.LE-TRAIN-BLEU.COM

MAP 9 MONTMARTRE

LE CAFÉ QUI PARLE *CAFÉ • FRENCH $$*
This homey dining spot on a leafy Montmartre corner serves hearty, stick-to-your-ribs fare like lamb roast, succulent steaks, and rustic country pâtés. Take a seat on the terrace if the sun is out and enjoy friendly service with quintessentially Parisian views.

MAP 9 C2 R 9 24 RUE CAULAINCOURT, 18E
01-46-06-06-88 WWW.CAFEQUIPARLE.COM

CHAMARRÉ MONTMARTRE *HOT SPOT • FUSION $$*
In French the name means "very colorful," and, indeed, Chamarré has brought a soft, spicy ornamentation to Montmartre, with its soulful and exotic Franco-Mauritian cuisine, in addition to one of the most charming terraces in Paris. Adventurous gourmets can't get enough.

MAP 9 A4 R 2 52 RUE LAMARCK, 18E
01-42-55-05-42 WWW.CHAMARRE-MONTMARTRE.COM

LE CHINON *CAFÉ • FRENCH $*
This laid-back café serves food until midnight and coffee, beer, wine, and hot chocolate until 2 A.M. Live music every other Sunday attracts a youngish bohemian crowd to this part of Montmartre, not yet taken over by souvenir shops.

MAP 9 D3 R 18 49 RUE DES ABBESSES, 18E
01-42-62-07-17

LE TRAIN BLEU

MILK

HÔTEL AMOUR *AFTER HOURS • FRENCH $*
Dim lighting, flickering candles, and a bevy of good-looking customers; the owners of the Hôtel Amour have created the perfect combination for a romantic evening. The kitchen specializes in comfort food *extraordinaire*, offering dressed-up dishes like mac and cheese and *pain perdu* (French toast).

MAP 9 F5 R 36 8 RUE NAVARIN, 9E
01-48-78-31-80 WWW.HOTELAMOURPARIS.FR

MILK *BREAKFAST AND BRUNCH • FRENCH $*
Milk isn't what's on the menu; it's an acronym for Mum In her Little Kitchen, and the homey smells wafting out of this tiny space make you feel like you really have come home. Have a seat at one of the vintage Formica tables and tuck into simple tarts, crumbles, and clafoutis served with tasty 1950s flair.

MAP 9 D5 R 22 62 RUE D'ORSEL, 18E
01-42-59-74-32 WWW.MILK-LEPICERIE.COM

ROSE BAKERY *BREAKFAST AND BRUNCH • FUSION $$*
Since 2002, locals with British sensibilities have flocked to Rose Bakery for simple organic meals and tasty pastries washed down with a fine cuppa. The weekend brunch is particularly popular; come early to avoid a wait.

MAP 9 F6 R 37 46 RUE DES MARTYRS, 9E
01-42-82-12-80

MAP 10 CANAL ST-MARTIN

BOB'S JUICE BAR *QUICK BITES • VEGETARIAN $*
Bob's introduced the juice bar concept to the City of Light, but the menu isn't limited to liquid elixirs. Daily specials include bagels, soups, and sushi, and you can always count on a tasty selection of freshly baked sweets, many of which are gluten-free.

MAP 10 E2 R 19 15 RUE LUCIEN SAMPAIX, 10E
09-50-06-36-18 WWW.BOBSJUICEBAR.COM

LE GALOPIN *HOT SPOT • FRENCH $$*
Hybrid gastronomy-bistro fare is the specialty of chef Romain

PINK FLAMINGO PIZZA   RESTAURANT PIERRE SANG BOYER

Tischenko, a past winner of TV's *Top Chef*. The seven-course fixed-price menu is a satisfying steal, and the warm, friendly service is a refreshing change of pace.

MAP 10 C4 R 7   34 RUE STE-MARTHE, 10E
01-42-06-05-03   WWW.LE-GALOPIN.COM

HELMUT NEWCAKE *BREAKFAST AND BRUNCH • FRENCH $*
At first glance, this patisserie and *salon du thé* (teahouse) looks like so many others, but what isn't immediately evident is that each colorful tart, pastry, and pizza is gluten-free. Sunday brunch is a full-on feast, and the *épicerie* (food shop) section vends gluten-free products to go.

MAP 10 D3 R 18   36 RUE BICHAT, 10E
09-82-59-00-39   WWW.HELMUTNEWCAKE.COM

DU PAIN ET DES IDÉES *QUICK BITES • BAKERY $*
Stepping through the centuries-old doorway at this corner *boulangerie* (bakery) gives the sensation of stepping backward in time. Vintage decor and the timeless aroma of butter, flour, and yeast permeate the air, and the dazzling pastries and rustic breads are a carb-lover's dream made real.

MAP 10 E2 R 20   34 RUE YVES TOUDIC, 10E
01-42-40-44-52   WWW.DUPAINETDESIDEES.COM

LE PETIT CAMBODGE *HOT SPOT • ASIAN $*
Get here early to secure a table before the line reaches around the corner. The specialty is the rice-noodle meal-in-bowl, *bo bun*, but curries and rice plates are worth a taste, too. Wash your spicy meal down with a carafe of wine, and if there's room for dessert, the banana tapioca is divine.

MAP 10 D3 R 17   20 RUE ALIBERT, 10E
01-42-45-80-88   WWW.LEPETITCAMBODGE.FR

PINK FLAMINGO PIZZA *QUICK BITES • FUSION $*
Organic pizzas with quirky names like The Obama (bacon and pineapple chutney) or The Bjork (smoked salmon and crème fraîche) are the draw here. Eat in or have your pie delivered to your alfresco dining spot along the canal.

MAP 10 D2 R 10   67 RUE BICHAT, 10E
01-42-02-31-70   WWW.PINKFLAMINGOPIZZA.COM

RESTAURANT PIERRE SANG BOYER *HOT SPOT • FUSION $$*
France meets South Korea at this no-reservations restaurant launched by the young Mr. Boyer, a 2011 *Top Chef* finalist. The fixed menu changes daily but might include pigeon ravioli with cabbage, pickled onions, and preserved-lemon oil, or seared girolle mushrooms and haricots verts in an apricot emulsion.

MAP 10 F5 R 24 55 RUE OBERKAMPF, 10E WWW.PIERRESANGBOYER.COM

TEN BELLES *CAFÉ • FRENCH $*
A common complaint among non-French visitors to the capital is the dearth of quality coffee. At Ten Belles, there's only room for compliments. Locally roasted beans translate to rich and tasty brews. Simple salads, sandwiches, and peanut butter brownies hit the midday hunger spot.

MAP 10 D2 R 9 10 RUE DE LA GRANGE AUX BELLES, 10E
01-42-40-90-78 WWW.TENBELLES.COM

LA VERRE VOLÉ *HOT SPOT • FRENCH $$*
A delectable selection of natural wines and well-rounded menu of small, meaty plates, such as *boudin noir* (blood sausage) and veal terrine, give this casual neighborhood bistro/wine shop its homey appeal. Discovered a wine you like? Buy a bottle to go for tomorrow's picnic in the park.

MAP 10 D2 R 14 67 RUE DE LANCRY, 10E
01-48-03-17-34 WWW.LEVERREVOLE.FR

YOUPI ET VOILÀ *HOT SPOT • FRENCH $$$*
An unmarked doorway and surprise fixed-price menu are just a couple of the exclusive features diners will discover at this chic and welcoming restaurant. The focus is on seasonal foods hand-selected by chef Patrice Gelbart and served with colorful, artistic flair.

MAP 10 C3 R 5 34 8 RUE VICQ D'AZIR, 10E
01-83-89-12-63 WWW.YOUPIETVOILA.COM

OVERVIEW MAP

ABRI *HOT SPOT • FUSION $$*
Chef Katsuaki Okiyama honed his chops at some of the city's best restaurants before launching Abri, a gourmet sandwich shop by day, Asian-fusion neobistro by night. Come for the casual vibe, down-to-earth prices, and the sublime seafood.

OVERVIEW MAP **C4** 92 FAUBOURG-POISSONNIÈRE, 10E
01-83-97-00-00

LE BARATIN *HOT SPOT • FRENCH $$*
Argentinean Raquel Carena has put the Baratin, known to be the restaurant of choice for many of Paris's top chefs, on the map with her take on traditional French cuisine, along with an oenophile's dream selection of natural wines. Reservations are essential.

OVERVIEW MAP **C5** 3 RUE JOUYE-ROUVE, 20E
01-43-49-39-70

EPICURE

PÉTRELLE

CHEZ ALINE *QUICK BITES • WINE BAR $*

Chef Delphine Zampetti has transformed this former horse-meat butcher shop into a locavore's dream of a lunch spot. Natural wines and a casual atmosphere attract local diners, but the inventive sandwiches are the major draw.

OVERVIEW MAP **D5** 85 RUE DE LA ROQUETTE, 11E
01-43-71-90-75

LA CLOSERIE DES LILAS *HOT SPOT • FRENCH $$$*

Follow greats like Picasso through these doors, which first opened in 1808. Today La Closerie packs in hip professionals who opt for unfussy dishes, pricey and well made. Its discreet, dark bar is a throwback to another age.

OVERVIEW MAP **D3** 171 BD. DU MONTPARNASSE, 14E
01-40-51-34-50 WWW.CLOSERIEDESLILAS.FR

EPICURE *HOT SPOT • CONTEMPORARY FRENCH $$$*

Refinement and luxury abound at this haute cuisine restaurant in Le Bristol Paris hotel. Chef Eric Frechon was elected Meilleur Ouvrier de France in 1993, a prestigious recognition involving three years of preparation and a final judging in front of France's most glorious chefs, and the awards continue to come.

OVERVIEW MAP **C3** 112 RUE DU FAUBOURG ST-HONORÉ, 8E
01-53-43-43-40 WWW.LEBRISTOLPARIS.COM

L'OFFICE *HOT SPOT • FUSION $$*

Kitchen personnel changes haven't diminished the quality or the taste of the plates gliding out of this American-owned Right Bank bistro. Expect bright-tasting, seasonal produce and locally farmed meat, and a helpful English-speaking sommelier to help you choose the perfect wine to accompany your meal.

OVERVIEW MAP **C4** 3 RUE RICHER, 9E
01-47-70-67-31

LES PAPILLES *HOT SPOT • FRENCH $$*

This popular bistro – whose name means "taste buds" – has won a loyal Parisian following for its deftly executed southwestern French dishes, such as candied pork cheek with gnocchi. Choose a wine from the market on premises and pay only for the amount you drink.

OVERVIEW MAP **D4** 30 RUE GAY LUSSAC, 5E
01-43-25-20-79 WWW.LESPAPILLESPARIS.FR

PÉTRELLE *ROMANTIC • FRENCH $$*
Local and in-season are the buzzwords at this charming bistro. Vegetables take the starring roles here, and expertly prepared meat, fish, and poultry are the award-winning support players.

OVERVIEW MAP **B4** 34 RUE PÉTRELLE, 9E
01-42-82-11-02 WWW.PETRELLE.FR

ROSEVAL *HOT SPOT • CONTEMPORARY FRENCH $$*
Ever since this tiny, noisy neobistro opened its doors in 2012, foodies-in-the-know have flocked to its north Paris location with dreams of degustation menus in their heads. Splurge on the food-and-wine pairing option, and you'll see what all the fuss is about.

OVERVIEW MAP **C5** 1 RUE D'EUPATORIA, 20E
09-53-56-24-14 WWW.ROSEVAL.FR

NIGHTLIFE

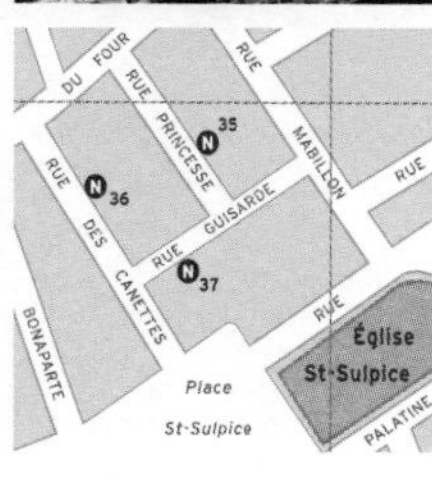

Best English pub: **THE BOMBARDIER,** p. 54

Best place to be seen: **LE MONTANA,** p. 55

Best bar to spot a former French president:
LA RHUMERIE, p. 55

Best bubbly bar: **LE DOKHAN'S BAR,** p. 57

Best cocktails: **BALLROOM DU BEEF CLUB,** p. 57

Best lounge: **ANDY WAHLOO,** p. 60

Best music: **LES TAULIÈRES,** p. 63

Best beer and bowling: **BOWLING MOUFFETARD,** p. 64

MAP 1 QUARTIER LATIN/LES ÎLES

THE BOMBARDIER *PUB*

Looking for an authentic English pub in Paris? The Bombardier, with its classic pub grub and ale on tap, is one of the best. It's also a great place to watch sports.

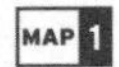
E4 N 25 2 PL. DU PANTHÉON, 5E
01-43-54-79-22 WWW.BOMBARDIERPUB.FR

CAVEAU DE LA HUCHETTE *JAZZ CLUB*

Since it opened in 1946, this jazz bar has welcomed many musical greats, including Count Basie and Sidney Bechet. Today, the energy still jumps with dance-till-you-drop live jazz.

MAP 1 B2 N 7 5 RUE DE LA HUCHETTE, 5E
01-43-26-65-05 WWW.CAVEAUDELAHUCHETTE.FR

CURIO PARLOR *BAR*

Curio Parlor, an intimate and cozy bar, serves up some of Paris's best mixed cocktails. It also stays open late for electro-pop DJ evenings.

MAP 1 C4 N 13 16 RUE DES BERNARDINS, 5E
01-44-07-12-47 WWW.CURIOPARLOR.COM

LA LUCHA LIBRE *BAR*

Margaritas and Mexican wrestling are the draw at this spirited, student-filled watering hole. Grab a bite of bar food at the upstairs restaurant, then head downstairs for your entertainment fix.

MAP 1 D4 N 22 10 RUE DE LA MONTAGNE SAINTE-GENEVIÈVE, 5E
01-43-29-59-86 WWW.LALUCHALIBRE.COM

MAP 2 ST-GERMAIN-DES-PRÉS

BAR DU MARCHÉ *LOUNGE*

Treat yourself to a truly Parisian address, from the Edith Piaf posters and the red banquettes to the traditionally uniformed waiters. Everyone comes here sooner or later.

MAP 2 C3 N 18 75 RUE DE SEINE, 6E
01-43-26-55-15

CASTEL *CLUB*

Since the 1960s, Castel has been a bastion of jet-set-aristo chic. Though the club never officially went out of style, today it enjoys a revival with their aptly named Prince and Princess parties.

MAP 2 E3 N 35 15 RUE PRINCESSE, 6E
01-40-51-52-80 WWW.CASTELPARIS.COM

CHEZ GEORGES *BAR*

This bar remains a quintessential stop for the under-25 crowd. Dancing and singing along to French *chanson* music in the vaulted cave below will transport you to Paris during the 1960s.

E3 N 36 11 RUE DES CANETTES, 6E
01-43-26-79-15

CURIO PARLOR

CASTEL

LE DIX BAR *BAR*

Low-key and cozy, this sangria bar popular with Sorbonne students is the ideal place to unwind after a long day on the sightseeing circuit. Carry coins to fuel the eclectic jukebox.

 D5 N 33 10 RUE DE L'ODÉON, 6E
01-43-26-66-83 HTTP://10BAR.PAGESPERSO-ORANGE.FR

L'ECHELLE DE JACOB *LOUNGE*

A sophisticated piano bar overflowing with classic elegance, L'Echelle de Jacob is known for welcoming well-dressed professionals who hail from the chic quarters of Paris.

 C3 N 15 10-12 RUE JACOB, 6E
01-46-34-00-29 WWW.ECHELLEDEJACOB.COM

LE MONTANA *LOUNGE*

More intimate than a nightclub, Le Montana has become the hottest nightspot around, welcoming celebrities and fashion models. This is the place to be during Paris Fashion Week.

 D2 N 25 28 RUE ST-BENOÎT, 6E
01-45-44-60-60

LE POUSSE-AU-CRIME *BAR*

Chatty folk and friendly service bring a bevy of young travelers, students, and the congenitally social to this easygoing place.

 E3 N 37 15 RUE GUISARDE, 6E
01-46-33-36-63 WWW.LEPOUSSEAUCRIME.FR

PRESCRIPTION COCKTAIL CLUB *BAR*

Resembling a 19th-century library, this atmospheric bar prescribes trendy cocktails to cure all ailments. The treatment seems to agree with the hip, young crowds who flock here.

 C4 N 19 23 RUE MAZARINE, 6E
01-45-08-88-09 WWW.PRESCRIPTIONCOCKTAILCLUB.COM

LA RHUMERIE *BAR*

Man Ray frequented this family-run bar back in the 1930s, and today, you might see Rhumerie regular Jacques Chirac in the corner sipping a rum cocktail.

 D3 N 31 166 BD. ST-GERMAIN, 6E
01-43-54-28-94 WWW.LARHUMERIE.COM

LE SHOWCASE

LE BAR DU PLAZA ATHÉNÉE

MAP 3 INVALIDES

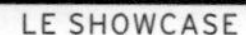

NIGHTLIFE

BAR DU LUTETIA *LOUNGE*

Your mixed drink in this hotel bar comes steeped in history and culture. It's a classic literary hangout, and the cool atmosphere and live piano still attract writers, politicians, and thespians.

MAP 3 D6 41 HÔTEL LUTETIA, 45 BD. RASPAIL, 6E
01-49-54-46-09 WWW.LUTETIA-PARIS.COM

THE CLUB *BAR*

At this "chaotic chic" bar, scrumptious club sandwiches are served alongside inventive cocktails and whiskeys from around the world. For intimate conversation, brave the slippery staircase and settle into the downstairs lounge.

MAP 3 C1 25 24 RUE SURCOUF, 7E
01-45-50-31-54 WWW.THECLUB-PARIS.COM

LE SHOWCASE *CLUB*

Located under the illustrious Pont Alexandre III, Le Showcase is best known for its packed calendar of live club nights and a fun-loving Parisian clientele.

MAP 3 A2 7 UNDER THE PONT ALEXANDRE III, PORT DES CHAMPS-ELYSÉES, 8E
01-45-61-25-43 WWW.SHOWCASE.FR

MAP 4 TOUR EIFFEL/ARC DE TRIOMPHE/TROCADÉRO

LE BAR DU PLAZA ATHÉNÉE *BAR*

This is a classic hotel bar, with comfortable chairs, wood paneling, and a modern twist that includes a bar lit from within. It's the summit of chic in a neighborhood dripping with riches.

MAP 3 B5 18 HÔTEL PLAZA ATHÉNÉE, 25 AV. MONTAIGNE, 8E
01-53-67-66-00 WWW.PLAZA-ATHENEE-PARIS.COM

LE BARON *CLUB*
Le Baron remains one of the most exclusive clubs in Paris. Party people and celebrities press to be seen at this nightspot for the elite.

MAP 4 C4 Ⓜ 21 6 AV. MARCEAU, 8E
01-47-20-04-01 WWW.CLUBLEBARON.COM

 **LE DOKHAN'S BAR** *CHAMPAGNE BAR*
Choose among 60 bottles of bubbly poured by an impossibly professional staff. Eiffel Tower views and a crackling fireplace encourage lingering for more than one *coupe* (glass).

MAP 4 D1 Ⓜ 23 117 RUE LAURISTON, 16E
01-53-65-66-99 WWW.RADISSONBLU.COM/DOKHANHOTEL-PARISTROCADERO

SIR WINSTON *BAR*
Old London style reigns at this homey lounge in the shadow of the Arc de Triomphe. Sink into a leather club chair and sip your cocktail while the DJ spins soothing R&B.

MAP 4 B2 Ⓜ 14 5 RUE DE PRESBOURG, 16E
01-40-67-17-37 WWW.SIRWINSTON.FR

MAP 5 GRANDS BOULEVARDS

BUDDHA BAR *CLUB*
The luxe, Asian decor might transport you to old Hong Kong – or a movie-set approximation. Count on the invigorating tunes and an interesting crowd to keep you entertained while sipping your mai tai.

MAP 5 E1 Ⓜ 43 8-BIS RUE BOISSY D'ANGLAS, 8E
01-53-05-90-00 WWW.BUDDHA-BAR.COM

HARRY'S NEW YORK BAR *BAR*
At Harry's, you can pretend you're Hemingway or another grizzled journalist newly back from the Spanish Civil War. Chances are you won't be the only one, though. Drink your Scotch straight here.

MAP 5 B4 Ⓜ 8 5 RUE DAUNOU, 2E
01-42-61-71-14 WWW.HARRYS-BAR.FR

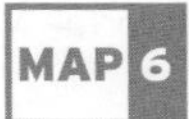

MAP 6 LOUVRE/LES HALLES

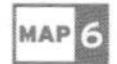 **BALLROOM DU BEEF CLUB** *BAR*
The folks behind successful Paris bars Curio Parlor and Experimental Cocktail Club have struck gold again with this modern speakeasy where old-time absinthe cocktails meet hipster cool. Beef Club, the restaurant upstairs, is a meat-eater's mecca.

MAP 6 C3 Ⓜ 22 58 RUE JEAN-JACQUES ROUSSEAU, 1ER
09-54-37-13-65

HOTEL BARS

If you're cutting costs by staying in a modestly priced hotel, splurge your spare euros on a bit of indulgent hotel bar-hopping. With the closing of the Hemingway Bar while the Ritz gets a facelift, Le Bar 228 at **Hótel Le Meurice (p. 117)** is the new go-to. The see-and-be-seen vibe is hottest at the stylish **Le Bar du Plaza Athénée (p. 56)** in Hótel Plaza Athénée, but the fickle fashion pack can also be found posing late into the night at Le Bar du Bristol in **Le Bristol Paris (p. 121).** The Champagne and caviar set will find more of their kind, along with some really fabulous bubbly, at the elegant **Le Dokhan's Bar (p. 57)** at the Radisson Blu Le Dokhan's Hotel, Paris Trocadéro.

CAB *CLUB*

Exotic and beautiful urbanites flock to this exclusive, immense bar/restaurant that comes alive with DJ pulses. For an intimate archway table, reserve in advance. Brace yourself for pricey, bottle-only orders.

2 PL. DU PALAIS ROYAL, 1ER
01-58-62-56-25 WWW.CABARET.FR

CLUB 18 *QUEER*

The oldest gay club in Paris might also be the smallest gay club in Paris, but the dance-inspiring techno music and shimmering disco balls will help you forget about the lack of space.

18 RUE DE BEAUJOLAIS, 1ER
01-42-97-52-13 WWW.CLUB18.FR

LE DUC DES LOMBARDS *JAZZ CLUB*

A famous jazz haunt, the Duc welcomes international stars and local favorites. Reserve a table in advance for prime jazz-listening.

 D6 N 36

42 RUE DES LOMBARDS, 1ER
01-42-33-22-88 WWW.DUCDESLOMBARDS.COM

EXPERIMENTAL COCKTAIL CLUB *LOUNGE*

This is rated as one of the best cocktail bars in Paris. The ambiance is hip and friendly, while the cocktail list is long and worth experimentation.

 A4 N 4

37 RUE ST-SAUVEUR, 2E
01-45-08-88-09 WWW.EXPERIMENTALCOCKTAILCLUB.COM

LE FUMOIR *BAR*

When not used as a canteen for the fashion shows at the neighboring Louvre, this restaurant/bar and its cozy library draw stylish Parisians in search of a perfectly poured cocktail.

 E3 N 40

6 RUE DE L'AMIRAL DE COLIGNY, 1ER
01-42-92-00-24 WWW.LEFUMOIR.COM

CLUB 18

1979

LA GARDE ROBE *WINE BAR*

Locals in the know come for the natural wines and rustic cheese plates served late into the night. Table seating is limited, but advance bookings are accepted and encouraged.

 E4 Ⓝ 41 41 RUE DE L'ABRE SEC, 2E
01-49-26-90-60

KONG *BAR*

Carrie Bradshaw was one of the first to try Kong, in the final season of *Sex and the City*. Since then, it has been a classic nightspot for enjoying a late meal or an early cocktail.

 F4 Ⓝ 46 1 RUE DU PONT NEUF, 1ER
01-40-39-09-00 WWW.KONG.FR

LE MAGNIFIQUE *LOUNGE*

Belle-Mondo and the Atomic Kitten are two of the popular mixed drinks created by Colin Field for Le Magnifique, a discreet lounge with a 1970s playboy appeal.

MAP 6 D1 Ⓝ 28 25 RUE DE RICHELIEU, 1ER
06-19-71-37-26 WWW.LEMAGNIFIQUE.FR

1979 *BAR*

Restaurant by day, funk-filled music party by night, 1979 attracts a vibrant young crowd keen on dancing until dawn – literally. The fun doesn't end here until 6 A.M.

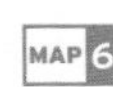 D3 Ⓝ 32 49 RUE BERGER, 1ER
01-40-41-08-78
WWW.MILLENEUFCENTSOIXANTEDIXNEUF.FR

LE SOCIAL CLUB *CLUB*

The dance floor is the draw at this steamy club where local and international DJs spin the fiercest grooves in town.

 A2 Ⓝ 1 142 RUE MONTMARTRE, 2E
06-79-97-85-48 WWW.PARISSOCIALCLUB.COM

SUNSET/SUNSIDE *JAZZ CLUB*

The tiny jazz club Sunset, a dark and intimate cellar, has a street-level venue, Sunside. Both fill up quickly, but get there early and you can often nab a free spot.

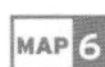 D6 Ⓝ 35 60 RUE DES LOMBARDS, 1ER
01-40-26-46-60 WWW.SUNSET-SUNSIDE.COM

NIGHTLIFE

ANDY WAHLOO

WANDERLUST

MAP 7 MARAIS

ANDY WAHLOO *LOUNGE*

In this Moroccan souk atmosphere, the beautiful people and fashion types come to start their evening. Andy Wahloo was launched by the owners of the famous Momo Club in London.

 MAP 7 B1 N 10
69 RUE DES GRAVILLIERS, 3E
01-42-71-20-38 WWW.MOMORESTO.COM

LA BELLE HORTENSE *WINE BAR*

Feel like an old friend immediately in this small bookstore and wine bar, where vintages and titles are lovingly chosen by a discerning staff. Literary discussions flow easily at the bar.

 MAP 7 D4 N 37
31 RUE VIEILLE DU TEMPLE, 4E
01-48-04-71-60

CANDELARIA *BAR*

From the outside, it's merely a hip Marais taco shop; push through the doors at the back of this tiny eatery and enter a dark and moody bar where tasty mixed cocktails reign.

 MAP 7 A4 N 5
52 RUE SAINTONGE, 3E
01-42-74-41-28 WWW.CANDELARIAPARIS.COM

DERNIER BAR AVANT LA FIN DU MONDE *BAR*

Sci-fi kitsch and imaginative tipples (try the Pan Galactic Gargle Blaster if you dare) make for a fun night at this end-of-the-world-themed bar.

 MAP 7 E1 N 46
19 AV. VICTORIA, 1ER
01-53-00-98-95 WWW.DERNIERBAR.COM

LE DUPLEX *QUEER*

Small, smoky, arty, and so Parisian, this is a neighborhood fixture and bar with character. Expect an eclectic, mainly gay crowd, cheap drinks, and cool music that's never too loud.

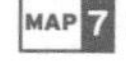 MAP 7 B2 N 11
25 RUE MICHEL LE COMTE, 3E
01-42-72-80-86 WWW.DUPLEX-BAR.COM

MIXER BAR *BAR*

Among the many bars in the Marais, Mixer stands out for its good music. DJs spin the latest electro for an appropriately mixed crowd.

MAP 7 D3 N 33 23 RUE STE-CROIX DE LA BRETONNERIE, 4E
01-48-87-55-44 WWW.MIXERBAR.COM

LA PERLE *BAR*

Despite the rather nondescript appeal of this neighborhood bar, La Perle has become a favorite with the fashion pack, who often hold court late into the night.

MAP 7 C4 N 22 78 RUE VIEILLE DU TEMPLE, 3E
01-42-72-69-93

LE 3W KAFÉ *QUEER*

One of the most happening lesbian bars in the city, the 3W Kafé is known for its specialty cocktails and menu of accompanying aphrodisiacs.

MAP 7 D4 N 41 8 RUE DES ECOUFFES, 4E
01-47-87-39-26

MAP 8 BASTILLE

BOTTLE SHOP *BAR*

Music lovers will feel at home at one of the many electro-pop DJ evenings held here. Clients are trendy 20-somethings who appreciate the warm and friendly vibe.

MAP 8 B5 N 19 5 RUE TROUSSEAU, 11E
01-43-14-28-04 WWW.CHEAPBLONDE.COM

RED HOUSE *BAR*

In true Texas style, this Southwest-themed watering hole is equipped with two bars spread across two rooms, offering room to spread out and enjoy the spicy cocktails.

MAP 8 A6 N 9 1-BIS RUE DE LA FORGE ROYALE, 11E
01-43-67-06-43

LE RÉSERVOIR *CLUB*

Nightly musical performances span the spectrum from 1980s pop (The Cure played here) to folk to reggae, but the popular Sunday brunch is always backed by a live jazz soundtrack.

MAP 8 A6 N 7 16 RUE DE LA FORGE ROYALE, 11E
01-43-56-39-60 WWW.RESERVOIRCLUB.COM

LE VIADUC CAFÉ *LOUNGE*

A mellow vibe keeps this place going long past the rest of the sleepy neighborhood – late-night snackers can dine until 2 A.M. The terrace is much coveted on summer nights.

MAP 8 C5 N 28 43 AV. DAUMESNIL, 12E
01-44-74-70-70 WWW.LEVIADUC-CAFE.COM

WANDERLUST *CLUB*

Dancing until dawn is what's on at this lime-green behemoth on the banks of the Seine. You'll find a young, vibrant crowd and fresh DJs mixing inspired grooves.

MAP 8 F5 N 32 32 QUAI D'AUSTERLITZ, 13E
01-76-77-25-30 WWW.WANDERLUSTPARIS.COM

MAP 9 MONTMARTRE

LE CARMEN *CLUB*

Composer George Bizet wrote the opera *Carmen* while living in this Montmartre house-turned-nightclub. The belle époque charm is as intoxicating as the house cocktails.

F3 N 33 34 RUE DUPERRÉ, 9E
01-45-26-50-00 WWW.LE-CARMEN.FR

CHEZ MOUNE *CLUB*

Located in a former lesbian cabaret, Chez Moune has relaunched with a new crowd of party-goers, thanks to nightclub impresarios André and Lionel, owners of the trendsetting club Le Baron.

MAP 9 F4 N 35 54 RUE JEAN-BAPTISTE PIGALLE, 9E
01-45-26-64-64

LE CHOPE DU CHÂTEAU ROUGE *BAR*

The unpretentious, welcoming feel of this hilltop bar is aided and abetted by happy-hour drinks and free couscous nights. After dark, the neighborhood can feel rough around the edges but still retains its charm.

MAP 9 A6 N 3 40 RUE DE CLIGNANCOURT, 18E
01-46-06-20-10

LE DIVAN DU MONDE *CLUB*

Baudelaire, Toulouse-Lautrec, and Picasso were illustrious regu-

RUE OBERKAMPF

Far from the beaten path of most tourist destinations, rue Oberkampf has developed into one of the city's most vibrant nightlife destinations. **Nouveau Casino (p. 65)** welcomes international DJs for all-night music sessions, while its sister restaurant next door, Le Café Charbon (109 rue Oberkampf, 11E, 01-43-57-55-13), is a good place to enjoy cocktails until 4 A.M. on weekends. Not far away is **Ave Maria (p. 64),** a festive bar lined with garlands and tiki decor, much-loved for its authentic *mojitos* and late-night South American cuisine. L'Alimentation Générale (64 rue Jean-Pierre Timbaud, 11E, 01-43-55-42-50) attracts night-loving crowds for mixed programs such as live concerts, funk and soul DJs, and artistic film projections.

LE CARMEN

CHEZ PRUNE

lars at this club. Today the Divan is a concert hall, club venue, and host to various events, including talks with filmmakers like David Lynch.

 E5 N29 75 RUE DES MARTYRS, 18E
01-44-92-77-66 WWW.DIVANDUMONDE.COM

L'ELYSÉE-MONTMARTRE *LIVE MUSIC*

The French can-can was born within these celebrated walls, and the metallic framework found inside was designed by Gustav Eiffel. DJs spin each weekend, while the week welcomes big artists on the international music scene.

 D6 N26 72 BD. DE ROCHECHOUART, 18E
01-44-92-45-36 WWW.ELYSEEMONTMARTRE.COM

LA FOURMI *BAR*

Its charm may be hard to define, but a mix of hard-living and better-groomed Parisians still stream in for late-night hobnobbing – perhaps as a warm-up to neighboring clubs.

MAP 9 E5 N30 74 RUE DES MARTYRS, 18E
01-42-64-70-35

MARLUSSE ET LAPIN *BAR*

Quirky (tables made from vintage sewing machines) and hip (a perpetually young and good-looking crowd), this tiny bar boasts tasty cocktails, beer, and wine at down-to-earth prices. Come early or call to reserve a table.

 E4 N28 4 RUE GERMAIN PILON, 18E
01-42-59-17-97

LES TAULIÈRES *BAR*

Owners Cath and Nath are local favorites in the Montmartre scene, greeting new visitors like old friends. Their loyal, hip clientele appreciates their superb cocktail creations as well as the DJ music.

 A3 N1 10 RUE DE LA FONTAINE DU BUT, 18E
01-42-58-60-64 WWW.LESTAULIERES.COM

MAP 10 CANAL ST-MARTIN

AVE MARIA *BAR*

An evening at this colorful bar/restaurant is almost as good as a trip to the tropics. Fruity cocktails, vivid decor, and warm service form the perfect Friday night trifecta.

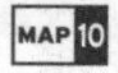 F5 Ⓝ 25 1 RUE JACQUARE, 11E
01-47-00-61-73

CHEZ PRUNE *BAR*

This no-frills café/bar's secret allure draws the thirsty hordes. Stay for the late-night pints of beer, and return in the morning for a *café crème* (coffee with cream) on the sunny sidewalk terrace.

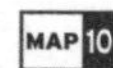 E3 Ⓝ 21 36 RUE BEAUREPAIRE, 10E
01-42-41-30-47

LE COMPTOIR GÉNÉRAL *BAR*

Part of the new wave of hybrid venues, this café/cinema/museum is a mishmash of amusements. Come for Sunday brunch, a late-night film, or a refreshing drink before dinner at a local brasserie.

 D3 Ⓝ 16 80 QUAI DE JEMAPPES, 10E
01-44-88-24-46 WWW.LECOMPTOIRGENERAL.COM

HÔTEL DU NORD *BAR*

The Hôtel du Nord's latest incarnation as a low-key restaurant and bar might be its best. The upstairs library is yours to explore, and chess, backgammon, and dice can be found in the small salon.

 D2 Ⓝ 8 102 QUAI DE JEMMAPES, 10E
01-40-40-78-78 WWW.HOTELDUNORD.ORG

POINT ÉPHÉMÈRE *BAR*

Give a dilapidated factory a modern makeover, then add a dash of youth culture and you've got Point Éphémère. Seven days a week, this contemporary arts venue serves drinks, music, art, and dance on tap.

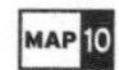 B2 Ⓝ 4 200 QUAI DE VALMY, 10E
01-40-34-02-48 WWW.POINTEPHEMERE.ORG

OVERVIEW MAP

BOWLING MOUFFETARD *PUB*

This subterranean house of fun isn't just for the kids, despite the pinball machines and *minifoot* (foosball) tables. Besides bowling and billiards by the hour, a fully stocked bar keeps adults happy until 2 A.M. every night.

OVERVIEW MAP D4 73 RUE MOUFFETARD, 5E
01-43-31-09-35 WWW.BOWLINGMOUFFETARD.FR

FAVELA CHIC *CLUB*

Claustrophobics should stay clear of this legendary jam-packed

POINT ÉPHÉMÈRE

BOWLING MOUFFETARD

Brazilian restaurant and club. It has some of the best beats in Paris – down a raspberry caipirinha and start shaking.

OVERVIEW MAP C5 18 RUE DU FAUBOURG DU TEMPLE, 10E
01-40-21-38-14 WWW.FAVELACHIC.COM

NOUVEAU CASINO *LIVE MUSIC*

Behind Le Café Charbon, this concert and club space hosts some of the capital's newest and best in techno, pop, and rock. It's a hub of the rue Oberkampf night scene.

OVERVIEW MAP C5 109 RUE OBERKAMPF, 11E
01-43-57-57-40 WWW.NOUVEAUCASINO.NET

LE POMPON *CLUB*

Before it was a nightclub, it was a synagogue, which might explain the heavenly beats pumping through the sound system. Wear your dancing shoes and bring your Parisian swagger.

OVERVIEW MAP C4 39 RUE DES PETITES ECURIES, 10E
01-53-34-60-85

ROSA BONHEUR *BAR*

Known as a *guinguette*, literally a place where all walks of life come to eat, drink, and dance, Rosa Bonheur overflows with enthusiastic scenesters, especially during the warmer months.

OVERVIEW MAP B5 2 ALLÉE DE LA CASCADE, PARC DES BUTTES-CHAUMONT, 19E
01-42-00-00-45 WWW.ROSABONHEUR.FR

SHOPS

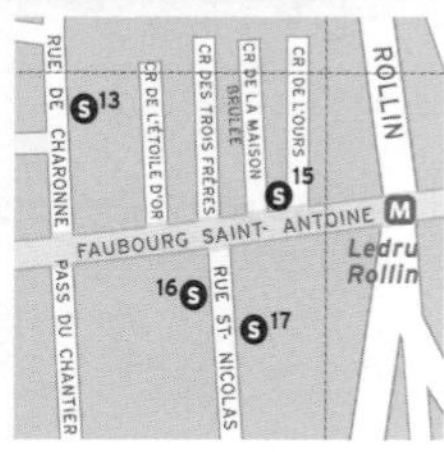

Best selection of unusual books: **ASSOULINE,** p. 68

Best candles: **CIRE TRUDON,** p. 69

Most interesting perfumes:
EDITIONS DE PARFUM FRÉDÉRIC MALLE, p. 71

Best selection of gourmet goodies under one roof:
LA GRANDE EPICERIE DU BON MARCHÉ, p. 71

Best pastry selection: **LA PÂTISSERIE DES RÊVES,** p. 71

Sexiest lingerie: **SABBIA ROSA,** p. 72

Most luxurious spa: **ANNE FONTAINE,** p. 74

Best for shabby chic decor: **ASTIER DE VILLATTE,** p. 74

Best mustard boutique: **BOUTIQUE MAILLE,** p. 74

Best French Fashion Experience: **COLETTE,** p. 75

Best French beauty products: **BY TERRY,** p. 77

Best French kitchen gear: **E. DEHILLERIN,** p. 78

Best place to browse during a rainstorm:
GALERIE VIVIENNE, p. 78

Best concept store: **THE BROKEN ARM,** p. 80

Best shopping street for Sunday strolling:
RUE DES FRANCS-BOURGEOIS, p. 81

Best place to meet the green fairy:
VERT D'ABSINTHE, p. 81

MAP 1 QUARTIER LATIN/LES ÎLES

LE BONBON AU PALAIS *GOURMET GOODIES*
It's not just the kids who salivate over the vintage glass decanters brimming with bonbons. Fill up on artisanal marshmallows, chewy caramels, and fruit-flavored jellies from every corner of France.

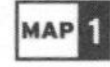 D5 Ⓢ 23 19 RUE MONGE, 5E
01-78-56-15-72 WWW.BONBONSAUPALAIS.FR

DIPTYQUE *GIFT AND HOME*
The famed perfumery's flagship boutique is more than just a retail store; it's a mood-lifting experience. Choose from candle scents like brioche, leather, and fig, which come in both standard and portable travel sizes.

 C4 Ⓢ 14 34 BD. ST-GERMAIN, 6E
01-43-26-77-44 WWW.DIPTYQUEPARIS.FR

MARCHÉ AUX FLEURS/ MARCHÉ AUX OISEAUX *GIFT AND HOME*
This oft-painted flower market is one of the last in Paris. Come to enjoy the colors and fragrances any day. Songbirds join the fray on Sundays.

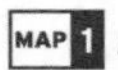 A2 Ⓢ 3 PL. LOUIS LÉPINE, 4E

SHAKESPEARE AND CO. *BOOKS*
A landmark of literary Paris, this cultish bookstore has hosted great American expats, from the Lost Generation to today's poets. Cozy up with a book in the upstairs library.

 B2 Ⓢ 8 37 RUE DE LA BÛCHERIE, 5E
01-43-25-40-93 WWW.SHAKESPEARECO.ORG

MAP 2 ST-GERMAIN-DES-PRÉS

ADELLINE *JEWELRY*
A staple of Left Bank fashion, Adelline has built a very Parisian clientele by offering a delicate range of jewelry made from semi-precious stones in fashionable gold settings.

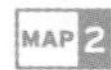 C1 Ⓢ 9 54 RUE JACOB, 6E
01-47-03-07-18 WWW.ADELLINE.COM

ASSOULINE *BOOKS*
French publisher Assouline has conquered the international jet-set with books on everything from fashion and the arts to culture and lifestyle. This boutique bookstore also sells a selection of home objects and novelties.

 D2 Ⓢ 22 35 RUE BONAPARTE, 6E
01-43-29-23-20 WWW.ASSOULINE.COM

LA CERISE SUR LE CHAPEAU *ACCESSORIES*
Create your own panama hat for summer or felt fedora for winter.

SHAKESPEARE AND CO.

MARIE MERCIÉ

Designer Cerise Bentz will guide you through her three-step process to customize your own personal look.

 F3 Ⓝ48 11 RUE CASSETTE, 6E
01-45-49-90-53 WWW.LACERISESURLECHAPEAU.COM

CIRE TRUDON *GIFT AND HOME*

Founded in 1643, Cire Trudon was the candle maker for the kings of France. Relaunched in 2007, it has become the smart choice for fashionable scented gifts.

 E4 Ⓢ40 78 RUE DE SEINE, 6E
01-43-26-46-50 WWW.CIRETRUDON.COM

LADURÉE BEAUTÉ *GIFT AND HOME*

Its macaroons are a cult favorite, and now, the celebrated house of Ladurée is generating a new legion of fans with its line of decadent candles, perfumes, and lotions.

 21 RUE BONAPARTE, 6E
01-44-07-64-87 WWW.LADUREE.FR

MAISON DE FAMILLE *GIFT AND HOME*

Maison de Famille carries upscale home decor and accessories in the French *maison de campagne* style for those who have ever dreamed of owning a French country house.

 E4 Ⓢ43 29 RUE ST-SULPICE, 6E
01-46-33-99-91 WWW.MAISONDEFAMILLE.FR

MARIE MERCIÉ *CLOTHING AND ACCESSORIES*

Celebrity milliner Marie Mercié's fanciful, feminine hats have adorned the heads of everyone from Princess Diana to Kristin Scott Thomas. Try one on for a shot of instant glamour.

 E4 Ⓢ41 24 RUE ST-SULPICE, 6E
01-43-26-45-83 WWW.MARIEMERCIE.COM

MONA *CLOTHING AND ACCESSORIES*

Mona is a one-stop boutique offering the ultimate in luxury designer women's clothing and accessories. Brands like Chloé, Lanvin, and Pierre Hardy keep the ladies of St-Germain in high fashion.

 C2 Ⓢ12 17 RUE BONAPARTE, 6E
01-44-07-07-27

LA GRANDE EPICERIE DU BON MARCHÉ

LA PÂTISSERIE DES RÊVES

PAUL & JOE *CLOTHING AND ACCESSORIES*
Named after the designer's two young sons, this French brand is known for well-cut jeans, flowing tops, and hip little dresses for the younger crowd.

 66 RUE DES STS-PÈRES, 7E
01-42-22-47-01 WWW.PAULANDJOE.COM

SHOPS

PIERRE HERMÉ *GOURMET GOODIES*
At first glance, this gourmet patisserie looks like a jewelry boutique, with star chef Hermé's beautiful pastries lined up like gems. Look for inventive flavor combinations and seasonally changing ingredients.

 72 RUE BONAPARTE, 6E
01-43-54-47-77 WWW.PIERREHERME.COM

POILÂNE *GOURMET GOODIES*
In France, it's not just bread, it's "Poilâne." Although the famed baker died in 2002, his daughter has sworn to uphold the family's reputation.

 8 RUE DU CHERCHE MIDI, 6E
01-45-48-42-59 WWW.POILANE.FR

VANESSA BRUNO *CLOTHING AND SHOES*
Funky fashion for 20-somethings with fabulous figures, these pieces reconcile comfort, taste, and modernity. Bruno excels in little T-shirts, floaty layers, and asymmetric hems.

 25 RUE ST-SULPICE, 6E
01-43-54-41-04 WWW.VANESSABRUNO.COM

MAP 3 INVALIDES

BARTHÉLEMY *GOURMET GOODIES*
This is considered to be the haute couture shop of French cheese, so let yourself be guided by the experts into gourmet specialties such as farmhouse brie and goat cheese in olive oil.

 51 RUE DE GRENELLE, 7E
01-42-22-82-24

BONTON *KIDS STUFF*
This concept store bathes the world of little ones in colorful duds and fun things for their bedrooms. The under-10s and their parents will find bright, modern, and straightforward styles.

MAP 3 C5 S 30 82 RUE DE GRENELLE, 7E
01-44-39-09-20 WWW.BONTON.FR

DEBAUVE ET GALLAIS *GOURMET GOODIES*
Chocolate maker to kings of France and other fortunate folk for over 200 years, this historic shop serves up old-fashioned "medicinal" chocolates and delicious modern concoctions.

MAP 3 B6 S 22 30 RUE DES STS-PÈRES, 7E
01-45-48-54-67 WWW.DEBAUVE-ET-GALLAIS.COM

EDITIONS DE PARFUM FRÉDÉRIC MALLE *BATH AND BEAUTY*
Malle, the grandson of the creator of Dior perfumes, has created an exquisite shop for his "editions" of original scents. The staff will patiently help you find the right scent.

MAP 3 C6 S 35 37 RUE DE GRENELLE, 7E
01-42-22-77-22 WWW.EDITIONSDEPARFUMS.COM

LA GRANDE EPICERIE DU BON MARCHÉ *GOURMET GOODIES*
Paris's oldest department store is as grand and captivating as when Zola wrote about it in the 1880s. Live out your gourmet fantasy in the cavernous grocery store (La Grande Epicerie), adjacent to the main store.

MAP 3 D6 S 42 38 RUE DE SÈVRES, 7E
01-44-39-81-00 WWW.LEBONMARCHE.COM

LIBRAIRIE STUDIO 7L *BOOKS*
When not designing clothing, fashion guru Karl Lagerfeld sketches, takes photographs, and reads voraciously. This bookstore, crammed ceiling to floor with art tomes, celebrates his inner bibliophile.

MAP 3 B6 S 18 7 RUE DE LILLE, 7E
01-42-92-03-58 WWW.LIBRAIRIE7L.COM

MODA *SHOES*
Situated on a street known for its designer discount shops, Moda is heaven for bargain-hunting shoe lovers. Last season's Chloé and Marc Jacobs are among the draw, with a wide selection of models and sizes.

MAP 3 E6 S 49 45 RUE ST-PLACIDE, 6E
01-45-49-32-60

1 ET 1 FONT 3 *CLOTHING AND ACCESSORIES*
Think "yummy mummy" at the maternity boutique favored by French celebrities and their growing bumps. The starter kit, with five sartorial essentials, makes a practical yet thoughtful gift.

MAP 3 B4 S 11 3 RUE DE SOLFÉRINO, 7E
01-40-62-92-15 WWW.1ET1FONT3.COM

LA PÂTISSERIE DES RÊVES *GOURMET GOODIES*
Philippe Conticini has been making dreams come true with his reinterpretation of classic French pastries, like his Saint-Honoré

cream pastry and *mille-feuille du dimanche* (layered puff pastry with vanilla cream). Tasting is believing.

MAP 3 D5 S 40 93 RUE DU BAC, 7E
01-42-84-00-82 WWW.LAPATISSERIEDESREVES.COM

LES PRAIRIES DE PARIS *CLOTHING AND ACCESSORIES*
A women's collection of basic French classics, which, depending on the season, could be the perfect-fitting woolen pea-coat or the striped navy shirt of your dreams.

MAP 3 B6 S 21 6 RUE DU PRÉ AUX CLERCS, 7E
01-40-20-44-12 WWW.LESPRAIRIESDEPARIS.COM

PRINCE JARDINIER AND MAISON DEYROLLE *GIFT AND HOME*
Prince Louis-Albert de Broglie has brought his chic "gentleman farmer" garden accessories to the historic house of Deyrolle: a taxidermy boutique and museum, adored by Parisians.

MAP 3 B5 S 17 46 RUE DU BAC, 7E
01-42-22-30-07 WWW.DEYROLLE.COM

SABBIA ROSA *CLOTHING*
Step into this boudoir-style boutique – it feels naughty but so nice to indulge in the flirty silk lingerie and dresses that are its trademark pieces.

MAP 3 C6 S 34 73 RUE DES STS-PÈRES, 6E
01-45-48-88-37

SENTOU *GIFT AND HOME*
Sentou offers modern, fresh French design objects and furniture from big interior design names and from the boutique's own label.

MAP 3 C6 S 36 26 BD. RASPAIL, 7E
01-45-49-00-05 WWW.SENTOU.FR

MAP 4 TOUR EIFFEL/ARC DE TRIOMPHE/TROCADÉRO

CHAMPS-ELYSÉES *SHOPPING DISTRICT*
If it's couture you're looking for, head to Champs-Elysées and its side streets, avenue George V and avenue Montaigne. This ultra-exclusive shopping quarter, nicknamed the Golden Triangle, is home to the top fashion houses in the city.

MAP 4 A3 S 8 AV. DES CHAMPS-ELYSÉES, AV. GEORGE V, AND AV. MONTAIGNE WWW.CHAMPSELYSEES.ORG

GRÉGORY RENARD CHOCOLATIER: CACAO ET MACARONS *GOURMET GOODIES*
It's a tight race for the title of best *macaron* in Paris, but the chocolate variety concocted at this tantalizing boutique is a front-runner. The bitter chocolate caramels aren't too bad, either.

MAP 4 E5 S 38 120 RUE ST-DOMINIQUE, 7E
01-47-05-19-17 WWW.CACAOETMACARONS.COM

GUERLAIN *BATH, BEAUTY, AND SPA*
This magnificent flagship store alone may justify a trip to Paris.

LADURÉE

LOUIS VUITTON

You'll find rare fragrances, beauty-artist Olivier Echaudmaison's makeup line, and the added luxury of an unparalleled day spa.

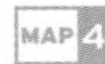 A4 S 11 68 AV. DES CHAMPS-ELYSÉES, 8E
01-45-62-52-57 WWW.GUERLAIN.FR

LADURÉE *GOURMET GOODIES*
Step back in time when you enter the gilded, sumptuous decor at this branch of the renowned Paris tearoom. Come for lunch or simply a pastry, and be sure to taste one of the famous macaroon cookies.

 A4 S 12 75 AV. DES CHAMPS-ELYSÉES, 8E
01-40-75-08-75 WWW.LADUREE.FR

LOUIS VUITTON *CLOTHING AND ACCESSORIES*
There is often a line to enter this flagship store on the Champs-Elysées. Handbags and clothes bearing the famous Louis Vuitton monogram mix effortlessly alongside installations by artists like Olafur Eliasson.

 A3 S 9 101 AV. DES CHAMPS-ELYSÉES, 8E
01-53-57-52-00 WWW.LOUISVUITTON.COM

RUE CLER *SHOPPING DISTRICT*
Cobbled Rue Cler turns into a pedestrian-friendly marketplace lined with boutiques that meld the quaint with the practical. Wine shops and *fromageries* (cheese shops) sidle up to Italian delis and fragrant *boulangeries* (bakeries).

 E6 S 40 RUE CLER BETWEEN RUE DE GRENELLE AND RUE DE LA MOTTE PICQUET

MAP 5 GRANDS BOULEVARDS

ALICE CADOLLE *CLOTHING*
Founded in 1889 by Herminie Cadolle, this boutique abounds in luxury lingerie and the movie stars who appreciate it.

 D2 S 35 4 RUE CAMBON, 1ER
01-42-60-94-22 WWW.CADOLLE.COM

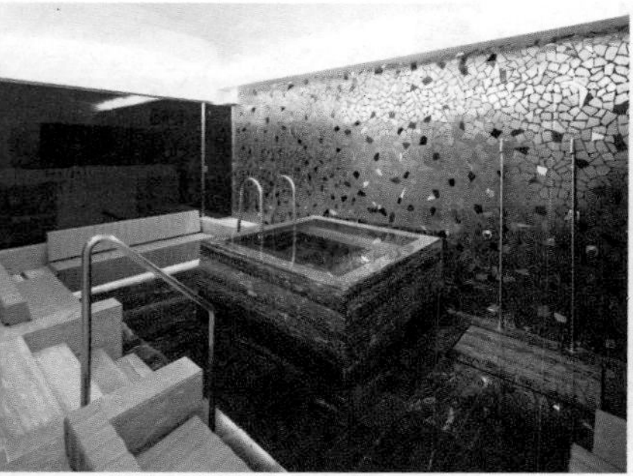

ANNE FONTAINE

FAUCHON

ANNE FONTAINE *SPA*

Anne Fontaine has added a spa to her specialty shirt boutique, and it is no ordinary destination. It offers some of the best treatments and massages in Paris, conjuring pure luxurious bliss.

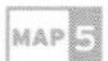 D5 41
270 RUE ST-HONORÉ, 1ER
01-42-61-03-70 WWW.ANNEFONTAINE.COM

ASTIER DE VILLATTE *GIFT AND HOME*

This is the ultimate boutique for lovers of French shabby chic, best known for its selection of rustic white tableware, although chic beauty and decoration objects are also sold.

 D5 42
173 RUE ST-HONORÉ, 1ER
01-42-60-74-13 WWW.ASTIERDEVILLATTE.COM

ATELIER DU BRACELET PARISIEN *ACCESSORIES*

Artisan Jean-Claude Perrin is considered to be the worldwide reference concerning matters of luxury watchbands. At A.B.P. each band has been carefully handmade in a range of leathers and exotic skins.

 C4 27
28 PL. DU MARCHÉ ST-HONORÉ, 1ER
01-42-86-13-70 WWW.ABP-PARIS.COM

ATELIERS D'ART DE FRANCE *GIFT AND HOME*

Works by over 300 French artisans are exhibited and sold by the Studios of French Art, from deco objects to lighting, tableware, jewelry, and fashion accessories: Items are either unique pieces or limited editions.

 B3 6
1 RUE SCRIBE, 9E
01-40-17-94-15 WWW.ATELIERSDART.COM

BOUTIQUE MAILLE *GOURMET GOODIES*

Spicy, sweet, piquant, truffled – however you like your mustard, there's a variety on tap (literally) to suit every palate. The ceramic jars are refillable, so pack yours on your return visit.

 C1 19
6 PL. DE LA MADELEINE, 8E
01-40-15-06-00 WWW.MAILLE.COM

CHANEL *CLOTHING*

A classic French fashion address, Chanel has expanded its collection to include fashion-forward sportswear, but the mood remains ever elegant.

 C2 21
29 RUE CAMBON, 1ER
01-42-86-28-00 WWW.CHANEL.COM

COLETTE *GIFT AND HOME*
A trendy boutique that doubles as a museum, Colette has become a Paris style landmark for chic knickknacks and clothing for men and women. The fashionable Water Bar in the basement sells a large selection of designer water.

MAP 5 D4 S 40 213 RUE ST-HONORÉ, 1ER
01-55-35-33-90 WWW.COLETTE.FR

FAUCHON *GOURMET GOODIES*
Glorious goodies in all shapes and sizes can be found at this venerable house of epicurean delight. Their most recent hit, the Mona Lisa éclair, is an arty delicacy.

MAP 5 C1 S 13 24-26 PL. DE LA MADELEINE, 8E
01-70-39-38-00 WWW.FAUCHON.COM

LA GALERIE DE L'OPÉRA DE PARIS *CLOTHING AND ACCESSORIES*
The boutique for little girls, and not-so-little girls, who dream of one day becoming ballerinas. Clothing, accessories, books, and many wonderful gifts connected to the world of ballet and opera.

MAP 5 A3 S 3 PALAIS GARNIER, RUE HALÉVY, 9E
08-92-89-90-90 WWW.OPERADEPARIS.FR

GALIGNANI *BOOKS*
The first English bookstore on the Continent (established 1802) offers nibbles of all subjects, in French and English, and a browser's feast of fine-art books.

MAP 5 E3 S 50 224 RUE DE RIVOLI, 1ER
01-42-60-76-07 WWW.GALIGNANI.FR

HÉDIARD *GOURMET GOODIES*
Offering French gourmet and exotic products for more than 150 years, this upscale gastronomic boutique sells a wide range of delicious items, such as French condiments, gourmet tea, coffee, and biscuits.

MAP 5 C1 S 12 21 PL. DE LA MADELEINE, 8E
01-43-12-88-88 WWW.HEDIARD.FR

HERMÈS *CLOTHING AND ACCESSORIES*
Famed for its signature silk scarves and ties, Hermès offers myriad delights and very expensive temptations in its large, beautifully appointed flagship store.

MAP 5 D1 S 32 24 RUE DU FAUBOURG ST-HONORÉ, 8E
01-40-17-47-17 WWW.HERMES.COM

LAVINIA *GOURMET GOODIES*
A mega wine store that challenges its gourmet neighbors, Lavinia offers thousands of bottles, with an impressive selection of foreign labels as well.

MAP 5 C1 S 15 3 BD. DE LA MADELEINE, 1ER
01-42-97-20-20 WWW.LAVINIA.COM

MAISON DE LA TRUFFE *GOURMET GOODIES*
The earthy smell of the treasured fungus permeates the air at this boutique. Truffled pastas, oils, and cheeses are just a few of the pungent possibilities.

MAP 5 C1 S 14 19 PL. DE LA MADELEINE, 8E
01-42-65-53-22 WWW.MAISON-DE-LA-TRUFFE.COM

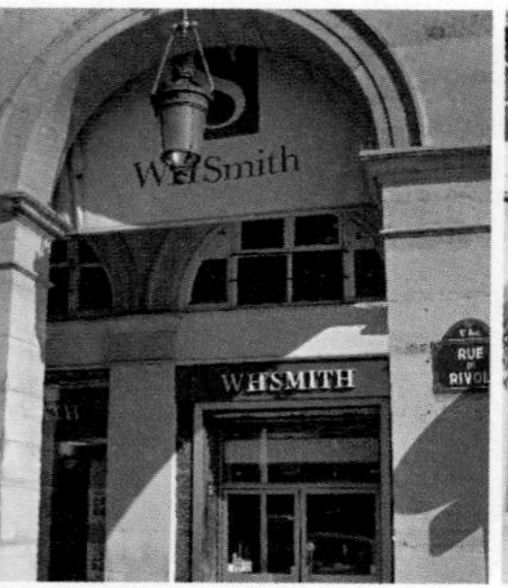

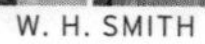
W. H. SMITH AGNÈS B.

LA MAISON DU CHOCOLAT *GOURMET GOODIES*
Chocoholics must make a solemn pilgrimage here to taste the handmade chocolates and divinely rich truffles, and to admire the artful wrapping jobs.

 MAP 5 C2 S 20
8 BD. DE LA MADELEINE, 9E
01-47-42-86-52 WWW.LAMAISONDUCHOCOLAT.COM

MAÎTRE PARFUMEUR ET GANTIER *BATH AND BEAUTY*
Step inside and breathe in the refinement of the Old World in this re-creation of a 17th-century perfume salon. Choose your own personal or home scents from the original line.

 MAP 5 C3 S 23
5 RUE DES CAPUCINES, 1ER
01-42-96-35-13 WWW.MAITRE-PARFUMEUR-ET-GANTIER.COM

MINA POE *CLOTHING AND ACCESSORIES*
Designer Mina d'Ornano references her Slavic roots and a passion for theater in her line of unique accessories and clothing. It's for luxury lovers who like uncommon and imaginative pieces, many with opulent hand-embroidered touches.

 MAP 5 D2 S 34
382 RUE ST-HONORÉ, 1ER
01-42-61-06-41 WWW.MINAPOE.COM

MORGANNE BELLO *JEWELRY*
We dare you not to be charmed by Morganne Bello's line of whimsical jewelry: semiprecious stone charms sold in heart and "lucky" four-leaf clover shapes, paired with cord or gold-plated bracelets.

 MAP 5 D4 S 39
3 RUE DU MARCHÉ ST-HONORÉ, 1ER
01-42-60-14-04 WWW.MORGANNEBELLO.COM

AU NAIN BLEU *KIDS STUFF*
Opened in 1836, the Nain Bleu (Blue Dwarf) was originally famous for its exquisite couture dolls and clothing; nowadays, its three stories offer a wide range of modern and old-fashioned toys.

 MAP 5 C1 S 17
5 BD. MALESHERBES, 8E
01-42-65-20-20 HTTP://BOUTIQUE.AUNAINBLEU.COM

PIERRE CORTHAY *SHOES*
While the sultan of Brunei might be one of his best custom-order clients, Pierre Corthay still manages to make the average man feel like a king with his classic line of men's shoes.

 MAP 5 C3 S 22
1 RUE VOLNEY, 2E
01-42-61-08-89 WWW.CORTHAY.FR

REPETTO *SHOES*
From the ballerinas of the Opéra Garnier to the feet of Brigitte Bardot, Repetto ballet slippers have become a benchmark of Parisian chic. Here, the walls are dripping with shoes.

MAP 5 B3 S 7 22 RUE DE LA PAIX, 2E
01-44-71-83-12 WWW.REPETTO.COM

RUE DU FAUBOURG ST-HONORÉ *SHOPPING DISTRICT*
Old French fashion houses like Hermès and Lanvin line this high-end shopping street – a window-shopper's paradise. Serious fashionistas find their way here.

MAP 5 D1 S 33 RUE DU FAUBOURG ST-HONORÉ W. FROM RUE ROYALE, 8E

W. H. SMITH *BOOKS*
This excellent bookstore is a locus for English-speakers in Paris and indispensable for news junkies desperate for a media fix.

MAP 5 E2 S 45 248 RUE DE RIVOLI, 1ER
01-44-77-88-99 WWW.WHSMITH.COM

WORKSHOP ISSÉ *GOURMET GOODIES*
Step across the threshold and enter the refined world of gourmet Japan. Let the super sake selection and fine green teas tempt you, or take an afternoon class in tempura or Japanese tapas.

MAP 5 B5 S 10 11 RUE ST-AUGUSTIN, 2E
01-42-96-26-74

MAP 6 LOUVRE/LES HALLES

AGNÈS B. *CLOTHING AND SHOES*
Agnès B.'s various collections of high-quality lines for office, evening, and weekend wear sum up French style for many. Children's and men's stores are just down the street.

MAP 6 C3 S 25 6 RUE DU JOUR, 1ER
01-45-08-56-56 WWW.AGNESB.COM

UN APRÈS-MIDI DE CHIEN *ACCESSORIES*
Try on a retro feel (think 1940s), or dabble in pretty, feminine handbags and accessories at this small, original boutique. The two designers who created the label assure a strong, consistent style.

MAP 6 B4 S 10 32 RUE ETIENNE MARCEL, 2E
01-40-39-00-07 WWW.UNAPRESMIDIDECHIEN.FR

L'ARTISAN PARFUMEUR *BATH AND BEAUTY*
Specializing in fresh, original fragrances, L'Artisan is particularly prized for its selection of perfumed candles and interior scents. Stop in for a bit of sensual self-indulgence.

MAP 6 F3 S 44 2 RUE L'AMIRAL DE COLIGNY, 1ER
01-44-88-27-50 WWW.ARTISANPARFUMEUR.COM

BY TERRY *BEAUTY AND SPA*
Creator of the world's first couture makeup line, Terry de Gunzburg has created a line of high-quality beauty products

KILIWATCH

ANNA RIVKA

famous for their glowing results. Facial treatments are also available here.

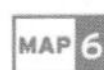 D2 30 36 PASSAGE VÉRO-DODAT, 1ER
01-44-76-00-76 WWW.BYTERRY.COM

CHRISTIAN LOUBOUTIN *SHOES*

For the shoe-obsessed, Louboutin's flagship boutique is fashion mecca. A pair of the signature red-soled stilettos makes a stylish souvenir, and bespoke services are available on-site for the well-heeled clientele.

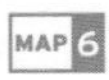 D3 31 19 RUE JEAN-JACQUES ROUSSEAU, 1ER
01-42-36-05-31 WWW.CHRISTIANLOUBOUTIN.COM

DIDIER LUDOT *VINTAGE*

Owner Didier Ludot sells mint-condition, vintage haute-couture treasures (Chanel, Dior, Balmain, Hermès) to museums and private collectors.

 D1 27 24 GALERIE DE MONTPENSIER, 1ER
01-42-96-06-56 WWW.DIDIERLUDOT.COM

E. DEHILLERIN *GIFT AND HOME*

Gourmet and novice chefs alike have been coming to Dehillerin since 1820 to stock up on professional cooking and baking equipment, like piles of copper pots, casseroles, knives, gadgets, and more.

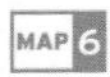 C3 23 18 RUE COQUILLIÈRE, 1ER
01-42-36-53-13 WWW.E-DEHILLERIN.FR

GALERIE VIVIENNE *SHOPPING CENTER*

Inaugurated in 1826, this elegant covered passageway has welcomed tourists and window-shoppers under its glass-topped arcade ever since. Come here to enjoy a wide range of boutiques, a bite to eat, or just to admire the architecture.

 B1 5 ENTER AT 6 RUE DES PETITS CHAMPS OR 4 RUE VIVIENNE, 2E
WWW.GALERIE-VIVIENNE.COM

GAS BIJOUX *ACCESSORIES AND JEWELRY*

Stop by this boutique to stock up on charming and trendy jewelry that will add a colorful French touch to any basic outfit.

 C3 21 44 RUE ETIENNE MARCEL, 2E
01-45-08-49-46 WWW.GASBIJOUX.FR

KILIWATCH *CLOTHING AND ACCESSORIES*

Hip students and cutting-edge fashionistas know to visit Kiliwatch for the latest must-have. An edited selection of thrift and vintage clothing is also available in this boutique bursting with treasures.

 B4 S9 64 RUE TIQUETONNE, 2E
01-42-21-17-37 WWW.ESPACEKILIWATCH.FR

LEGRAND FILLES ET FILS *GOURMET GOODIES*

Legrand is a lovely wine shop tucked into the Galerie Vivienne. Sample the wide selection of fruits of the vine at the wine bar.

 C1 S16 1 RUE DE LA BANQUE, 2E
01-42-60-07-12 WWW.CAVES-LEGRAND.COM

SPA NUXE *SPA*

Treat yourself to an afternoon of pampered bliss at one of the hippest spas in the city, from the French body-care line Nuxe. Asian-inspired minimalist luxury and total discretion make it a refuge for calm-seeking patrons.

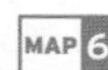 C4 S26 32 RUE MONTORGUEIL, 1ER
01-55-80-71-40 WWW.NUXE.COM

STOHRER *GOURMET GOODIES*

Serving royalty alongside the common people in the same location since 1730, this gilded, delectable patisserie is famous for creating the *baba au rhum*, a rum-soaked cake.

 B4 S7 51 RUE MONTORGUEIL, 2E
01-42-33-38-20 WWW.STOHRER.FR

MAP 7 MARAIS

ANNA RIVKA *JEWELRY*

Acquire the look of a chic and modern Marais girl with a beautiful bauble rendered in metal, beads, and stones.

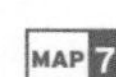 B4 S13 104 RUE VIEILLE DU TEMPLE, 3E
01-40-23-92-84 WWW.ANNARIVKA.FR

ANTIK BATIK *CLOTHING AND SHOES*

Step into this airy boutique for elegant and worldly duds for chic guys and gals who wish to cultivate a bourgeois bohemian look. This brand is a favorite of young, hip fashionistas.

 D6 S45 18 RUE DE TURENNE, 4E
01-44-78-02-00 WWW.ANTIKBATIK.FR

LES ARCHIVES DE LA PRESSE *GIFT AND HOME*

Browse through a mind-boggling treasure trove of old magazines and journals from the early 19th century to the present day: fashion, sports, and cinema, as well as period posters and advertising.

 C3 S20 51 RUE DES ARCHIVES, 3E
01-42-72-63-93 WWW.LESARCHIVESDELAPRESSE.COM

VA-VA-VA VINTAGE

Parisians do vintage the way they do everything else: subtly and discreetly rather than working a head-to-toe look. To acquire old-school chic like a local, the first stop should be the Marais, which is bursting at the seams with vintage stores. You'll find by-the-kilo warehouses (www.kilo-shop.com) and designer label boutiques like La Jolie Garde Robe (01/42-72-13-90, 15 Rue Commines, 3E). Girlie-girls go apoplectic at the sight of Chez Sarah's garden party frocks at **Les Puces de St-Ouen (p. 85),** the city's northernmost flea market. Prices begin at around €100, but the quality and selection are above par. Fifties Sound (www.fiftiessound.fr) orchestrates roving vintage bazaars where the city's best vintage vendors converge under one roof. Burlesque diva Dita Von Teese is a regular.

LES BAINS DU MARAIS *SPA*

Stepping into this Asian-inspired day spa will instantly relax you, as will their *hammam* (steam room) and full line of spa treatments.

 D3 S 32
31-33 RUE DES BLANCS MANTEAUX, 4E
01-44-61-02-02 WWW.LESBAINSDUMARAIS.COM

BENSIMON AUTOUR DU MONDE *GIFT AND HOME*

Follow the rainbow of colors spread out among housewares that range from bedding, candles, and cushions to comfy clothing in natural fabrics.

 D5 S 43
12 RUE DES FRANCS-BOURGEOIS, 3E
01-42-77-16-18 WWW.BENSIMON.COM

BHV *SHOPPING CENTER*

Whether on the prowl for lingerie or a lasagna pan, odds are better than good you'll find what you need at this historic department store spanning six floors.

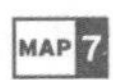 D2 S 31
52 RUE DE RIVOLI, 4E
09-77-40-14-00 WWW.BHV.FR

THE BROKEN ARM *CLOTHING AND SHOES*

This hip hybrid store features designer duds and good, strong coffee in a chic, minimalist showroom. Jewelry and one-of-a-kind treasures from independent artists make memorable souvenirs.

 A3 S 2
12 RUE PERRÉE, 3E
01-44-61-53-60 WWW.THE-BROKEN-ARM.COM

CHEZ IZRAEL *GOURMET GOODIES*

Like a Turkish bazaar, every corner of this international *épicerie* (food shop) is crammed with preserved fruits, tangy olives, and jar after jar of mystery condiments and sauces.

 E4 S 50
30 RUE FRANÇOIS MIRON, 3E
01-42-72-66-23

THE BROKEN ARM

MERCI

MARIAGE FRÈRES *GOURMET GOODIES*

Employees dressed as colonial dandies invite you to savor the scents of hundreds of excellent teas. An appropriately elegant teapot or two may be too tempting to resist.

D3 Ⓢ 35 30 RUE DU BOURG-TIBOURG, 4E
01-42-72-28-11 WWW.MARIAGEFRERES.COM

MERCI *CLOTHING AND ACCESSORIES*

Leading the socially conscious trend in Paris, the owners of Merci give 100 percent of their profits to charity. Their fashion friends have jockeyed to participate, making Merci one of the hippest shops of the moment.

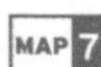

B6 Ⓢ 16 111 BD. BEAUMARCHAIS, 3E
01-42-77-00-33 WWW.MERCI-MERCI.COM

RUE DES FRANCS-BOURGEOIS *SHOPPING DISTRICT*

This quaint shopping street in the historic Marais district provides easy access between museums and clothing boutiques. With most shops open on Sundays, it's a local favorite.

C4 Ⓢ 23 RUE DES FRANCS-BOURGEOIS BTWN. RUE DES ARCHIVES AND RUE DE TURENNE

SURFACE TO AIR *CLOTHING AND ACCESSORIES*

Cutting-edge fashionable shoppers looking for affordable mid-range clothes for both men and women should head to Surface to Air, perpetual darling of the Marais fashion scene.

B4 Ⓢ 14 108 RUE VIEILLE DU TEMPLE, E2
01-44-61-76-27 WWW.SURFACETOAIR.COM

VERT D'ABSINTHE *GOURMET GOODIES*

Fans of *la fée verte* (the green fairy) pop in to stock up on the potent wormwood elixir that's seduced French artists and writers for centuries.

D5 Ⓢ 44 11 RUE D'ORMESSON, 4E
01-42-71-69-73 WWW.VERTDABSINTHE.COM

VILLAGE ST-PAUL *SHOPPING DISTRICT*

Meander the medieval streets of this ancient neighborhood and discover its treasure trove of upmarket antiques shops, artists' ateliers, and secret courtyards.

E5 Ⓢ 52 RUE ST-PAUL, 4E WWW.LEVILLAGESAINTPAUL.COM

MAP 8 BASTILLE

CARAVANE CHAMBRE 19 *GIFT AND HOME*
Devoted to sleep and well-being, this vast and airy shop in a former furniture warehouse offers stylish beds, linens, PJs, and all things related to the bedroom.

 B4 S 16 19 RUE ST-NICOLAS, 12E
01-53-02-96-96 WWW.CARAVANE.FR

LE CHOCOLAT ALAIN DUCASSE *GOURMET GOODIES*
Superstar chef Alain Ducasse made dreams come true when he opened his bean-to-bar chocolate factory and boutique in 2013. The old-fashioned pralines and gourmet ganaches should come with warning labels.

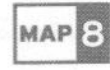 A3 S 4 40 RUE DE LA ROQUETTE, 11E
01-48-05-82-86 WWW.LECHOCOLAT-ALAINDUCASSE.COM

ISABEL MARANT *CLOTHING AND SHOES*
Very much in vogue with fashionable Parisiennes, Isabel Marant is considered one of the best of the new fashion generation. Her of-the-moment styles are urban and feminine.

 B4 S 13 16 RUE DE CHARONNE, 11E
01-49-29-71-55 WWW.ISABELMARANT.TM.FR

LILLI BULLE *KIDS STUFF*
Shop here for fun, funky, bright, and slightly offbeat clothes created by various local designers for babies and kids. This shop on a tiny side street also carries a small selection of toys, gadgets, and furniture.

 A6 S 8 3 RUE DE LA FORGE ROYALE, 11E
01-43-73-71-63 WWW.LILLIBULLE.COM

LOUISON *ACCESSORIES*
Louison was founded by a former accessories designer for the House of Céline. Jacques Choï and his wife, Agnès, have conquered Paris with their line of eye-catching sparkling bags and accessories.

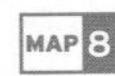 B4 S 17 20 RUE ST-NICOLAS, 12E
01-43-44-02-62 WWW.LOUISONPARIS.COM

MUJI *GIFT AND HOME*
Tokyo and Paris collide at this eco-friendly concept store where function and style reign. Shop for trendy striped T-shirts, the perfect pen, and travel accoutrements for 21st-century globetrotters.

 B4 S 15 91-93 RUE DU FAUBOURG ST-ANTOINE, 11E
01-53-33-48-48 WWW.MUJI.EU

VIADUC DES ARTS *SHOPPING DISTRICT*
In the archways below a former railway line dating from 1859, the pink brick viaduct is now home to boutiques and ateliers, all dedicated to preserving fine arts and craftsmanship. Above the viaduct is a garden-filled pedestrian promenade.

 C4 S 25 1-129 AV. DAUMESNIL, 12E WWW.VIADUC-DES-ARTS.FR

MUJI

BA&SH

MAP 9 MONTMARTRE

A.P.C. SURPLUS *CLOTHING AND SHOES*
Tweed, denim, and preppy classics are the principal components of the A.P.C. house style. This surplus boutique, selling past seasons' items at 50 percent off, affords views of nearby Basilique Sacre-Coeur and bargains galore.

 B6 S 7 20 RUE ANDRÉ DEL SARTE, 18E
01-42-62-19-76 WWW.APC.FR

BA&SH *CLOTHING AND SHOES*
Just since 2003, this hometown label has morphed into one of the most sought-after women's clothing brands in Europe. At the Montmartre outpost, a friendly, helpful staff will help you acquire that oh-so-elusive Parisian chic.

MAP 9 D5 S 23 1-BIS RUE DES ABBESSES, 18E
01-46-06-20-46 WWW.BA-SH.COM

EMMANUELLE ZYSMAN *ACCESSORIES AND JEWELRY*
Parisienne to the tips of her toes, Emmanuelle Zysman creates discreet and elegant jewelry that has a handmade bohemian look – bracelets with tiny madeleine-shaped charms and delicate semiprecious stone or enamel rings.

MAP 9 D5 S 25 81 RUE DES MARTYRS, 18E
01-42-52-01-00 WWW.EMMANUELLEZYSMAN.FR

GENERATION 1962 *CLOTHING AND ACCESSORIES*
Modern, wearable pieces with a timeless flair hold court at this adorable boutique. Snag a stylish Orla Kiely bag and fill it with souvenirs from Montmartre.

MAP 9 D3 S 15 3 RUE THOLOZÉ, 18E
01-83-56-21-17 WWW.BOUTIQUE1962.COM

GRAND HERBORISTERIE MÉDICALE DE LA PLACE DE CLICHY *BATH AND BEAUTY*
This frozen-in-time apothecary dispenses herbal formulas to heal most ailments. The friendly medical professionals guide you to tinctures, creams, and teas that soothe without side effects.

 F1 S 32 87 RUE D'AMSTERDAM, 8E
01-48-74-83-32 HTTP://HERBORISTERIEPARIS.COM

ROSE BUNKER

ANTOINE ET LILI

L'OBJET QUI PARLE *VINTAGE*
This is a charming vintage shop for picking up the retro objects one would find at the home of a French *grand-mère* (grandmother): spice jars and café au lait bowls, linens, glassware, and more.

 D5 24
86 RUE DES MARTYRS, 18E
06-09-67-05-30

ROSE BUNKER *GIFT AND HOME*
"Eclectic" best describes the contents of this upstairs-downstairs boutique bursting with vibrant colors. It's a great place to score contemporary art and vintage knickknacks without busting your budget.

 D3 17
10 RUE ARISTIDE BRUANT, 18E
01-42-57-90-62 WWW.ROSE-BUNKER.FR

SPREE *CLOTHING AND ACCESSORIES*
Mix a selection of the coolest designers of the moment with a healthy helping of Scandinavian-designed furniture and try not to be tempted to go on your own spree.

 D5 21
16 RUE LA VIEUVILLE, 18E
01-42-23-41-40 WWW.SPREE.FR

MAP 10 CANAL ST-MARTIN

ANTOINE ET LILI *CLOTHING AND ACCESSORIES*
You can't miss the trio of candy-colored shops shining like a beacon of retail therapy beside the canal. Inside the clothing, housewares, and kids' boutiques, brightly colored, high-quality treasures await.

 D2 13
95 QUAI DE VALMY, 10E
01-40-37-41-55 WWW.ANTOINEETLILI.COM

ARTAZART *BOOKS*
Prepare to be sucked into a visually stimulating vortex at this bookshop stuffed with books on art and design. In-house art shows and an interesting selection of functional gift ideas round out the retail possibilities.

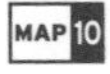 D2 15
83 QUAI DE VALMY, 10E
01-40-40-24-00 WWW.ARTAZART.COM

CARMEN RAGOSTA *CLOTHING AND ACCESSORIES*
The eponymous Italian proprietor and her dachshund, Pippo, welcome you into their one-of-a-kind boutique that melds food and fashion. Look for unique sartorial treasures, then indulge in some to-die-for tiramisu.

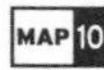
MAP 10 D2 Ⓢ 11 8 RUE DE LA GRANGE AUX BELLES, 10E
01-42-49-00-71 WWW.CARMENRAGOSTA.COM

LA TÊTE DANS LES OLIVES *GOURMET GOODIES*
Cédric Casanova has become a superstar on the Paris food scene with his Italian boutique selling vintages and specialty flavors of his now-famous extra-virgin olive oils.

MAP 10 C3 Ⓢ 6 2 RUE STE-MARTHE, 10E
09-51-31-33-34 WWW.LATETEDANSLESOLIVES.COM

OVERVIEW MAP

LES GRANDS MAGASINS *SHOPPING DISTRICT*
On this boulevard dedicated to French temples of fashion Galeries Lafayette and Printemps, you'll find an impressive selection of objects to desire from home to clothing to food.

OVERVIEW MAP **C4** 40 AND 64 BD. HAUSSMANN, BTWN. RUE DE LA CHAUSSÉE D'ANTIN AND RUE DU HAVRE, 9E WWW.GALERIESLAFAYETTE.COM, WWW.PRINTEMPS.FR

LES PUCES DE ST-OUEN *GIFT AND HOME*
On the northern rim of Paris, the world's largest flea market bustles across several acres. Tourists and antiques dealers comb 15 separate markets for everything from perfume bottles to Picassos. Bargaining is expected.

OVERVIEW MAP **A4** 17 AV. DE LA PORTE DE CLIGNANCOURT, 18E
08-92-70-57-65
WWW.MARCHEAUXPUCES-SAINTOUEN.COM

RÉCIPROQUE *CLOTHING AND ACCESSORIES*
Ever wonder where the grande dames of Paris send their clothing once the season is over? Réciproque is the consignment shop just bursting with their designer hand-me-downs, many only lightly used.

OVERVIEW MAP **C2** 89-101 RUE DE LA POMPE, 16E
01-47-04-30-28 WWW.RECIPROQUE.FR

ROGER VIVIER *SHOES*
Vivier was the creator of the stiletto heel. His signature buckle shoe, famously worn by Catherine Deneuve in the movie *Belle de Jour,* is iconic to this day.

OVERVIEW MAP **C3** 29 RUE DU FAUBOURG ST-HONORÉ, 8E
01-53-43-00-85 WWW.ROGERVIVIER.COM

RUE D'ALÉSIA *CLOTHING AND ACCESSORIES*
Rue d'Alésia is best known for its designer outlets and stock boutiques; brands like Sonia Rykiel and Cacharel have discreetly set up shop to sell last season's items at more than 50 percent off.

OVERVIEW MAP **E3** 64-114 RUE D'ALÉSIA, 14E

ARTS AND LEISURE

Most romantic museum: **MUSÉE RODIN,** p. 90

Best contemporary art: **PALAIS DE TOKYO – SITE DE CRÉATION CONTEMPORAINE,** p. 91

Best small museum: **MUSÉE DE L'ORANGERIE,** p. 92

Best museum gift shop:
MUSÉE DES ARTS DÉCORATIFS, p. 92

Best free museum: **MUSÉE CARNAVALET,** p. 93

Best modern art: **MUSÉE NATIONAL D'ART MODERNE – CENTRE POMPIDOU,** p. 94

Best all-night movies with breakfast: **LE CHAMPO,** p. 97

Best bet for English-language theater:
THÉÂTRE DU CHÂTELET (THÉÂTRE MUSICAL DE PARIS), p. 99

Best cabaret: **BAL DU MOULIN ROUGE,** p. 100

Most variety of performances: **LE BATACLAN,** p. 101

Best all-weather activity: **BATOBUS,** p. 103

Best bike tours:
FAT TIRE BIKE AND CITY SEGWAY TOURS, p. 106

Best family park: **PARC DE LA VILLETTE,** p. 107

Best panoramic view of the city:
TOUR MONTPARNASSE, p. 109

MUSEUMS AND GALLERIES

MAP 1 QUARTIER LATIN/LES ÎLES

CONCIERGERIE

Paris's first prison, the Conciergerie became notorious during the Revolution as the last stop for many before the guillotine. Marie Antoinette's dungeon, among others, has been restored and preserved.

2 BD. DU PALAIS, 1ER
01-53-40-60-93 WWW.CONCIERGERIE.MONUMENTS-NATIONAUX.FR
ADMISSION: €8.50

INSTITUT DU MONDE ARABE

This Seine-side architectural wonder exhibits Arabic and Islamic art and artifacts. The building's south side is covered with shutters that open and close automatically like a camera, and the roof terrace offers great views.

1 RUE DES FOSSÉS ST-BERNARD, 5E
01-40-51-38-38 WWW.IMARABE.ORG
ADMISSION: €8

MUSÉE NATIONAL DU MOYEN AGE – THERMES ET HÔTEL DE CLUNY

See SIGHTS, p. 2.

6 PL. PAUL PAINLEVÉ, 5E
01-53-73-78-00 WWW.MUSEE-MOYENAGE.FR
ADMISSION: €8

MAP 2 ST-GERMAIN-DES-PRÉS

MUSÉE DE LA MONNAIE

When it reopens in late 2014 after major renovations, the French mint will offer a gourmet dining experience at its on-site restaurant, as well as expos on French coins and their history from Roman times to the present.

B3 5

11 QUAI DE CONTI, 6E
01-40-46-55-35 WWW.MONNAIEDEPARIS.FR
ADMISSION: €8.50

MUSÉE DU LUXEMBOURG

Next to the French Senate, facing the Jardin du Luxembourg, this museum hosts powerhouse temporary exhibits that draw crowds, such as a Marc Chagall expo in 2013.

F4 49

19 RUE DE VAUGIRARD, 6E
01-40-13-62-00 WWW.MUSEEDULUXEMBOURG.FR
ADMISSION: €11

CONCIERGERIE

INSTITUT DU MONDE ARABE

MUSÉE NATIONAL EUGÈNE DELACROIX

Artist Eugène Delacroix's mid-19th-century home now exhibits his lesser-known works, enhancing the major displays in the Louvre and Musée d'Orsay.

 C3 A 16
6 RUE DE FURSTENBERG, 6E
01-44-41-86-50 WWW.MUSEE-DELACROIX.FR
ADMISSION: €5

MAP 3 INVALIDES

GALERIES NATIONALES DU GRAND PALAIS

Built for the 1900 World's Fair, the Grand Palais boasts intricate art nouveau architecture. The museum holds big-name temporary exhibits, such as an exposition in 2010 examining the works of Claude Monet.

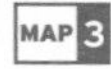 A1 A 2
GRAND PALAIS, 3 AV. DU GÉNÉRAL EISENHOWER, 8E
01-44-13-17-17 WWW.GRANDPALAIS.FR
ADMISSION: VARIES

MUSÉE DE L'ARMÉE

Specialists and laity alike should enjoy this huge collection of weaponry, armor, flags, uniforms, and other military artifacts. Many moving and beautiful objects are on display.

 D3 A 37
129 HÔTEL DES INVALIDES, RUE DE GRENELLE, 7E
01-44-42-37-72 WWW.INVALIDES.ORG ADMISSION: €9.50

MUSÉE DES BEAUX-ARTS DE LA VILLE DE PARIS

The Petit Palais, little brother to the Grand Palais, exhibits a wide range of art, from antiquity to the 20th century. It also offers workshops for children and adults.

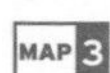 A2 A 6
PETIT PALAIS, AV. WINSTON CHURCHILL, 8E
01-53-43-40-00 WWW.PETIT-PALAIS.PARIS.FR
ADMISSION: €5-€11, DEPENDING ON EXHIBIT

MUSÉE DES LETTRES ET MANUSCRITS

Writers and readers love this private museum for its vast and interesting permanent collection of historic documents from literary and historical greats, including Napoléon and Oscar Wilde.

 C6 A 33
222 BD. ST-GERMAIN, 6E
01-42-22-48-48 WWW.MUSEEDESLETTRES.COM
ADMISSION: €7

MUSÉE RODIN

PALAIS DE LA DÉCOUVERTE

MUSÉE D'ORSAY

See SIGHTS, p. 9.

1 RUE DE LA LEGION D'HONNEUR, 7E
01-40-49-48-14 WWW.MUSEE-ORSAY.FR
ADMISSION: €9

MUSÉE MAILLOL – FONDATION DINA VIERNY

Several works by Catalan sculptor Aristide Maillol are on public display around Paris. This charming museum, opened by his muse, Dina Vierny, houses more of his fine work.

59-61 RUE DE GRENELLE, 7E
01-42-22-59-58 WWW.MUSEEMAILLOL.COM
ADMISSION: €11.50

MUSÉE RODIN

Auguste Rodin's last home now houses his best works, including *The Thinker* and *The Kiss,* plus his private collection, including works by Van Gogh, Renoir, and Monet.

 D3 A 38

77 RUE DE VARENNE, 7E
01-44-18-61-10 WWW.MUSEE-RODIN.FR
ADMISSION: €10.80

PALAIS DE LA DÉCOUVERTE

This hands-on science museum invites the young and young-at-heart to discover starlit galaxies, microscopic worlds, and cybercultures in interactive "ateliers" for kids. It has excellent temporary exhibits.

 A1 A 3

GRAND PALAIS, AV. FRANKLIN DELANO ROOSEVELT, 8E
01-56-43-20-20 WWW.PALAIS-DECOUVERTE.FR
ADMISSION: €8

 TOUR EIFFEL/ARC DE TRIOMPHE/TROCADÉRO

AQUARIUM DU TROCADÉRO

Massive tanks with sharks and exotic fish have made this aquarium a favorite with family groups. The children's program includes a dancing pirate show and balloon sculpture workshops.

 D3 A 26

5 AV. ALBERT DE MUN, 16E
01-40-69-23-23 WWW.CINEAQUA.COM
ADMISSION: €19.90

MUSÉE D'ART MODERNE DE LA VILLE DE PARIS

In the Palais de Tokyo, a grotesquely grand 1937 building, this 20th- and 21st-century collection includes work by Dufy, Matisse, Modigliani, and others.

PALAIS DE TOKYO, 13 AV. DU PRÉSIDENT WILSON, 16E
01-53-67-40-00 WWW.MAM.PARIS.FR
ADMISSION: FREE

MUSÉE DE L'HOMME

When this museum, famous for its 18,000 skulls (including that of philosopher Descartes) reopens in 2015, highlights will include a new program dedicated to humanity and its relationship to nature.

 E2 A 30

PALAIS DE CHAILLOT, 17 PL. DU TROCADÉRO, 16E
01-44-05-72-72 WWW.MUSEEDELHOMME.FR
ADMISSION: VARIES

MUSÉE DU QUAI BRANLY

Designed by famed architect Jean Nouvel, this museum houses a permanent collection dedicated to the indigenous arts, cultures, and civilizations of Africa, Asia, Oceania, and the Americas.

 E4 A 36

37 QUAI BRANLY, 7E
01-56-61-70-70 WWW.QUAIBRANLY.FR
ADMISSION: €10.10

MUSÉE GALLIERA (MUSÉE DE LA MODE DE LA VILLE DE PARIS)

After three years of renovations, this museum focused on all things fashion-related reopened in September 2013 with a splashy retrospective dedicated to the work of French-Algerian couturier Azzedine Alaïa.

 C3 A 19

10 AV. PIERRE 1ER DE SERBIE, 16E
01-56-52-86-00 WWW.PARISMUSEES.PARIS.FR
ADMISSION: VARIES

MUSÉE GUIMET

Some 45,000 items make up one of the world's largest collections, with the largest Khmer collection outside Southeast Asia. In short, it's a marvel.

 D3 A 25

6 PL. D'IÉNA, 16E
01-56-52-53-00 WWW.GUIMET.FR
ADMISSION: €7.50

MUSÉE NATIONAL DE LA MARINE

The spirit of booming cannons and swelled sails is best captured in the old-ship models at this maritime history museum. A must for sailing enthusiasts, pirates, and other seafaring types.

 E2 A 34

PALAIS DE CHAILLOT, 17 PL. DU TROCADÉRO, 16E
01-53-65-69-69 WWW.MUSEE-MARINE.FR
ADMISSION: €7

PALAIS DE TOKYO – SITE DE CRÉATION CONTEMPORAINE

Inaugurated in 2001, this lab for new art has dropped jaws, mostly over the improbable mix of shapes and sounds now dominating a warehouse-like chunk of the Palais de Tokyo.

 C4 A 22

13 AV. DU PRÉSIDENT WILSON, 16E
01-47-23-54-01 WWW.PALAISDETOKYO.COM
ADMISSION: €10

MAP 5 GRANDS BOULEVARDS

JEU DE PAUME

Once the tennis court for the Tuileries palace, this small building shows outstanding photo exhibits, which have included retrospectives of work by Martin Parr, Richard Avedon, and Lee Miller.

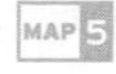 E2 Ⓐ46
1 PL. DE LA CONCORDE, 8E
01-47-03-12-50 WWW.JEUDEPAUME.ORG
ADMISSION: €8.50

MUSÉE DE LA MODE ET DU TEXTILE

At last, Paris exhibits its most prized commodity: fashion. From the 17th century to the present, whether powdered and petticoated or provocative Gaultier, you'll find it here.

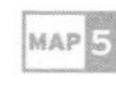 E5 Ⓐ52
107 RUE DE RIVOLI, 1ER
01-44-55-57-50 WWW.LESARTSDECORATIFS.FR
ADMISSION: €9.50; INCLUDES MUSÉE DE LA PUBLICITÉ AND MUSÉE DES ARTS DÉCORATIFS

MUSÉE DE LA PUBLICITÉ

This museum devotes itself to the "art of the ephemeral," with exhibits of posters from the 1700s to today and a most extraordinary database of promotional materials.

 E6 Ⓐ53
107 RUE DE RIVOLI, 1ER
01-44-55-57-50 WWW.LESARTSDECORATIFS.FR
ADMISSION: €9.50; INCLUDES MUSÉE DE LA MODE ET DU TEXTILE AND MUSÉE DES ARTS DÉCORATIFS

MUSÉE DE L'ORANGERIE

Located in the orangery of the Tuileries palace, this museum houses Claude Monet's *Nymphéas* (Water Lilies) series, which is of major importance to the world of art.

 F2 Ⓐ55
JARDIN DES TUILERIES, 1ER
01-44-77-80-07 WWW.MUSEE-ORANGERIE.FR
ADMISSION: €7.50

MUSÉE DES ARTS DÉCORATIFS

From the Middle Ages to today's contemporary works, the decorative arts are avidly represented at this world-renowned museum. The re-creation of fashion couturier Jeanne Lanvin's apartment is just one of the amazing exhibits.

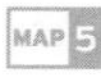 E6 Ⓐ54
107 RUE DE RIVOLI, 1ER
01-44-55-57-50 WWW.LESARTSDECORATIFS.FR
ADMISSION: €9.50; INCLUDES MUSÉE DE LA PUBLICITÉ AND MUSÉE DE LA MODE ET DU TEXTILE

MAP 6 LOUVRE/LES HALLES

MUSÉE DU LOUVRE

See SIGHTS, p. 15.

COUR NAPOLÉON, 34 QUAI DU LOUVRE, 1ER
01-40-20-50-50 WWW.LOUVRE.FR
ADMISSION: €11

JEU DE PAUME

MUSÉE DES ARTS DÉCORATIFS

MAP 7 MARAIS

MAISON EUROPÉENNE DE LA PHOTOGRAPHIE

This 18th-century Marais mansion with a modern annex exhibits an impressive, changing collection of photographic work, both old and new, and videography.

MAP 7 E5 A 51 5-7 RUE DE FOURCY, 4E
01-44-78-75-00 WWW.MEP-FR.ORG
ADMISSION: €8

MUSÉE CARNAVALET

Sprawling through two beautiful Marais mansions, this museum rambles through the history of Paris in a disorganized but charming collection of paintings, fine art, and impressive furniture.

MAP 7 C5 A 26 23 RUE DE SÉVIGNÉ, 3E
01-44-59-58-58 WWW.CARNAVALET.PARIS.FR
ADMISSION: FREE

MUSÉE COGNACQ-JAY

This private collection of 18th-century fine art, donated to the state by the founders of the La Samaritaine department store, reverently displays work by Rembrandt, Rubens, and Canaletto.

MAP 7 C5 A 25 8 RUE ELZÉVIR, 3E
01-40-27-07-21 WWW.PARIS.FR
ADMISSION: FREE

MUSÉE D'ART ET D'HISTOIRE DU JUDAÏSME

In a fine 1650 Marais mansion, the story of the Jewish community in Paris and beyond is told through art and craft works, books, letters, and even anti-Semitic cartoons.

MAP 7 C2 A 19 71 RUE DU TEMPLE, 3E
01-53-01-86-53 WWW.MAHJ.ORG
ADMISSION: €6.80

MUSÉE DE LA MAGIE

The young and young-at-heart will enjoy this fun collection of magic tricks and optical illusions. Enthusiasts can also take lessons at the École de Magie (School of Magic).

MAP 7 E6 A 53 11 RUE ST-PAUL, 4E
01-42-72-13-26 WWW.MUSEEDELAMAGIE.COM
ADMISSION: €9

MUSÉE NATIONAL D'ART MODERNE

ESPACE MONTMARTRE DALÍ

MUSÉE DES ARTS ET MÉTIERS

Founded in 1794 and housed in a medieval abbey, this science museum is filled with machines, models, and automatons from 1500 to the present.

 A1 Ⓐ1
60 RUE RÉAUMUR, 3E
01-53-01-82-20 WWW.ARTS-ET-METIERS.NET
ADMISSION: €6.50

MUSÉE NATIONAL D'ART MODERNE – CENTRE POMPIDOU

Spanning two floors of the Centre Pompidou, this wide collection includes good surrealist and Picasso exhibits, plus Matisse, Pollock, and a host of other style-setters.

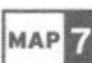 C2 Ⓐ18
PL. GEORGES POMPIDOU, 19 RUE BEAUBOURG, 4E
01-44-78-12-33 WWW.CENTREPOMPIDOU.FR
ADMISSION: €13

MUSÉE NATIONAL PICASSO

After several years of renovation, this museum is set to open in Spring 2014. Its collection is devoted exclusively to the works of Pablo Picasso. Many of the more than 213 paintings and 158 sculptures come from the private collection of his heirs.

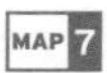 C5 Ⓐ24
5 RUE DE THORIGNY, 3E
01-42-71-25-21 WWW.MUSEE-PICASSO.FR
ADMISSION: TBD

MAP 8 BASTILLE

MAISON DE VICTOR HUGO

Formerly the great novelist's residence, this Marais mansion now houses original furniture, manuscripts, paintings, Hugo's lesser-known photographic work, and personal mementos.

 B2 Ⓐ10
6 PL. DES VOSGES, 4E
01-42-72-10-16 WWW.PARIS.FR
ADMISSION: FREE

MAP 9 MONTMARTRE

ESPACE MONTMARTRE DALÍ

Idiosyncratic and stylish like the artist himself, this network of basement rooms displays Dalí's lesser-known works, including sculptures and book illustrations. Some items are for sale.

MAP 9 C4 Ⓐ10 11 RUE POULBOT, 18E
01-42-64-40-10 WWW.DALIPARIS.COM ADMISSION: €11

MUSÉE DE LA VIE ROMANTIQUE

A throwback to the time of those quintessential romantics, writers Georges Sand and Alfred de Musset, this *hôtel particulier* (mansion) nestled in a quaint garden houses tidbits and artworks that are true to theme.

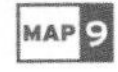 F3 Ⓐ34 16 RUE CHAPTAL, 9E
01-55-31-95-67 WWW.PARIS.FR ADMISSION: FREE

MUSÉE DE MONTMARTRE

Once a studio for the likes of Renoir and Utrillo, this 17th-century house now displays a charming collection of documents, paintings, and memorabilia from old Montmartre.

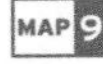 B4 Ⓐ5 12 RUE CORTOT, 18E
01-46-06-61-11 WWW.MUSEEDEMONTMARTRE.FR
ADMISSION: €8

OVERVIEW MAP

CITÉ DES SCIENCES ET DE L'INDUSTRIE

A giant silver geode marks the spot of this hands-on, kid-friendly museum where art and science merge.

OVERVIEW MAP **B5** 30 AV. CORENTIN-CARIOU, 19E
01-40-05-80-00 WWW.CITE-SCIENCES.FR
ADMISSION: €8

CITÉ NATIONAL DE L'HISTOIRE DE L'IMMIGRATION

Paris is a city of immigrants, and this museum tells their stories through photographs, film, and interactive exhibits. It's a fascinating detour for history buffs.

OVERVIEW MAP **E6** 293 AV. DAUMESNIL, 12E
01-53-59-58-60 WWW.HISTOIRE-IMMIGRATION.FR
ADMISSION: €4.50

FONDATION CARTIER POUR L'ART CONTEMPORAIN

Designed by Jean Nouvel, this foundation for the contemporary arts was launched in 1994. It has managed to stay on the cutting edge of the contemporary art world – no mean feat.

OVERVIEW MAP **E4** 261 BD. RASPAIL, 14E
01-42-18-56-50 WWW.FONDATION.CARTIER.COM
ADMISSION: €9.50

MUSÉE CERNUSCHI – MUSÉE DES ARTS DE L'ASIE

Named after the man who donated his mansion and extensive

MUSÉE MARMOTTAN

MUSÉE NATIONAL D'HISTOIRE NATURELLE

Asian art collection to the city of Paris, this museum houses a remarkable collection of ancient Chinese art.

OVERVIEW MAP **B3** 7 AV. VÉLASQUEZ, 8E
01-53-96-21-50 WWW.CERNUSCHI.PARIS.FR
ADMISSION: €7

MUSÉE GREVIN

This wax museum showcases French and international figures from showbiz, sports, politics, and more. Even if you don't know who all the figures are, it's a magical maze, fun for both kids and adults.

OVERVIEW MAP **C4** 10 BD. MONTMARTRE, 9E
01-47-70-85-05 WWW.GREVIN.COM
ADMISSION: €22.50

MUSÉE JACQUEMART-ANDRÉ

In this magnificent 19th-century mansion, guests are privy to a private collection of works by Rembrandt, Van Dyck, and Botticelli, along with a glimpse into a grander lifestyle.

OVERVIEW MAP **C3** 158 BD. HAUSSMANN, 8E
01-45-62-11-59 WWW.MUSEE-JACQUEMART-ANDRE.COM
ADMISSION: €11

MUSÉE MARMOTTAN – CLAUDE MONET

Based on a vast collection bequeathed to the artist's son, this assemblage has been enhanced by other Impressionist works by Gauguin, Renoir, and Pissarro.

OVERVIEW MAP **C1** 2 RUE LOUIS BOILLY, 16E
01-44-96-50-33 WWW.MARMOTTAN.COM
ADMISSION: €10

MUSÉE NATIONAL D'HISTOIRE NATURELLE

Situated in the 400-year-old Jardin des Plantes, the National Museum of Natural History consists of four historic buildings housing the museums of paleontology, botanical, mineralogy, and the stunning Grand Gallery of Evolution.

OVERVIEW MAP **D4** 36 RUE GEOFFROY-ST-HILAIRE, 5E; ACCESS GARDENS VIA QUAI ST-BERNARD, RUE BUFFON, OR RUE CUVIER
01-40-79-54-79 WWW.MNHN.FR ADMISSION: €7

MUSÉE NISSIM DE CAMONDO

Set in Count Camondo's mansion on the border of the chic Parc Monceau, this museum offers a glimpse into a wealthy art collector's life at the turn of the 20th century.

OVERVIEW MAP **C3** 63 RUE DE MONCEAU, 8E
01-53-89-06-40 WWW.LESARTSDECORATIFS.FR
ADMISSION: €7.50

PERFORMING ARTS

MAP 1 QUARTIER LATIN/LES ÎLES

LE CHAMPO *MOVIE HOUSE*

Around since 1938, this theater plays indie/art films, plus retrospectives from some of film's biggest directors, all in VO (*"version originale,"* meaning their original language).

MAP 1 D2 Ⓐ 20 51 RUE DES ÉCOLES, 5E
01-43-54-51-60 WWW.LECHAMPO.COM

MAP 3 INVALIDES

LA PAGODE *MOVIE HOUSE*

Brought to Paris a century ago, this stunning Japanese building with sumptuous silks, carvings, and paintings offers movies from the East and the West.

MAP 3 E4 Ⓐ 46 57-BIS RUE DE BABYLONE, 7E
01-45-55-48-48 WWW.ETOILE-CINEMAS.COM/PAGODE

MAP 4 TOUR EIFFEL/ARC DE TRIOMPHE/TROCADÉRO

LE CRAZY HORSE *CABARET*

A bit racier than the other cabarets of the same ilk, Le Crazy Horse features celebrity guest performers like Dita von Teese and Pamela Anderson.

MAP 4 C4 Ⓐ 20 12 AV. GEORGE V, 8E
01-47-23-32-32 WWW.LECRAZYHORSEPARIS.COM

LE LIDO *CABARET*

Since 1946, this family-owned cabaret has been putting on the glitz with its elaborate shows and risqué showgirls (some are topless). Partly cheesy, partly over-the-top, it's a rite of passage for many first-timers in Paris.

MAP 4 A3 Ⓐ 7 116-BIS AV. DES CHAMPS-ELYSÉES, 8E
01-40-76-56-10 WWW.LIDO.FR

LES MARIONNETTES DU CHAMPS DE MARS *PUPPET SHOW*

French children love to watch the escapades of Guignol, a naughty

BEST BETS FOR NON-FRENCH SPEAKERS

With hundreds of plays, operas, musicals, and performances a night, there is simply no shortage of entertainment to be found in the City of Light. The daunting task for non-French speakers can be just where to find the information.

Start with your hotel concierge, who can help you consult one of the weekly guides, like the *Pariscope*, a valuable directory for events and movie times in the city.

Best bets include ballet performances at the magnificent **Opéra Garnier (p. 14);** the Marc Chagall ceiling is breathtaking. **L'Olympia (p. 98)** is a well-known venue for international musicians and has welcomed artists like the Rolling Stones and Madonna. **Salle Pleyel (p. 102)** is one of the foremost concert halls in Europe, and will already be a familiar name to those interested in classical music. Musical theater lovers should try their luck at the **Théâtre du Châtelet (p. 99).**

puppet, and his friends. There's lots of action, so even with the language difference youngsters will be amused.

 F5 Ⓐ43 ALLÉE DU GÉNÉRAL MARGUERITE, CHAMPS DE MARS, 7E
01-48-56-01-44
WWW.GUIGNOLDUCHAMPDEMARS.CENTERBLOG.NET

THÉÂTRE NATIONAL DE CHAILLOT *THEATER*

Non-francophones will enjoy the translation system in this 1930s theater, which hosts large-scale musicals and other grand productions.

 E2 Ⓐ31 1 PL. DU TROCADÉRO, 16E
01-53-65-31-00 WWW.THEATRE-CHAILLOT.FR

MAP 5 GRANDS BOULEVARDS

L'OLYMPIA *THEATER/CONCERTS*

Once a music hall, then a concert venue (the Beatles played here), l'Olympia is now home to a range of music and drama productions.

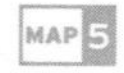 B2 Ⓐ5 28 BD. DES CAPUCINES, 2E
08-92-68-33-68 WWW.OLYMPIAHALL.COM

LE CRAZY HORSE

OPÉRA GARNIER

OPÉRA GARNIER
See SIGHTS, p. 14.

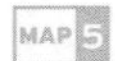 A3 ✪2 PL. DE L'OPÉRA, 9E
01-40-01-22-63 OR 08-92-89-90-90 (TICKETS)
WWW.OPERADEPARIS.FR

MAP 6 LOUVRE/LES HALLES

COMÉDIE FRANÇAISE (SALLE RICHELIEU) *THEATER*
Based here for more than 200 years, France's oldest theater company puts on the grand classics of French and international drama.

MAP 6 E1 Ⓐ37 2 RUE DE RICHELIEU, 1ER
08-25-10-16-80 WWW.COMEDIE-FRANCAISE.FR

THÉÂTRE DU CHÂTELET (THÉÂTRE MUSICAL DE PARIS) *VARIOUS*
Known as the "Châtelet" for its location, the home of Diaghilev mixes world-class ballet, music, and opera. It also presents popular musicals with subtitles, often with the original English-speaking casts.

MAP 6 F6 Ⓐ48 1 PL. DU CHÂTELET, 1ER
01-40-28-28-40 WWW.CHATELET-THEATRE.COM

MAP 7 MARAIS

CAFÉ DE LA GARE *VARIOUS*
If you want to sample Paris's café-theater scene, this Marais courtyard setting is one of the best, with offerings of drama, comedy, cabaret, and stand-up – in French.

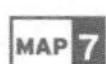 D2 Ⓐ30 41 RUE DU TEMPLE, 4E
01-42-78-52-51 WWW.CAFE-DE-LA-GARE.FR.ST

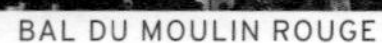

BAL DU MOULIN ROUGE LA CINÉMATHÈQUE FRANÇAISE

MAP 8 BASTILLE

OPÉRA NATIONAL DE PARIS BASTILLE *OPERA/CONCERTS*
Opened in 1989 to enhance the Garnier, this theater lacks the soul of the original but presents top-notch opera, symphony, and ballet. Performances take place September through mid-July.

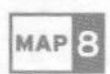 120 RUE DE LYON, 12E
01-71-25-24-23 WWW.OPERADEPARIS.FR

MAP 9 MONTMARTRE

LES ABBESSES *VARIOUS*
Modern drama, dance, and world music productions share the stage in this neoclassical theater tucked into a quiet corner of charming old Montmartre.

 31 RUE DES ABBESSES, 18E
01-42-74-22-77 WWW.THEATREDELAVILLE-PARIS.COM

BAL DU MOULIN ROUGE *CABARET*
Drink in the razzle-dazzle of this legendary cabaret – a show-stopper with more than 60 dancers in 1,000 sequined and feathered costumes.

 82 BD. DE CLICHY, 18E
01-53-09-82-82 WWW.MOULINROUGE.FR

LA CIGALE *CABARET*
This cabaret theater first opened in 1887, and it has presented a broad mix of music and drama ever since. In 2011, it doubled as the Moulin Rouge in Woody Allen's film *Midnight in Paris*.

 120 BD. DE ROCHECHOUART, 18E
01-46-06-59-29 OR 01-49-25-89-99 (TICKETS)
WWW.LACIGALE.FR

CINÉMA STUDIO 28 *MOVIE HOUSE*
Intimate and dripping with art deco charm, this single-screen the-

LE BATACLAN

CABARET SAUVAGE

ater shows oldies and new releases in every genre. Come early to sip a glass of wine at the in-house café before the show.

D3 A 14 10 RUE THOLOZE, 18E
01-46-06-36-07 WWW.CINEMASTUDIO28.COM

AU LAPIN AGILE *CABARET*
The setting in Steve Martin's fictional play about Picasso, this atmospheric, legendary Montmartre cabaret may not spell a wild night out, but it's a great place to hear old French *chansons* sung by an enthusiastic group of young singers.

B3 A 4 22 RUE DES SAULES, 18E
01-46-06-85-87 WWW.AU-LAPIN-AGILE.COM

MAP 10 CANAL ST-MARTIN

LE BATACLAN *CONCERTS*
Music fans line up for 1980s New Wave, modern French pop, and the occasional heavy metal show at this venue built in 1864. The Bataclan Café next door dishes up pre-concert drinks and tapas.

F5 A 26 50 BD. VOLTAIRE, 11E
01-43-14-35-35 WWW.BATACLAN.FR

OVERVIEW MAP

LA BELLEVILLOISE *VARIOUS*
On any given night, you might find cabaret or theater performances upstairs, caffeine and jazz downstairs, or an art happening on the uppermost floor. Events are eclectic and fun, and pull a mixed crowd.

OVERVIEW MAP **B6** 19-21 RUE BOYER, 20E
01-46-36-07-07 WWW.LABELLEVILLOISE.COM

CABARET SAUVAGE *CONCERTS*
Artists from all over the world perform concerts under the enormous

red circus tent at this canal-side hot spot. A veritable circus of sights and sounds in a magical setting.

OVERVIEW MAP B5 PEDESTRIAN ACCESS AT 59 BD. MACDONALD IN PARC DE LA VILLETTE, 19E
01-42-09-03-09 WWW.CABARETSAUVAGE.COM

LA CINÉMATHÈQUE FRANÇAISE *MOVIE HOUSE*
The Cinémathèque boasts the largest movie archives in the world, with a full program of classic films, many rare. Movie types like Wim Wenders and David Lynch have appeared in the past for Q & A sessions on their works.

OVERVIEW MAP E5 51 RUE DE BERCY, 12E
01-71-19-33-33 WWW.CINEMATHEQUE.FR

CITÉ DE LA MUSIQUE *CONCERTS*
Part of Parc de la Villette, this music complex hosts concerts and performances of dazzling variety, from a famed jazz festival in July to world music concerts.

OVERVIEW MAP B5 221 AV. JEAN JAURÉS, 19E
01-44-84-44-84 WWW.CITE-MUSIQUE.FR

FLÈCHE D'OR *CONCERTS*
A belle époque train station has been reborn as an intimate concert hall that welcomes the best indie bands from across Europe. It provides easy access to nightlife for guests at hip hotel Mama Shelter, directly across the street.

OVERVIEW MAP D6 102-BIS RUE DE BAGNOLET, 20E
01-44-64-01-02 WWW.FLECHEDOR.FR

LE GRAND REX *MOVIE HOUSE*
Open since 1932, one of the biggest cinemas in Europe hosts movies, premieres, big-name concerts, and more. It also offers guided tours of the theater, some combining visits to other tourist sites or special courses for children.

OVERVIEW MAP C4 1 BD. POISSONIÈRE, 2E
08-92-68-05-96 WWW.LEGRANDREX.COM

SALLE PLEYEL *CONCERTS*
Home to the Orchestra of Paris and the Philharmonic Orchestra of Radio France, the Salle Pleyel has stunning acoustics and is regarded as one of the best concert halls in Europe.

OVERVIEW MAP C2 252 RUE DU FAUBOURG ST-HONORÉ, 8E
01-42-56-13-13 WWW.SALLEPLEYEL.FR

THÉÂTRE DE LA BASTILLE *DANCE*
This is one of the city's leading dance venues for cutting-edge contemporary work, experimental music, and drama.

OVERVIEW MAP D5 76 RUE DE LA ROQUETTE, 11E
01-43-57-42-14 WWW.THEATRE-BASTILLE.COM

LE TRABENDO *CONCERTS*
At this compact club in the Parc de la Villette, fans can sidle right up to the low stage for close contact with their favorite musicians. A super spot to see up-and-coming bands.

OVERVIEW MAP B5 211 AV. JUAN JUARES, 19E
01-42-06-05-52 WWW.LATRABENDO.NET

RECREATION

MAP 1 QUARTIER LATIN/LES ÎLES

PISCINE PONTOISE
Made famous by Juliette Binoche in the movie *Blue*, this art deco swimming pool has been classified a historical monument by the City of Paris.

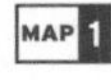 C5 Ⓐ16 17 RUE DE PONTOISE, 5E
01-55-42-77-88 WWW.EQUIPEMENT.PARIS.FR

ST-GERMAIN-DES-PRÉS

VEDETTES DU PONT NEUF
Holding up to 550 passengers at a time (smaller than the *bateaux-mouches*), these water cruisers ply the Seine all year, letting you see many Paris sights from a spectacular vantage point.

 A3 Ⓐ2 SQUARE DU VERT GALANT (BENEATH PONT NEUF), 1ER
01-46-33-98-38 WWW.VEDETTESDUPONTNEUF.COM

TOUR EIFFEL/ARC DE TRIOMPHE/TROCADÉRO

BATEAUX-MOUCHES
With capacities of 600–1,400 passengers, these large boats offer lunch and dinner cruises as well as standard-issue Seine excursions with recorded commentary in multiple languages.

 D4 Ⓐ28 PONT DE L'ALMA, 7E
01-40-76-99-99 WWW.BATEAUX-MOUCHES.FR

BATOBUS
Hop on and off at key landmarks (e.g., Tour Eiffel, Musée d'Orsay, Musée du Louvre, Notre-Dame) with a day pass for this commuter boat used by Parisians. Unlike boat cruises, these are commentary-free, which can be a blessing.

 E3 Ⓐ35 PORT DE LA BOURDONNAIS, 7E
08-25-05-01-01 WWW.BATOBUS.COM

I HEART HANIF CABS
Whirl around Paris in a Thai-style *tuk-tuk* (auto rickshaw), chasing

SOME LIKE IT HOT

If words like "chiffonade" and *"déglacer"* (to deglaze) whet your appetite, consider sinking your teeth into French culinary culture at a local cooking course. **Le Cordon Bleu (p. 106)** teaches novices to sauté, julienne, and *désosser* (to bone), but short courses in macaroon-making or bread-baking hold a definitive Franco-appeal. At La Cucina di Terresa (www.lacucina-diterresa.com), crash courses in organic vegetables and natural wines commence with a charming American hostess in her authentic Paris apartment, and the icing on the cake is eating your efforts at the end of class. In tree-shaded Montmartre, cozy culinary academy Cook'n with Class (01/42-57-22-84, 21 rue Custine, 18E, www.cooknwithclass.com) gives primers on French desserts and (swoon!) chocolate for beginners.

all the must-see sights and a few lesser-known insider spots. Photo breaks and custom music amp up the adventure.

 A2 Ⓐ5 01-79-46-94-71 WWW.HANIF-TUKTUK-PARIS.COM

GRANDS BOULEVARDS

CITROËN TOURS OF PARIS – 4 ROUES SOUS 1 PARAPLUIE
Grab your beret and take a trip back in time from the backseat of a vintage convertible Citroën 2CV. Friendly chauffeurs in striped T-shirts fulfill the French fantasy component with style.

 E2 Ⓐ47 DEPARTURES FROM PLACE DE LA CONCORDE, 8E
08-00-80-06-31 WWW.4ROUES-SOUS-1PARAPLUIE.COM

MARAIS

PARIS PLAGES
Parisians in town during the summer and savvy tourists head to Paris Plages, the sandy beachfronts created along the Seine and, more recently, along the Bassin de la Villette, during the last week of July until the last week of August.

 F5 Ⓐ54 FROM THE PONT DES ARTS TO THE PONT DE SULLY

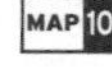 A2 Ⓐ1 FROM LA ROTONDE DE LEDOUX TO MAGASINS GÉNÉRAUX WWW.PARIS-PLAGES.FR

CITROËN TOURS OF PARIS

PROMENADE PLANTÉE

PARIS RANDO VÉLO

This volunteer-run operation leads a free three-hour bike excursion around Paris every Friday night from 10:30 P.M. The route changes every week, but the website has detailed instructions.

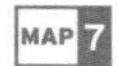 E2 Ⓐ 47 BEGINS IN FRONT OF HÔTEL DE VILLE, 4E
06-64-17-90-44 WWW.PARISRANDOVELO.COM

MAP 8 BASTILLE

DANCING ON THE SQUARE TINO ROSSI

Open-air dancing beside the Seine takes place in this square every night June-September, with "stages" for tango, salsa, and swing. All ages and abilities are welcome.

 E2 Ⓐ 30 QUAI ST-BERNARD, 5E

PROMENADE PLANTÉE

Stroll from the Gare de Lyon to the Bois de Vincennes through a park constructed atop an ancient train trestle and along paths alive with wild and cultivated vegetation.

 C5 Ⓐ 26 AV. DAUMESNIL, 12E
01-44-68-13-48 WWW.PROMENADE-PLANTEE.ORG

MAP 10 CANAL ST-MARTIN

CANAUXRAMA

These small boats float at a leisurely pace down the canal and through each of its locks, offering a glimpse of Paris's lesser-known neighborhoods.

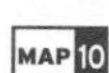 A2 Ⓐ 2 13 QUAI DE LA LOIRE, 19E
01-42-39-15-00 WWW.CANAUXRAMA.COM

OVERVIEW MAP

BOATING IN THE BOIS DE VINCENNES AND BOIS DE BOULOGNE

There's nothing more romantic than rowing around the scenic lakes of Paris's two great "woods," the Bois de Vincennes and the Bois de Boulogne. Boat rentals are available March-October for up to four adults. Bring a picnic.

OVERVIEW MAP **E6** BOIS DE VINCENNES, LAC DAUMESNIL, 12E WWW.PARIS.FR

OVERVIEW MAP **C1** BOIS DE BOULOGNE, LAC INFÉRIEUR, 16E WWW.PARIS.FR

CIAO PARIS

Earn bragging rights and cool cred with a freewheelin' spin through the cobbled streets on a classic Vespa scooter. Candy-colored machines are delivered to your door, along with suggested itineraries and that all-important helmet.

SCOOTERS DELIVERED TO YOUR HOTEL WWW.CIAOPARIS.FR

LE CORDON BLEU

Special courses at the prestigious Cordon Bleu cookery school include two-hour workshops for children and three-hour workshops for adults, covering subjects ranging from how to perfect your own soups to creating classic desserts.

OVERVIEW MAP **E2** 8 RUE LÉON DELHOMME, 15E 01-53-68-22-50 WWW.CORDONBLEU.EDU

FAT TIRE BIKE AND CITY SEGWAY TOURS

Enjoy a leisurely day or evening bike tour in English around Paris, or day trips to Versailles and Monet's gardens. Segway and skip-the-line museum tours are also available.

OVERVIEW MAP **D2** 24 RUE EDGAR FAURE, 15E 01-56-58-10-54 WWW.FATTIREBIKETOURSPARIS.COM WWW.CITYSEGWAYTOURS.COM

FRIDAY NIGHT FEVER SKATE

This weekly phenomenon attracts up to 20,000 skaters for about three hours of fast-paced blading. It's also an amusing spectator sport for less-expert enthusiasts. It starts Friday nights at 10 P.M.

OVERVIEW MAP **D3** MEET AT TOUR MONTPARNASSE IN FRONT OF THE TRAIN STATION, 14E HTTP://PARI-ROLLER.COM

PARC ANDRÉ CITROËN

This contemporary, riverside park replaced a Citroën car factory with imaginative water features and room for up to 15 passengers at a time in a giant, anchored hot-air balloon.

OVERVIEW MAP **D1** QUAI ANDRÉ CITROËN, 15E WWW.PARIS.FR

PARC DE BELLEVILLE

Some of the best views of Paris can be seen from this contemporary, hillside park built on top of an old quarry. The cascading fountain is the longest in the city.

OVERVIEW MAP **C5** RUE COURONNES OR RUE JULIEN LACROIX, 20E WWW.PARIS.FR

FAT TIRE BIKE AND CITY SEGWAY TOURS

PARC DES BUTTES CHAUMONT

PARC DE BERCY

Drop in for a stroll beneath the century-old trees of this creatively designed contemporary park in Paris's former wine-bottling district next to Bercy Village.

OVERVIEW MAP **E5** 41 RUE PAUL BELMONDO, 12E
01-44-74-09-09 WWW.PARIS.FR

PARC DE LA VILLETTE

This modern, mixed-use green space built where the old city slaughterhouses once stood contains museums, restaurants, concert venues, and exposition halls. Summertime is high season, with concerts, outdoor cinema, and recreation possibilities for every generation.

OVERVIEW MAP **B5** 211 AV. JEAN JAURÉS, 19E
01-40-03-75-75 WWW.VILLETTE.COM

PARC DES BUTTES CHAUMONT

Ascend to wild nature in this hilltop park created in the 19th

PARIS ON TWO WHEELS

There are many activities in Paris for fans of two-wheeled diversions. With the advent of Vélib' (01/30-79-79-30, www.velib.paris.fr), the city-sponsored bicycle-hire system, cycling through the streets of Paris isn't as far-fetched as it may seem. Pick up your bike at one of 1,800 stations across the city, and for amazing views, take advantage of the bicycle lanes located along the Seine. For a more structured excursion, call the friendly guides at **Fat Tire Bike and City Segway Tours (p. 106),** who arrange regular outings for groups on one of their cushy cruisers or a Segway. And the volunteer-run **Paris Rando Vélo (p. 105)** offers free three-hour evening bike rides every Friday night at 10 P.M.

PARC DES PRINCES

PARC MONTSOURIS

century. You can picnic on its grassy lawns – a rarity in the city's manicured parks.

OVERVIEW MAP B5 ACCESS VIA RUE MANIN OR RUE BOTZARIS, 19E
WWW.PARIS.FR

PARC DES PRINCES

The home stadium for the Paris St-Germain football league hosts lively matches that steep game-goers in French sports culture. In the off-season, big-ticket concerts reign. Michael Jackson, the Rolling Stones, and Green Day have all played here.

OVERVIEW MAP E1 24 RUE DU COMMANDANT GUILBAUD, 16E
01-47-43-71-71 WWW.PSG.FR

PARC MONTSOURIS

Sweeping lawns perfect for sunbathing, 100-year-old trees, and a picturesque lake make this romantic English-style park a popular retreat with locals and university students.

OVERVIEW MAP E4 BD. JOURDAN AT RER CITÉ UNIVERSITAIRE, 14E
WWW.PARIS.FR

LE PETIT BAL MUSETTE

Rain, snow, or shine, accordionist Christian Bassoul hits the square every Sunday at 11 A.M. and the dancers follow. The decades-old tradition gives this already quaint quarter even more charm.

OVERVIEW MAP E4 PLACE DE L'EGLISE ST-MEDIARD, 5E
06-18-52-31-51 WWW.PETITBAL.COM

PISCINE BUTTE-AUX-CAILLES

These three pools – one indoors and two outdoors – are historically listed, art deco–era structures.

OVERVIEW MAP E4 5 PL. PAUL VERLAINE, 13E
01-45-89-60-05 WWW.PARIS.FR

ROLAND GARROS

This stadium plays host to the French Open. Tickets for the Grand Slam event may be hard to come by, but the Tenniseum, a multimedia tennis museum, offers behind-the-scenes tours of the stadium to the public year-round.

OVERVIEW MAP D1 2 AV. GORDON BENNETT (NEAR PORTE D'AUTEUIL), 16E
01-47-43-48-48 WWW.ROLANDGARROS.COM

LE PETIT BAL MUSETTE

TOUR MONTPARNASSE

TOUR MONTPARNASSE

A speedy elevator whisks passengers to the 56th-floor terrace of Paris's tallest high-rise, where *incroyable* (incredible) views across the urban landscape await.

OVERVIEW MAP **E3** 33 AV. DU MAINE, 15E
01-45-38-52-56 WWW.TOURMONTPARNASSE56.COM

HOTELS

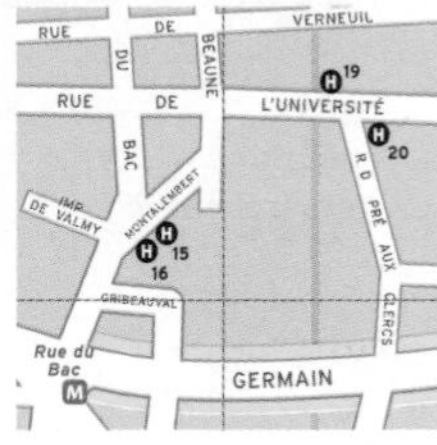

Best subterranean swimming pool: **L'HOTEL,** p. 112

Best bathrooms: **HÔTEL LE BELLECHASSE,** p. 114

Best value: **HÔTEL MAYET,** p. 115

Most luxurious spa: **FOUR SEASONS GEORGE V,** p. 116

Best revamp: **LE ROYAL MONCEAU – RAFFLES PARIS,** p. 116

Most historic atmosphere: **HÔTEL SAINT MERRY,** p. 119

Most romantic: **HÔTEL AMOUR,** p. 120

Best hostel: **PLUG-INN HOSTEL,** p. 120

Hippest hotel bar: **LE BRISTOL PARIS,** p. 121

Most space-age decor: **HÔTEL SEVEN,** p. 121

Most talked about: **MAMA SHELTER,** p. 122

Most peaceful: **SAINT JAMES PARIS,** p. 122

PRICE KEY

$ ROOMS UNDER $200

$$ ROOMS $200-300

$$$ ROOMS OVER $300

MAP 1 QUARTIER LATIN/LES ÎLES

HÔTEL DES GRANDS HOMMES *ROMANTIC $*
Friendly owners and a great location greet guests to this 18th-century building featuring brass beds, exposed beams, and a flower garden.

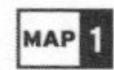
F3 29 17 PL. DU PANTHÉON, 5E
01-46-34-19-60 WWW.HOTELDESGRANDSHOMMES.COM

HÔTEL DESIGN DE LA SORBONNE *CHIC $$*
Modern decor livens up the Old World ambiance of this welcoming boutique hotel. All rooms feature state-of-the-art computers and free wireless Internet, and some rooms boast Eiffel Tour views and clawfoot bathtubs.

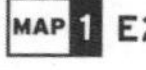
E2 24 6 RUE VICTOR COUSIN, 5E
01-43-54-58-08 WWW.HOTELSORBONNE.COM

HÔTEL DU JEU DE PAUME *QUAINT $$*
Retreat on the Île St-Louis in this 17th-century tennis court transformed into a well-lit and airy hotel with tiled floors, timbered ceilings, and a spacious garden.

A5 6 54 RUE ST-LOUIS-EN-L'ÎLE, 4E
01-43-26-14-18 WWW.JEUDEPAUMEHOTEL.COM

HÔTEL LE CLOS MEDICIS *CHIC $$*
Warm modern interiors and a wood-burning fireplace in the lobby make the Clos Medicis a truly welcoming home away from home. It's a short walk from the Jardin du Luxembourg.

F1 27 56 MONSIEUR LE PRINCE, 6E
01-43-29-10-80 WWW.CLOSMEDICIS.COM

HÔTEL LES DEGRÉS *QUAINT $*
Views over Notre Dame and a prime sightseeing location are two good reasons to choose this cozy hotel loaded with medieval charm. The breakfast croissants are another.

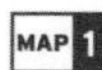
C3 11 10 RUE DES GRANDS DEGRÉS, 5E
01-55-42-88-88 WWW.LESDEGRESHOTEL.COM

MAP 2 ST-GERMAIN-DES-PRÉS

ARTUS *CHIC $$*
The art deco exterior has its own allure, but inside, it's a thoroughly modern experience. Smartly furnished rooms, a professional staff, and a hearty breakfast lure repeat clients.

D3 30 34 RUE DE BUCI, 6E
01-43-29-07-20 WWW.ARTUSHOTEL.COM

L'HÔTEL *CHIC $$$*
The enchantingly hip Jacques Garcia-designed hotel where Oscar Wilde took his last breath was a former *pavilion d'amour* (bordello),

HÔTEL LE CLOS MEDICIS

ARTUS

and it has since welcomed everyone from Princess Grace to Frank Sinatra.

MAP 2 B2 H 4 13 RUE DES BEAUX ARTS, 6E
01-44-41-99-00 WWW.L-HOTEL.COM

HÔTEL BEL AMI *CHIC $$*
Known for its minimalist chic design, the Bel Ami features rooms in calm pastels or citrus orange, with fresh orchids throughout, a fireplace lounge, and a Wellness Center.

MAP 2 D2 H 24 7-11 RUE ST-BENOÎT, 6E
01-42-61-53-53 WWW.HOTEL-BEL-AMI.COM

HÔTEL DE L'ABBAYE ST-GERMAIN *ROMANTIC $$*
A former convent, l'Abbaye's cobbled courtyard and fireplace lounge lead to well-appointed guest rooms with antique furnishings, designer floral fabrics, and flat-screen TVs.

MAP 2 F2 H 46 10 RUE CASSETTE, 6E
01-45-44-38-11 WWW.HOTEL-ABBAYE.COM

HÔTEL DES MARRONNIERS *ROMANTIC $*
Set back from the street by a cobbled courtyard, this adorable hotel has its own private garden shaded by chestnut trees. Rooms are small but quiet, with beautifully coordinated fabrics.

MAP 2 C2 H 14 21 RUE JACOB, 6E
01-43-25-30-60 WWW.HOTEL-MARRONNIERS.COM

HÔTEL RELAIS ST-GERMAIN *QUAINT $$*
This 17th-century building retains its historic mood with period furniture, luxurious fabrics, and antique prints. Each room is named for a different author.

MAP 2 D5 H 32 9 CARREFOUR DE L'ODÉON, 6E
01-44-27-07-97
WWW.HOTEL-PARIS-RELAIS-SAINT-GERMAIN.COM

HÔTEL SAINT THOMAS D'AQUIN *QUAINT $*
On a quiet shopping street, the Hôtel Saint Thomas d'Aquin is in a former private mansion with wonderful floor-length windows, and is known for its excellent service.

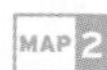 C1 H 10 3 RUE DU PRÉ AUX CLERCS, 7E
01-42-61-01-22 WWW.AQUIN-PARIS-HOTEL.COM

HÔTEL LE BELLECHASSE

HÔTEL LENOX

HÔTEL SAINT VINCENT *ROMANTIC* $
With Napoléon III-style decor mixed with modern amenities, the Saint Vincent has elegant Parisian features, like exposed wooden beams. Budget-friendly rates and the Left Bank location make this an ideal place to stay.

MAP 2 C1 H 11 5 RUE DU PRÉ AUX CLERCS, 7E
01-42-61-01-51 WWW.HOTELSAINTVINCENTPARIS.COM

RELAIS CHRISTINE *CHIC* $$$
This 16th-century convent has kept its medieval feel with rich colors and exposed wooden beams. Rooms are individually decorated in toile de Jouy and Louis XIII furnishings.

MAP 2 C4 H 20 3 RUE CHRISTINE, 6E
01-40-51-60-80 WWW.RELAIS-CHRISTINE.COM

MAP 3 INVALIDES

HÔTEL DE L'UNIVERSITÉ *QUAINT* $
Formerly a Benedictine convent, this Left Bank favorite near St-Germain-des-Prés has stone fireplaces, simple antique furnishings, and plenty of space – a rarity in Paris!

MAP 3 B6 H 19 22 RUE DE L'UNIVERSITÉ, 7E
01-42-61-09-39 WWW.PARIS-HOTEL-UNIVERSITE.COM

HÔTEL DUC DE ST-SIMON *ROMANTIC* $$
This peaceful French country-style retreat has elegantly appointed rooms and gorgeous tiled bathrooms, all set around a shaded central courtyard.

MAP 4 C5 H 29 14 RUE DE ST-SIMON, 7E
01-44-39-20-20 WWW.HOTELDUCDESAINTSIMON.COM

HÔTEL LE BELLECHASSE *CHIC* $$
Fashion designer Christian Lacroix is the mastermind behind the elegant and often quirky decor found at this designer hotel. Modern touches like flat-screen TVs and iPod docks are harmoniously included.

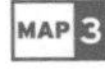
MAP 3 B4 H 12 8 RUE DE BELLECHASSE, 7E
01-45-50-22-31 WWW.LEBELLECHASSE.COM

CELEBRITY HOTELS

Paris hotels are notoriously good locations for celebrity encounters. Most stars stay either at **Hôtel Le Meurice (p. 117)** or the Hôtel de Crillon (closed until 2015 for renovations, 10 pl. de la Concorde, 8E, 01-44-71-15-00, www.crillon.com), both of which are venues for many international film junkets. Somewhat lesser known is **Hôtel Raphael (p. 116),** once home to Marlon Brando, and esteemed for being the more discreet choice for paparazzi-shy celebrities. Famous fashionistas and musicians tend to prefer **Hôtel Plaza Athénée (p. 116)** or **Le Bristol Paris (p. 121),** while those seeking an autograph from a tennis great should head to the **Hôtel de Sers (p. 116),** which enjoys a loyal following of world-class players competing in the French Open.

HÔTEL LENOX *ROMANTIC $$*

Within walking distance of the Musée d'Orsay and the Louvre, this cozy, stylish hotel is ideal for museum-goers. Nightcaps in the welcoming lounge are a nice way to end the day.

B6 H 20 9 RUE DE L'UNIVERSITÉ, 7E
01-42-96-10-95
WWW.HOTELPARISLENOXSAINTGERMAIN.COM

HÔTEL LUTETIA *GRAND $$$*

Built in 1911, this is the only true palace hotel on the Left Bank, with contemporary artwork throughout and a plush jazz bar frequented by chic Parisians.

MAP 3 D6 H 41 45 BD. RASPAIL, 6E
01-49-54-46-46 WWW.LUTETIA-PARIS.COM

HÔTEL MAYET *QUAINT $*

The rooms may be small at this budget boutique hotel, but each detail has been thoughtfully considered. Cheerful murals line the walls and a French breakfast is included in the price.

MAP 3 F5 H 50 3 RUE MAYET, 6E
01-47-83-21-35 WWW.MAYET.COM

HÔTEL PONT ROYAL *GRAND $$$*

Photos of Hemingway, Sartre, and other literary greats who've stayed here line the walls, rooting guests in the sense of regal Left Bank tradition. Room service comes courtesy of the attached Michelin-starred restaurant.

MAP 3 B5 H 16 5-7 RUE MONTALEMBERT, 7E
01-42-84-70-00
WWW.LESHOTELSDUROY.COM/EN/HOTEL-PONT-ROYAL

LE MONTALEMBERT *CHIC $$*

One of the earliest designer boutique hotels in Paris, the

Montalembert offers wildly contrasting styles of cool contemporary or cozy classic guest rooms just a few blocks from St-Germain-des-Prés.

MAP 3 B5 H 15 3 RUE MONTALEMBERT, 7E
01-45-49-68-68 WWW.HOTEL-MONTALEMBERT.FR

LE WALT *CHIC $$*
This contemporary boutique hotel near the Eiffel Tower features wooden floors, chocolate- and plum-colored fabrics, and enormous paintings above each bed.

MAP 3 E2 H 45 37 AV. DE LA MOTTE PICQUET, 7E
01-45-51-55-83 HTTP://LEWALTPARIS.COM

MAP 4 TOUR EIFFEL/ARC DE TRIOMPHE/TROCADÉRO

FOUR SEASONS GEORGE V *GRAND $$$*
A sumptuous palace hotel dripping with crystal, marble, silk, and antique furnishings, the George V is also renowned for its Versailles-style swimming pool and spa decorated in toile de Jouy and its Le Cinq restaurant.

MAP 4 B4 H 16 31 AV. GEORGE V, 8E
01-49-52-70-00 WWW.FOURSEASONS.COM/PARIS

HÔTEL DE SERS *GRAND $$$*
Minutes from the Champs-Elysées, 19th-century grandeur meets 21st-century chic. Rooms are spacious and luxurious. The hotel is also known for its superior fitness room.

MAP 4 B4 H 17 41 AV. PIERRE 1ER DE SERBIE, 8E
01-53-23-75-76 WWW.HOTELDESERS.COM

HÔTEL LANCASTER *GRAND $$$*
The Lancaster has long been a favored destination for those seeking comfortable seclusion. Enjoy the private art collection and Second Empire antiques.

MAP 4 A4 H 10 7 RUE DE BERRI, 8E
01-40-76-40-76 WWW.HOTEL-LANCASTER.FR

HÔTEL PLAZA ATHÉNÉE *GRAND $$$*
A favorite with fashionistas and visiting royalty, this hotel features opulently grand guest rooms, a stylish contemporary bar, and an haute-cuisine restaurant run by French superchef Alain Ducasse.

MAP 4 B5 H 18 25 AV. MONTAIGNE, 8E
01-53-67-66-65 WWW.PLAZA-ATHENEE-PARIS.COM

HÔTEL RAPHAEL *GRAND $$$*
Favored by U.S. presidents, including Ford and Bush Senior, the Raphael drips class. Its 90 rooms are crowded with antiques, and privacy is guaranteed.

MAP 4 B2 H 15 17 AV. KLÉBER, 16E
01-53-64-32-00 WWW.RAPHAEL-HOTEL.COM

LE ROYAL MONCEAU – RAFFLES PARIS *GRAND $$$*
Designer Philippe Starck was inspired by the 1940s and has created

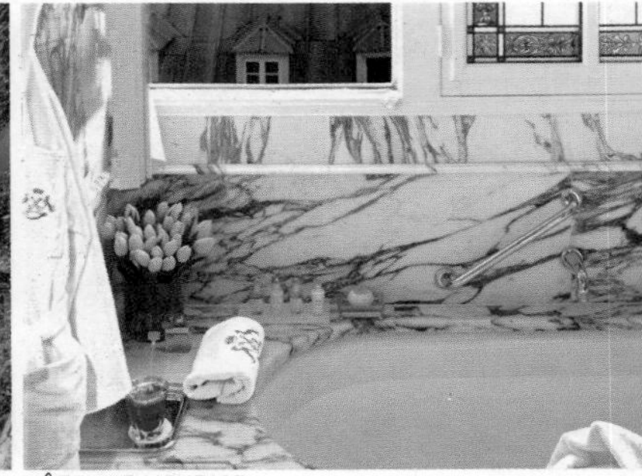

HÔTEL PLAZA ATHÉNÉE HÔTEL LE MEURICE

a luxurious bohemian decor, where rooms suggest the spontaneous creativity of an artist's atelier.

 A2 H1 37 AV. HOCHE, 8E
01-42-99-88-00 WWW.RAFFLES.COM

MAP 5 GRANDS BOULEVARDS

HÔTEL COSTES *CHIC $$$*

Statues of Roman gods hold court in the Costes's garden. The hotel's sumptuous velvety interior and indoor swimming pool attract jet-setting models and media types.

 D3 H36 239 RUE ST-HONORÉ, 1ER
01-42-44-50-00 WWW.HOTELCOSTES.COM

HÔTEL DES TUILERIES *QUAINT $*

Exceptionally located just off a market street near the Tuileries Garden, this 18th-century mansion is decorated with delicate antiques, gilt-framed paintings, and Persian carpets.

 D4 H38 10 RUE ST-HYACINTHE, 1ER
01-42-61-04-17 WWW.HOTEL-DES-TUILERIES.COM

HÔTEL GEORGE SAND *QUAINT $*

This cozy hotel combines crisp and contemporary decor with historic architectural details right around the corner from the Opéra Garnier and Parisian department stores.

 A1 H1 26 RUE DES MATHURINS, 9E
01-47-42-63-47 WWW.HOTELGEORGESAND.COM

HÔTEL LE MEURICE *GRAND $$$*

Built in 1817, this palace hotel overlooking the Tuileries is a kaleidoscope of mosaic tiling, marble, and crystal with enormous guest rooms decked out in Louis XVI furnishings.

 E3 H48 228 RUE DE RIVOLI, 1ER
01-44-58-10-10 WWW.LEMEURICE.COM

HÔTEL RITZ *GRAND $$$*

The legendary haunt of such luminaries as Ernest Hemingway and Coco Chanel closed for a two-year renovation project in mid-

HÔTEL THÉRÈSE

PARK HYATT PARIS-VENDÔME

2012 – the luxury hotel's first major closure since opening in 1898. The good news is that in addition to a room revamp, the pool and spa are getting a 21st-century makeover.

MAP 5 C3 H 25 15 PL. VENDÔME, 1ER
01-43-16-30-30 WWW.RITZPARIS.COM

HÔTEL THÉRÈSE *CHIC* *$*
Noble materials like deep velvets and rich wools are the inspiration for this mixture of period and modern decor. With the Louvre and the Opéra Garnier only a short walk away, the location can't be beat.

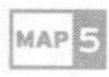 C6 H 30 5-7 RUE THÉRÈSE, 1ER
01-42-96-10-01 WWW.HOTELTHERESE.COM

HOTELS

PARK HYATT PARIS-VENDÔME *GRAND* *$$$*
Sleek mahogany, pale limestone, and rough bronze sculptures form the backdrop for high-tech luxuries like Bang & Olufsen TVs and under-floor heating.

 C3 H 24 5 RUE DE LA PAIX, 2E
01-58-71-12-34 HTTP://PARIS.VENDOME.HYATT.COM

MAP 6 LOUVRE/LES HALLES

HÔTEL BRITANNIQUE *ROMANTIC* *$*
The Britannique retains many of its attractive 19th-century features while also embracing modern facilities, such as Internet access, in its richly decorated rooms.

 E6 H 42 20 AV. VICTORIA, 1ER
01-42-33-74-59 WWW.HOTEL-BRITANNIQUE.FR

HÔTEL LE RELAIS DU LOUVRE *QUAINT* *$*
This typically Parisian hotel with views over the Louvre offers air-conditioned rooms decorated in colorful floral prints and exposed wooden beams.

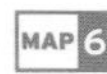 F3 H 45 19 RUE DES PRÊTRES ST-GERMAIN L'AUXERROIS, 1ER
01-40-41-96-42 WWW.RELAISDULOUVRE.COM

HÔTEL VICTOIRES OPÉRA *CHIC $$*
Redone in a tasteful minimalist style, the hotel's greatest charm is its location – on the bustling market street Montorgueil.

 B4 Ⓗ 8 56 RUE MONTORGUEIL, 2E
01-42-36-41-08 WWW.HOTELVICTOIRESOPERA.COM

MAP 7 MARAIS

HÔTEL BOURG TIBOURG *ROMANTIC $$*
This jewel-box hotel designed by Jacques Garcia features a voluptuous neo-Byzantine interior of mosaic tiling, exotic scented candles, and luxurious fabrics in rich colors.

 D3 Ⓗ 34 19 RUE DU BOURG-TIBOURG, 4E
01-42-78-47-39 WWW.BOURGTIBOURG.COM

HÔTEL CARON DE BEAUMARCHAIS *QUAINT $*
Named for the playwright Beaumarchais *(The Marriage of Figaro)*, who lived down the street, this charming hotel has exposed wooden beams and period furniture upholstered in fine floral fabrics.

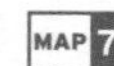 E4 Ⓗ 49 12 RUE VIEILLE DU TEMPLE, 4E
01-42-72-34-12 WWW.CARONDEBEAUMARCHAIS.COM

HÔTEL DU PETIT MOULIN *CHIC $$*
The 10 rooms in this historically listed building have been individually decorated by none other than French fashion designer Christian Lacroix.

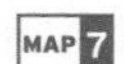 B4 Ⓗ 12 29-31 RUE DU POITOU, 3E
01-42-74-10-10 WWW.PARIS-HOTEL-PETITMOULIN.COM

HÔTEL SAINT MERRY *QUAINT $*
As if it stepped out of the Middle Ages, this former presbytery of the adjoining St-Merry Church is filled with authentic Gothic furnishings. The lack of TVs and an elevator adds to the monkish asceticism.

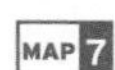 D1 Ⓗ 28 78 RUE DE LA VERRERIE, 4E
01-42-78-14-15 WWW.HOTELSAINTMERRYPARIS.COM

MAP 8 BASTILLE

LE PAVILLON DE LA REINE *ROMANTIC $$$*
Housed in a picture-perfect 17th-century mansion on Place des Vosges, this hotel has Louis XIII-style antiques, period tapestries, and fireplaces. Rooms feature four-poster beds, French windows, and views over a flowered courtyard.

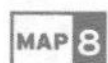 A1 Ⓗ 1 28 PL. DES VOSGES, 4E
01-40-29-19-19 WWW.PAVILLON-DE-LA-REINE.COM

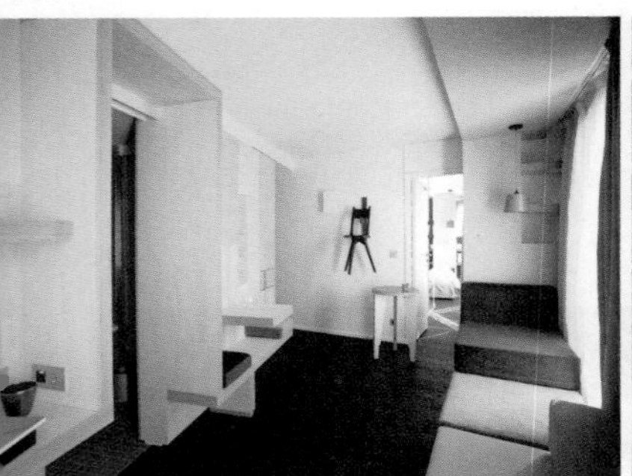
HOTEL LE CITIZEN DU CANAL PARIS

HÔTEL TAYLOR

MAP 9 MONTMARTRE

HÔTEL AMOUR *ROMANTIC $*

Read the love graffiti on the wall and you will understand why this amorous hotel has been such a hit. Each room has its own cheeky details just waiting to be discovered.

MAP 9 F5 H 36 8 RUE NAVARIN, 9E
01-48-78-31-80 WWW.HOTELAMOURPARIS.FR

HÔTEL PARTICULIER MONTMARTRE *ROMANTIC $$$*

A secret spot near the top of Montmartre, this former private mansion has been artfully turned into a unique and cozy hotel boasting gardens designed by Christian Louboutin's partner, Louis Benech.

MAP 9 C2 H 8 23 AV. JUNOT, 18E
01-53-41-81-40
WWW.HOTEL-PARTICULIER-MONTMARTRE.COM

PLUG-INN HOSTEL *QUAINT $*

Design and value reunite at the Plug-Inn, the only boutique-style hostel in Paris. Clean dormitory and triple accommodations are available for savvy budget travelers, with linens provided.

MAP 9 D3 H 16 7 RUE ARISTIDE BRUANT, 18E
01-42-58-42-58 WWW.PLUG-INN.FR

TERRASS HÔTEL *ROMANTIC $$*

One of the grandest hotels in Montmartre, this family-run hotel features breathtaking views from its upper rooms and a panoramic rooftop restaurant.

MAP 9 D2 H 13 12 RUE JOSEPH DE MAISTRE, 18E
01-44-92-34-14 WWW.TERRASS-HOTEL.COM

MAP 10 CANAL ST-MARTIN

HOTEL LE CITIZEN DU CANAL PARIS *CHIC $$*

This sleek hotel offers easy access to the neighborhood's best

HÔTEL 20 PRIEURE

AU SOURIRE DE MONTMARTRE

bars and eateries. Guests rave about the complimentary iPads and afternoon happy hour, but the hotel's highest marks are reserved for its stellar concierge services.

MAP 10 D2 H 12 96 QUAI DE JEMMAPES, 10E
01-83-62-55-50 WWW.LECITIZENHOTEL.COM

HÔTEL TAYLOR *ROMANTIC $*

On a calm street in a cool neighborhood, the Taylor makes a good home base for exploring the tree-lined canal and its eclectic wining-and-dining possibilities.

MAP 10 F2 H 22 6 RUE TAYLOR, 10E
01-42-40-11-01 WWW.PARIS-HOTEL-TAYLOR.COM

HÔTEL 20 PRIEURE *CHIC $*

Borrowing from Scandinavian design, this boutique hotel boasts bright, minimal rooms and a distinct coziness. A comfy urban escape for would-be bobos and arty types.

MAP 10 F4 H 23 20 RUE DE GRAND PRIEURE, 11E
01-47-00-74-14 WWW.HOTEL20PRIEURE.COM

OVERVIEW MAP

LE BRISTOL PARIS *GRAND $$$*

This 1925 palace boasts Louis XV- and Louis XVI-style luxury rooms. The magnificent gardens are topped only by the one-of-a-kind enclosed rooftop pool.

OVERVIEW MAP C3 112 RUE DU FAUBOURG ST-HONORÉ, 8E
01-53-43-43-00 WWW.LEBRISTOLPARIS.COM

HÔTEL DU MINISTÈRE *CHIC $$$*

Contemporary design and modern amenities (fitness room, organic toiletries) exude deluxe comfort. The natural wine bar and sumptuous breakfast spread are added bonuses.

OVERVIEW MAP C3 31 RUE DE SURENE, 8E
01-42-66-21-43 WWW.MINISTEREHOTEL.COM

HÔTEL SEVEN *CHIC $$*

Space-age and functional design converge at le Seven. Splurge

MAMA SHELTER

SAINT JAMES PARIS

on a glamorous suite with a fireplace and giant bathtub for the ultimate relaxing getaway.

OVERVIEW MAP D4 20 RUE BERTHOLLET, 5E
01-43-31-47-52 WWW.SEVENHOTELPARIS.COM

MAMA SHELTER *CHIC $*

Mama Shelter, designed by Philippe Starck, has created its own community on the outskirts of Paris. Guests are blown away by the quirky decor, like chalkboard designed ceilings, as well as the affordable rates.

OVERVIEW MAP C6 109 RUE DE BAGNOLET, 20E
01-43-48-48-48 WWW.MAMASHELTER.COM

SAINT JAMES PARIS *ROMANTIC $$$*

A stay at this luxe retreat is the next best thing to a weekend escape to a royal estate. Expect to be treated like visiting royalty during check-in, at the hotel spa, dining room, and everywhere in between.

OVERVIEW MAP C2 43 AV. BUGEAUD, 16E
01-44-05-81-82 HTTP://ST-JAMES-PARIS.COM

AU SOURIRE DE MONTMARTRE *QUAINT $$*

Morocco meets Montmartre at this inviting B&B. Rooms are a mélange of East and West, contemporary and classic, but the filling breakfast – croissants, fruit, coffee – is utterly French.

OVERVIEW MAP B4 64 RUE DE MONT CENIS, 18E
06-64-64-72-86
WWW.SOURIRE-DE-MONTMARTRE.COM

STANDARD DESIGN HÔTEL *CHIC $*

Modern and minimalist, this sleek hotel attracts a hip, urban clientele who want comfort and style with a dash of bohemia. The neighborhood is equally young and trendy.

OVERVIEW MAP B5 29 RUE DES TAILLANDIERS, 11E
01-47-00-29-26
WWW.STANDARD-DESIGN-HOTEL-PARIS.COM

SUBLIM EIFFEL *CHIC $$*

Outré design and a top-notch staff give this trendy hotel its edge. It's close enough to the Eiffel Tower and Invalides to feel connected, but distant enough to relax and unwind at the end of the day.

OVERVIEW MAP D3 94 BD. GARIBALDI, 15E
01-40-65-95-95 WWW.SUBLIMEIFFEL.COM

CITY ESSENTIALS

CHARLES DE GAULLE INTERNATIONAL AIRPORT

Most international flights land at Charles de Gaulle, which the French refer to as "Roissy," given its proximity to the village of Roissy-en-France, located 23 kilometers (14 miles) north of the city. To get to Paris from the airport there are several options.

The RER B train takes 45 minutes to central Paris (Châtelet-Les Halles), leaving from Terminal 2. If you arrive at Terminal 1, there is a free shuttle bus to Terminal 2.

Air France buses leave from both terminals every 15 minutes and stop at Porte Maillot and Place de l'Étoile (the Arc de Triomphe). The Roissybus runs every 15 minutes 6 A.M.-10:30 P.M. and every 20 minutes after 7 P.M. It will deposit you in central Paris at the Opéra Garnier.

You can also use a door-to-door shuttle service, which caters almost entirely to U.S.-based customers and has English-speaking staff. Prices are lower with two or more people. One reliable service is Airport Connection (01/43-65-55-55, www.airport-connection.com); you can make reservations in advance on the website.

A taxi takes 30 minutes to an hour, depending on traffic, so it's not necessarily faster. But it is probably the best option if you have a party of three and/or a lot of luggage. Keep in mind that French taxi drivers add an extra charge per article for luggage over 5 kg (roughly 11 lb.).

ARRIVING BY TRAIN

Paris has six main train stations, each providing service to different regions. These are: Gare d'Austerlitz (southwest France, Spain, and Portugal), Gare de l'Est (eastern France and Germany), Gare de Lyon (southern and eastern France, Switzerland, and Italy), Gare Montparnasse (Brittany and Bordeaux), Gare St-Lazare (Normandy), and Gare du Nord (Belgium, Holland, and England). Two types of trains serve each station: *grandes lignes* for long-distance trips and *banlieue* for suburban lines (both information lines can be reached at 08-90-36-10-10). The official website of SNCF (Société

Nationale des Chemins de Fer Français, www.sncf.com), the French train service, is notoriously difficult to use; however, it can be a cheaper option. Tickets can be sent to an address in France or picked up at the station using the same credit card used for purchase. Those looking to buy their tickets in person can do so at any of the several SNCF boutiques in central Paris, or at the train stations themselves.

Remember to *composter* (punch) your ticket in one of the yellow SNCF machines in the station before you board the train. If you haven't enough time, present yourself to an SNCF agent as soon as you board the train.

PUBLIC TRANSPORTATION

Paris has an extraordinary system of cheap public transportation. Métropolitain (Métro) lines link the entire city and run between 5:30 A.M. and about 1 A.M. weekly, and until 2:15 A.M. on Fridays and Saturdays. The lines are numbered and also identified by the final destination (for example, Line 1 westbound is indicated by La Défense, eastbound by Château de Vincennes). The same type of ticket can be used for buses and trams, where the ticket must be punched in the machine next to the driver or by the door. It is also possible to buy tickets directly from the bus driver; as a courtesy, try to use coins, because large bills are refused. To get off a bus, push the red button to signal that you would like to stop *(arrêt demandé)*. On the Métro you can transfer as many times as necessary using one ticket – just be certain to keep your ticket in a safe place, as inspections are commonplace and can mean large charges should you fail to produce your ticket. To transfer between buses or trams you must use a second ticket. If you miss the last Métro, you can catch the Noctilien "Noctambus" night bus (www.noctilien.fr), which runs 1-5:30 A.M. nightly, from the Châtelet area down the major roads of the city and into the suburbs. A bus on each Noctilien line is sent out every hour. A Métro ticket also allows you to ride on the RER (Réseau Express Régional) suburban trains within Paris city limits. To view Métro, bus, tram, or RER itineraries, visit the RATP (Régie Autonome des Transports Parisiens) site for transport options throughout Île-de-France, which encompasses more than 1,000 cities and towns in the greater Paris region (www.ratp.fr).

Vélib' (01/30-79-79-30, www.velib.paris.fr), a city-sponsored bicycle hire-service, allows cyclists to rent a bicycle from one of 1,800 terminals and to conveniently drop it off at any station of their choice. Customers have the option to apply for a year's subscription (€19-€39, depending on the type of subscription) or a short-term *abonnement*. Travelers should first check that they have the appropriate credit card: Visa, JCB, Mastercard, and American Express are accepted; however, cards must be a member of the GIE bank card network or have a microchip that meets EMV standards. Renting online allows you to use a non-chipped card. A short subscription costs €1.70 for one day (24 hours from when the bike was first taken from the terminal) and €8 for seven days. This subscription allows you to take the bicycle for free for the first half hour but costs €1 for the next half hour, €2 for the following half hour, and €4 for the third half hour. A deposit of €150 is pre-authorized from your card, but not cashed. When returning the bicycle to the terminal, make certain it has been properly attached, and that the red "locked" light is indicated. Also keep all receipts, should you need to make any claims.

TAXIS

Taxis are available throughout Paris, with taxi stands at most major intersections. A green light on the rooftop sign indicates that the taxi is free. A red light means it is occupied or has been engaged by a dispatcher. Taxi charges depend on the time of day and your location: Zone A is central Paris and Zone C takes you to the suburbs. There is a small extra charge for luggage weighing more than 5 kg (roughly 11 lb.). If you call for a taxi pickup, the fare will be counted from the moment the taxi heads in your direction. The *mairie* (office of the mayor) offers a taxi-stand directory service (01/45-30-30-30), which requires you to indicate the name of the arrondissement you wish to be retrieved in (in French) before you are transferred. Otherwise, reliable taxi services are Taxi Bleus (08/91-70-10-10) or Taxi G7 (01/47-39-47-39). If you are a group of more than three people it is recommended to call in advance to arrange a minivan, as many drivers will not take groups. If they do agree to take your group of more than three people, be aware there is a supplemental charge for the fourth person.

DRIVING AND RENTING A CAR

British, E.U., U.S., and Canadian driver's licenses are all valid in France. However, driving in Paris should be kept to a minimum unless you relish the challenges of contending with small one-way streets and somewhat rash drivers in congested traffic.

Street parking is metered in central Paris; you buy a ticket from a machine on the sidewalk and place it inside your windshield. There are public garages throughout the city that make the process more manageable and more expensive.

The major international rental companies are all represented in France, like Avis (08/20-05-05-05, www.avis.fr) and Hertz (01/41-91-95-25, www.hertz.fr), but there are also excellent European options, such as Europcar (08/25-35-83-58, www.europcar.fr). It is cheaper to shop around before you leave and, ideally, make car-rental arrangements in advance. Most major car-rental companies have offices at the airport and in or near central Paris, usually in the big train stations.

The newest public transportation system to hit Paris is the car-share program called Autolib'. Subscribing online (www.autolib.eu) for a period of a day, week, month, or year gives you access to a fleet of four-seat electric "Bluecars" stationed throughout Paris and the Île-de-France region. A valid driver's license and international permit are required for non-E.U. drivers, and charges average €10 to €14 per hour. This option is best for short, one-way trips.

CURRENCY EXCHANGE

France, as a member of the European Union, uses the euro (€) as its standard currency. Not all French banks change money, and their commissions vary. Banks are usually open Monday-Friday 9 A.M.-5 P.M. (some close at lunchtime) and often on Saturday mornings. Most of them will cash travelers checks, and some will give cash advances to Visa cardholders.

There are Travelex agencies in each of the two terminals at Charles de Gaulle airport. In addition, Thomas Cook maintains 50 branches in Paris, many of them in train stations. Look for the signs indicating a *bureau de change*.

AMERICAN EXPRESS

MAP 5 A2 11 RUE SCRIBE, 9E
01-47-14-50-00

BANQUE TRAVELEX

MAP 4 A4 52 AV. DES CHAMPS-ELYSÉES, 8E
01-42-89-80-33

EMBASSIES

BRITISH EMBASSY

OVERVIEW MAP **C3** 35 RUE DE FAUBOURG ST-HONORÉ, 8E
01-44-51-31-00

CANADIAN EMBASSY

MAP 4 B5 35 AV. MONTAIGNE, 8E
01-44-43-29-00

U.S. EMBASSY

OVERVIEW MAP **C3** 2 AV. GABRIEL, 8E
01-43-12-22-22

U.S. EMBASSY: AMERICAN CITIZEN SERVICES

MAP 5 D2 2 RUE ST-FLORENTIN, 1ER
01-43-12-22-22

VISITOR INFORMATION

The Office du Tourisme et des Congrès de Paris (Paris Convention and Visitors Bureau), the city's official tourist office, offers help with hotel reservations in French and

English, information about exhibitions, free maps and brochures, sightseeing information, and tour bookings. You can also buy here the Paris City Passport (a booklet of discount coupons), Paris Visite transport passes, and the Paris Museum-Monument Pass. The office is open Monday-Saturday 10 A.M.-7 P.M. and Sunday and public holidays 11 A.M.-7 P.M.

PARIS VISITORS BUREAU

MAP 5 D5 25 RUE DES PYRAMIDES
08-92-68-30-00 WWW.PARISINFO.COM

WEATHER

Paris is wet in spring, sometimes warm and humid, then suddenly chilly. The rain might be a drizzle or a torrential downpour. In winter, snow is rare, temperatures are cold, and skies are dark at 5 P.M. Summer days can be uncomfortably hot, but the long evenings compensate. Autumn weather is the most stable of the year.

HOURS

Paris is a late-night city, and can even be an all-night city in places like rue Oberkampf, the rue de Rivoli, and the Champs-Elysées. Otherwise, most restaurants, cafés, and wine bars shut their doors by 1 A.M., with many restaurants taking last orders at 10:30 P.M. and not after 2:30 P.M. for most lunch services. In general, Paris shops are open Monday-Saturday 10 A.M.-7 P.M. (some of the larger grocery stores, like Monoprix, are now open until 9 or 10 P.M.). Smaller shops and businesses sometimes close at lunch, usually 12:30-2 P.M., and on Mondays. Many family-owned shops and restaurants are closed all or part of August.

FESTIVALS AND EVENTS

JANUARY/FEBRUARY

Chinese New Year: Dragons and lanterns are on display from the Place d'Italie to the Porte de Choisy, the largest Chinese neighborhood in Paris. From the end of January to the beginning of February. (Pl. d'Italie to Porte de Choisy, 13E; www.paris.fr)

Retail Sales: Twice each year, for several weeks in January and June, France is thrown into a consumer frenzy with the start of *les soldes*, or sales. Throughout the country, boutiques, mom-and-pop shops, and giant department stores slash prices by 30, 50, or even 70 percent off the original prices. The first week offers the best selection. (Various locations)

MARCH

Salon du Livre: International literary lights descend on Paris for one week for this annual book fair. Mid-March. (Paris Porte de Versailles, Pavillon 1, Blvd. Victor, 15E; 01-47-56-64-36, www.salondulivreparis.com)

APRIL

Paris Marathon: The race starts at the Place de la Concorde and finishes on avenue Foch. The Champs-Elysées offers the best view. First week of April. (Pl. de le Concorde, 8E, to Av. Foch, 16E; 01-41-33-15-68, www.parismarathon.com)

MAY

French Open: This prestigious tennis tournament is one of the four Grand Slam events and draws big names. Last week of May/first week of June. (Stade Roland Garros, 08-25-16-75-16, www.rolandgarros.com)

JUNE

Designer's Days: Contemporary designers, showrooms, and cutting-edge boutiques open their doors for a showcase of exhibitions dedicated to design and fashion. Mid-June. (Various locations; 01-40-21-04-88, www.designersdays.com)

Festival de Saint-Denis: A classical and world music festival with a full program of concerts, held at the Basilique Cathédrale de Saint-Denis and venues across central Paris. All of June. (Basilique Cathédrale de Saint-Denis, 2 Pl. de la Légion d'Honneur 93200 St-Denis; 01-48-13-06-07, www.festival-saint-denis.com)

Fête de la Musique: In Paris, the longest day of the year is also the loudest. Singers of all stripes perform for free in parks and live bands jam in the streets. June 21. (Various locations; 01-40-03-94-70, www.fetedelamusique.culture.fr)

Fête du Cinéma: For three days, film buffs can see as many films as they want in any movie theater in Paris for €1.50 per ticket. End of June. (Various locations; www.feteducinema.com)

Garçons de Café: In this race, café waiters and waitresses run around carrying a tray with a bottle and glass, and any breaks mean they're out. Late June. (Location changes yearly; 08-92-68-31-12)

Gay Pride Parade: The annual gay and lesbian parade follows a different route every year, but it's a nonstop party in the Marais. Last Saturday in June. (Location changes yearly; www.gaypride.fr)

JULY

Bastille Day: The French national holiday is celebrated by an impressive military parade up the Champs-Elysées, fireworks by the Eiffel Tower, and festive balls at certain fire stations. July 14. (Various locations; www.paris.fr)

Cinéma en Plein Air: Outdoor-loving movie buffs live for the chance to watch films daily, outside at the Parc de la

Villette. All films are shown in their original version with subtitles. From mid-July to mid-August. (Parc de la Villette, Blvd. MacDonald, 19E; 01-40-03-75-75, www.villette.com)

Paris Plages: In late July stretching into late August, Paris gives its best approximation of a sunny seaside beach scene at two waterfront locations in Paris: the Seine and the Bassin de la Villette. Music, dancing, children's events, chaise longues, and summertime revelry reign, and the fun is free. (Various locations; www.paris.fr/parisplages)

Solidays: Solidays is a three-day concert featuring international music artists performing in support of AIDS charities. First week of July. (Hippodrome de Longchamp, Rte. des Tribunes, 16E; www.solidays.org)

Tour de France: Could the world's most famous bicycle race finish anywhere other than Paris? No matter where the three-week and 3,606-kilometer (2,240-mile) race begins, it always ends on the Champs-Elysées. July. (Various locations; 01-41-33-14-00, www.letour.fr)

AUGUST

Rock en Seine: International rock groups head the marquee at this three-day annual music festival held in the Parc de Saint-Cloud. Last week of August. (Parc de Saint-Cloud, 92210 St-Cloud; www.rockenseine.com)

SEPTEMBER

Festival d'Automne: This theater, dance, music, and arts festival welcomes Parisians back to the capital after the summer. Throughout the fall months. (Various locations; 01-53-45-17-00, www.festival-automne.com)

Jazz à la Villette: This world-renowned jazz festival attracts major players and soon-to-be stars. First half of September. (Various locations in Parc de la Villette, 19E; 01-44-84-44-84, www.jazzalavillette.com)

Les Journées du Patrimoine (Heritage Days): Some 300 historic sites – mainly fancy government buildings – usually off-limits to the public are open free of charge. Third weekend of September. (Various locations; www.journeesdupatrimoine.culture.fr)

Techno Parade: Techno music lovers take to the streets to dance to house and electro music. Last weekend in September. (Route from Pl. Denfert-Rochereau, 14E, to Pl. de la Bastille, 11E; 01-53-36-04-19, www.technoparade.fr)

OCTOBER

Fête des Vendanges de Montmartre: The oldest vineyard in Paris produces 500 bottles a year, a phenomenon celebrated with a street festival. First Saturday in October. (Various locations in Montmartre, 18E; 08-92-68-30-00, www.fetedesvendangesdemontmartre.com)

Nuit Blanche: Art lovers can roam free after hours, as a number of museums and galleries stay open for the night. First weekend in October. (Various locations; http://nuitblanche.paris.fr)

NOVEMBER

Illuminations de Noël: The trees along avenue Montaigne and the Champs-Elysées are adorned with white Christmas lights that glitter 5 P.M.-midnight. November 15-January 5. (Various locations; www.paris.fr)

Mois de la Photo: Paris Photo (www.parisphoto.fr), a photography festival, takes place in the Month of Photography. It's an annual opportunity to appreciate different purveyors of the art, in exhibitions across the city. All of November. (Various locations; www.mep-fr.org)

DECEMBER

Marchés de Noël: Beginning in late November, the Christmas season hops into high gear on the streets of Paris. Colorful Christmas markets spring up along the Champs-Elysées, atop Montmartre, and in full view of the Eiffel Tower at Place du Trocadero. Expect hot wine, regional treats, and tourists galore. (Various locations; www.paris.fr)

DISABLED ACCESS

In general, Paris does little to meet the needs of travelers with disabilities. The Paris Métro is not accessible; nor are the buses, now with a few exceptions. The intercity rail system has access in places (RER lines A, B, C, D, and E). Taxis are required by law to take passengers in wheelchairs if they can. Recently constructed and renovated museums and public buildings often have access, but it's best to check ahead of time. Public toilets with wheelchair accessibility are rare.

SAFETY

As in any city, visitors to Paris should travel smart, stay alert, and take precautionary safety measures. Pickpockets target tourists in train stations, busy tourist zones, and on the Métro. Rental cars are often broken into and valuable items should never be left inside. Avoid the Bois du Boulogne, Bois de Vincennes, and the Paris suburbs at night.

HEALTH AND EMERGENCY SERVICES

For immediate emergency services, call 15 for an ambulance (SAMU), 17 for the police, and 18 for the fire department. SOS Médecins (01/47-07-77-77) makes house calls (the fee is only slightly higher than at the office); SOS Dentaire (01/43-37-51-00) provides emergency dental treatment. Pharmacists are also trained in first aid and can arrange a visit to a local doctor or an ambulance.

Don't leave home without travel insurance that includes medical coverage. The standard of health care is high in Paris (lower in public hospitals and lower than U.S. private practice), but non-E.U. citizens are only covered if they have their own insurance.

PHARMACIES

There is a pharmacy – sometimes several – on nearly every block in Paris's downtown. Pharmacie Les Champs Dhéry is open 24 hours.

PHARMACIE DE LA MAIRIE DE PARIS

MAP 7 D3 9 RUE DES ARCHIVES, 4E
01-42-78-53-58

PHARMACIE DES INVALIDES

MAP 3 E2 25 BD. DE LA TOUR MAUBOURG, 7E
01-47-05-43-77

PHARMACIE LES CHAMPS DHÉRY

MAP 4 A4 84 AV. DES CHAMPS-ELYSÉES, GALERIE DES CHAMPS-ELYSÉES, 8E
01-45-62-02-41 WWW.PHARMACIELESCHAMPS.FR

MEDIA AND COMMUNICATIONS

All the phone numbers in this book are listed as they would be dialed within Paris. French telephone numbers have 10 digits. In Paris and the surrounding region (Île-de-France), all landline phone numbers begin with 01 and mobile phones begin with 06. Dial 118-710 or 118-712 for French telephone directory assistance, 3212 for international assistance. To dial overseas numbers from France, enter 00 followed by the country code and number.

The *télécarte* telephone card can be used in nearly all public telephones. They are sold at tobacco shops, post offices, Métro stations, supermarkets, and France Télécom stores. Each card has either 50 or 120 "units," which can be used from any phone booth *(cabine)* for local or international calls. A chip keeps track of the number of units left after each telephone call. There are also prepaid calling cards (with a toll-free number and PIN code) to use from any kind of phone, which is especially useful when the chip-slot doesn't work on streets. Keep in mind that when using these prepaid calling cards from a residential line, a standard local charge is still applied. For GSM-equipped mobile phones, you can also buy a pay-as-you-go SIM to use while in France, which gives you your own Paris mobile number and allows you to "top up" the credit on the phone. These chips can be bought at any mobile store. In some Paris neighborhoods you'll find telecommunications shops with Internet stations, fax machines, and pay-by-the-minute phone booths inside. Rates are generally fair, though the ambiance can vary greatly from place to place.

The French post office is known as "La Poste" (also PTT) and identified by a yellow sign. Normal hours are Monday-Friday 8 A.M.-7 P.M., Saturday 8 A.M.-noon. Most have photocopiers, fax machines, and outdoor cash points. In Paris, the central post and sorting office of the Louvre (52 rue du Louvre, 1ER) is open until midnight except on Sundays. All post offices are listed in the phone book under "Poste, La." The standard rate for a letter within France is €0.63; a letter to North America costs €0.95.

Paris is the epicenter of the French media, so there is a wealth of daily newspapers and weekly and monthly magazines in French. The best-known English-language publication is the *International Herald Tribune,* now fully owned by *The New York Times.* There is also the biweekly *FUSAC* (French USA Contacts) – available for free at anglophone bookshops, pubs, and churches.

INTERNET

A reliable chain with good rates and services is Milk Internet Café, favored by many gamers.

MILK INTERNET CAFÉ

28 RUE DU QUATRE SEPTEMBRE, 2E
01-40-06-00-78 WWW.MILKLUB.COM

SMOKING

As of January 2008, smoking is banned in all public places, bars, and restaurants. Some establishments may maintain special smoking rooms, but they are few and far between. Since this law was passed, many Parisians now pile onto chilly terraces and sidewalks to take their smoking breaks.

RESERVATIONS AND TIPPING

There are enough Michelin stars hovering over Paris restaurants to form a small constellation, and the gastronome's stay will twinkle with opportunity. But be aware of the serious need for reservations at many places. Trendy spots may require a few days to a week of advance notice; you may need to reserve months ahead for the best tables, depending on the season. If it's any consolation, it's usually worth the wait.

All French restaurants and cafés add 15 percent to the bill for service. Leave extra only if you want to – never more than 5 percent of the tab. It's customary to tip taxis by rounding up the fare, again to a maximum 5 percent.

DRY CLEANERS

PRESSING DE LA MADELEINE

MAP 5 B1 12 RUE ARCADE, 8E
01-42-65-30-11

SOS NET IMPEC BLANC

MAP 2 F3 31 RUE CASSETTE, 6E
01-42-22-34-03

TROCADÉRO PRESSING

MAP 4 D2 37 RUE DE LONGCHAMP, 16E
01-45-53-06-38

FRENCH PHRASES

Bienvenue à Paris! Despite the unflattering stereotypes you may have heard about Parisians, you'll find that many of them are happy to help you negotiate their city, and most speak at least rudimentary English. That said, however, please note that the friendliness of the locals increases exponentially when you initiate conversations in French. Even if you've never studied a word, just try. It's a clear sign of respect, and it will be appreciated. Politesse is also a must: Begin every interaction with *("Bonjour, monsieur/madame,"* and disperse thank yous *(merci)* liberally.

THE BASICS

ENGLISH	FRENCH	PRONUNCIATION
Good day	**Bonjour**	*bon-zhoor*
Good evening	**Bon soir**	*bon swahr*
Welcome	**Bienvenue**	*bee-an-veh-new*
Excuse me	**Excusez-moi**	*ex-kooh-zay mwah*
Pardon	**Pardon**	*par-dohn*
Sir	**Monsieur**	*muhs-yur*
Madam	**Madame**	*mah-dahm*
Miss	**Mademoiselle**	*mahd-mwah-zehl*
Do you speak English?	**Parlez-vous anglais?**	*parlay-voo ahn-glay*
I don't speak French.	**Je ne parle pas français.**	*zhuh nuh parl pah frahn-say*
How are you? (formal)	**Comment allez-vous?**	*koh-mohn tah-lay voo*
Very well, thank you.	**Très bien, merci.**	*tray bee-an, mehr-see*
How's it going? (informal)	**Ça va?**	*sah vah*
It's going fine.	**Ça va bien.**	*sah vah bee-an*
My name is...	**Je m'appelle...**	*zhuh mah-pehl...*
What's your name?	**Quel est votre nom?**	*kehl ay voh-treh nohm*
Please	**S'il vous plâit**	*seehl voo play*
Thank you	**Merci**	*mehr-see*
You're welcome.	**Je vous en prie.**	*zhuh voo zhan pree*
No problem	**De rien**	*duh ree-an*
I'm sorry	**Desolé**	*dehs-oh-lay*

Goodbye	**Au revoir**	*ohr-vwah*
Yes	**Oui**	*wee*
No	**Non**	*nohn*

GETTING AROUND

How do I get to...?	**Comment puis-je me rendre à...?**	*koh-mohn pwee-zheh muh rahn-druh ah*
Where is...?	**Où est...?**	*ooh ay*
the subway	**le Métro**	*luh may-troh*
the airport	**l'aéroport**	*lehr-oh-pohr*
the train station	**la gare**	*lah gayr*
the train	**le train**	*luh trahn*
the bus stop	**l'arrêt de bus**	*lah-ray duh boos*
the bus	**l'autobus**	*law-toh-boos*
the exit	**la sortie**	*lah sohr-tee*
the street	**la rue**	*lah roo*
the garden	**le jardin**	*luh zhar-dan*
a taxicab	**un taxi**	*uhn tak-see*
a hotel	**un hôtel**	*uhn oh-tehl*
a toilet	**une toilette**	*oohn twah-let*
a pharmacy	**une pharmacie**	*oohn far-mah-see*
a bank	**une banque**	*oohn bahnk*
a tourist office	**un bureau de tourisme**	*uhn byuh-roh duh tohr-ees-muh*
a telephone	**un téléphone**	*uhn teh-lay-fohn*

HEALTH AND EMERGENCY

Help!	**Au secours!**	*oh say-coor*
I am sick.	**Je suis malade.**	*zhuh swee mah-lahd*
I am hurt.	**Je suis blessé.**	*zhuh swee bleh-say*
I need...	**J'ai besoin de...**	*zhay buh-zwahn duh*
the hospital	**l'hôpital**	*loh-pee-tal*
the doctor	**le médicin**	*luh mayd-san*
an ambulance	**une ambulance**	*oohn am-bew-lahns*
the police	**la police**	*lah poh-lees*
medicine	**médicament**	*meh-dee-kah-mohn*

EATING

I would like...	**Je voudrais...**	*zhuh voo-dray*
a table for two	**une table pour deux**	*oohn tah-bluh poor duh*
the menu	**la carte**	*lah kahrt*
breakfast	**petit déjeuner**	*puh-tee day-zhuh-nay*
lunch	**déjeuner**	*day-zhuh-nay*
dinner	**dîner**	*dee-nay*
the bill	**l'addition**	*lah-dee-syon*
tip	**pourboire**	*poor-bwahr*
non-smoking	**non fumeur**	*nohn foo-muhr*
a drink	**une boisson**	*oohn bwah-sohn*
a glass of...	**une verre de...**	*oohn vehr duh*
water	**l'eau**	*low*
beer	**bière**	*bee-ehr*
wine	**vin**	*van*
I am...	**Je suis...**	*zhuh swee*
a vegetarian (male)	**végétarien**	*vay-zhay-teh-ree-yan*
a vegetarian (female)	**végétarienne**	*vay-zhay-teh-ree-yehn*
diabetic	**diabétique**	*dee-ah-bay-teek*
allergic	**allergique**	*ah-layr-zheek*
kosher	**kascher**	*kah-shehr*

SHOPPING

Do you have...?	**Avez-vous...?**	*ah-vay-voo*
Where can I buy...?	**Où puis-je acheter...?**	*ooh pwee-zhuh ash-tay*
May I try this?	**Peux-je l'essayer?**	*puh-zhuh leh-say-ay*
How much is this?	**Combien?**	*kohm-bee-an*
cash	**argent**	*ahr-zhahn*
credit card	**carte de crédit**	*kart duh kray-dee*
Too...	**Trop...**	*troh*
small	**petit**	*puh-tee*
large	**grand**	*grahn*
expensive	**cher**	*shehr*

TIME

What time is it?	**Quelle heure est-il?**	*kehl uhr ay teel*
It is...	**Il est...**	*eel ay*
eight o'clock	**huit heures**	*weet uhr*
half past ten	**dix heures et demi**	*deez uhr ay duh-mee*
quarter to five	**cinq heures moins quart**	*sank uhr mwahn kahr*
noon	**midi**	*mee-dee*
midnight	**minuit**	*meen-wee*
during the day	**pendant la journée**	*pehn-dahn lah zhur-nay*
in the morning	**le matin**	*luh mah-tan*
in the afternoon	**l'après-midi**	*lah-pray-mee-dee*
in the evening	**le soir**	*luh swahr*
at night	**la nuit**	*lah nwee*

DAYS OF THE WEEK

Monday	**Lundi**	*luhn-dee*
Tuesday	**Mardi**	*mahr-dee*
Wednesday	**Mercredi**	*mehr-kreh-dee*
Thursday	**Jeudi**	*zhuh-dee*
Friday	**Vendredi**	*vohn-druh-dee*
Saturday	**Samedi**	*sahm-dee*
Sunday	**Dimanche**	*dee-mansh*
this week	**cette semaine**	*sett suh-mehn*
this weekend	**ce weekend**	*suh week-end*
today	**aujourd'hui**	*oh-zhor-dwee*
tomorrow	**demain**	*duh-mah*
yesterday	**hier**	*ee-yayr*

MONTHS

January	**Janvier**	*zhahn-vee-yay*
February	**Février**	*fehv-ree-yay*
March	**Mars**	*mars*
April	**Avril**	*ahv-reel*
May	**Mai**	*may*
June	**Juin**	*zhwan*
July	**Juillet**	*zhwee-yay*

August	**Août**	*oot*
September	**Septembre**	*sep-tahm-bruh*
October	**Octobre**	*ohk-toh-bruh*
November	**Novembre**	*noh-vahm-bruh*
December	**Décembre**	*day-cehm-bruh*
this month	**ce mois**	*suh mwah*
this year	**cette année**	*seht ah-nay*
winter	**hiver**	*ee-vehr*
spring	**printemps**	*prehn-tahn*
summer	**été**	*ay-tay*
fall	**automne**	*oh-tuhn*

NUMBERS

zero	**zéro**	*zeh-roh*
one	**un**	*uhn*
two	**deux**	*duh*
three	**trois**	*twah*
four	**quatre**	*kah-truh*
five	**cinq**	*sank*
six	**six**	*sees*
seven	**sept**	*set*
eight	**huit**	*weet*
nine	**neuf**	*nuhf*
ten	**dix**	*deez*
eleven	**onze**	*ohnz*
twelve	**douze**	*dooz*
thirteen	**treize**	*trehz*
fourteen	**quatorze**	*kah-torz*
fifteen	**quinze**	*kanz*
sixteen	**seize**	*sehz*
seventeen	**dix-sept**	*deez-set*
eighteen	**dix-huit**	*deez-weet*
nineteen	**dix-neuf**	*deez-nuhf*
twenty	**vignt**	*vanh*
one-hundred	**cent**	*sahn*
one-thousand	**mille**	*meel*

Note: *J* sounds (spelled in the pronunciation key as zh) are pronounced like the g in massage.

STREET INDEX

Abbreviations Key
Av.: Avenue
Bd.: Boulevard
Carref.: Carrefour
Cr.: Cour
Imp.: Impasse
Pass.: Passage
Pl.: Place
Q.: Quai
R.: Rue
Sq.: Square
V.: Villa

C

D

E

F

H

I

JK

N

O

PQ

S

TU

VWXYZ

INDEX

RESTAURANT INDEX

NIGHTLIFE INDEX

SHOPS INDEX

HOTEL INDEX

ABOUT THE AUTHOR

AURELIA D'ANDREA

© SOPHIA PAGAN PHOTOGRAPHY

Journalist Aurelia d'Andrea's infatuation with Paris began in high school French class, but it was in 2004 – during a year-long adventure in the City of Light fueled by a steady diet of baguettes and Bordeaux – that she realized she was in love. Five years later, she packed up her San Francisco apartment and schlepped her husband, her dog, and seven bicycles back to the French capital. Today, bread, wine, and urban exploration still dominate her daily to-do list.

Besides being a source of non-stop creative inspiration, the city is a feast for the senses – and that's what keeps this expat's passion for Paris alive. After years of dedicated research, she can now share where to go for the best views of the city, which Louvre entrance has the shortest line, and which boulangerie bakes the best *pain au chocolat*.

CONTRIBUTORS TO THE PREVIOUS EDITIONS

D'Arcy Flueck, Alan Brent Gregston, Anthony Grant, Mike Gerard, M. K. Hoffman, Mia Lipman, Rebecca Perry Magniant, Helen Sillett, Heather Stimmler-Hall

PHOTO CREDITS

Page III (Sights) Tour Eiffel, © Fat Tire Bike and City Segway Tours; (Restaurants) L'Arpège, Courtesy of Restaurant L'Arpège, Paris; (Nightlife) Castel, Courtesy of Club Castel; (Shops) Marie Mercié, © Anne Roman; (Arts and Leisure) Musée d'Art Moderne de La Ville de Paris, Courtesy of Musée d'Art Moderne de La Ville de Paris/ Christophe /; (Hotels) Hôtel Bristol, © Roméo Balancourt / © Jean-Baptiste Leroux; Page VI, Paris skyline, © Roland Nagy/123rf.com; Page IX, Moulin Rouge, © Lucian Milasan/123rf.com; Page X, (Breizh Café) Courtesy of Breizh Café; (Marché Aux Fleurs) © adrianhancu/123rf.com; (Sacre Coeur) © Paul Prescott; Page XII (Pierre Hermé) Courtesy of Pâtisserie Pierre Hermé Paris; (Mariage Frères) © Mariage Frères; (Epicure) © Romeo Blancourt; Page XIV (Cite de la Mode et du Design) © Docks-Cité de la Mode et du Design-Jakob+McFarlane-Les Barbus; (Musée des Arts Décoratifs) © Jean-Marie Del Moral/ Musée des Arts Décoratifs; (Jardin des Tuileries) © Roger C. Lakhan; Map 1 (top) Pantheon, © Roger C. Lakhan; (bottom left) Sainte-Chapelle, © Luciano Mortula/123rf.com; (bottom right) Notre-Dame de Paris, © sborisov/123rf.com; Map 2 (top) Palais du Luxembourg, © rmcguirk /istockphoto.com; (bottom left) Pont Alexandre III, © 2013 Elissa V. Shaw; (bottom right) Vedettes de Pont Neuf, © Roger C. Lakhan; Map 3 (top) the Pont Alexander III Bridge, © Valerijs Kostreckis/123rf.com; (bottom left) Invalides statue of Napoleon, © 2013 Elissa V. Shaw; (bottom right) antique French railway clock in the Musee d'Orsay, © Jan Kranendonk/123rf.com; Map 4 (top) Tour Eiffel, © Frederic Prochasson/123rf.com; (bottom left) detail of high-relief on Arc de Triomphe, Triumph of Napoleon, © Rubens Alarcon/123rf.com; (bottom right) Arc de Triomphe, © Tomas Marek/123rf.com; Map 5 (top) Hediard, © Aurelia d'Andrea; (bottom left) Tuileries Gardens, © Ievgenii Fesenko/123rf.com; (bottom right) Fauchon, © Aurelia d'Andrea; Map 6 (top) Louvre, © Roger C. Lakhan; (bottom left) the crossroad of Rue de Rohan and Rue de Rivoli, © Pavel Losevsky/123rf.com; (bottom right) Galerie Vivienne, © Aurelia d'Andrea; Map 7 (top) Centre Pompidou, © Valery Voennyy/123rf.com; (bottom left) Mariage Frères, Courtesy of Mariage Frères; (bottom right) Le Renard, Courtesy of Le Renard / Franklin Azzi Architecture; Map 8 (top) Place Des Vosges, © Aurelia d'Andrea; (bottom left) Viaduc des Arts; (bottom right) Museum of Natural History, © Patrick Lafaite/Museum Nationa ID'Historie Naturelle; Map 9 (top) old carousel and Basilique Sacre Coeur in Paris, © Alexander Chaikin/www.123rf.com; (bottom left) Studio 28, © Aurelia d'Andrea; (bottom right) Moulin Rouge, © Paul Prescott; Map 10 (top) Canal St. Martin, © Aurelia d'Andrea; (bottom left) Antoine et Lili, © Paul Prescott; (bottom right) Helmut Newcake, © Helmut Newcake; Page 1 (top) Notre-Dame De Paris, © 2013 Elissa V. Shaw; (middle) Tour Eiffel, © Fat Tire Bike and City Segway Tours; Page 3 (Notre-Dame De Paris) © Oleksandr Dibrova/123rf.com; (Pantheon) © Roger C. Lakhan; Page 4 (Rue Mouffetard) © Roger C. Lakhan; (Sainte-Chapelle) © Juergen Schonnop/123rf.com; Page 6 (Pont des Arts) © Fat Tire Bike and City Segway Tours; (Pont Neuf) © 2013 Elissa V. Shaw; Page 8 (Les Invalides) © gregobagel/istockphoto.com; (Musée D'Orsay) © piccaya/123rf.com; Page 10 (Pont Alexandre III) © Valery Voennyy/123rf.com; (Arc De Triomphe) © Fat Tire Bike and City Segway Tours; Page 12 (Tour Eiffel) © Fat Tire Bike and City Segway Tours; (Jardin des Tuileries) © Fat Tire Bike and City Segway Tours; Page 15 (Opéra Garnier) © tupungato /123rf.com; (Musée du Louvre) © hugon/www.123rf.com; Page 16 (Palais Royal) © compassandcamera /istockphoto.com; (Centre Pompidou) © Valery Voennyy/123rf.com; Page 18 (Hotel de Ville) © Aurelia d'Andrea; (Rue des Rosiers) © Valery Voennyy/123rf.com; Page 19 (Jardin des Plantes) © Aurelia d'Andrea; (Place des Vosges) © atm2003/123rf.com; Page 21 (La

Basilique Sacré-Coeur de Montmartre) © Alexander Chaikin/ www.123rf.com; (Cimetière de Montmartre) © Aurelia d'Andrea; Page 24 (Parc Des Buttes Chaumont) © Paul Prescott; (Bois de Vincennes) © Aurelia d'Andrea; Page 25 (Les Catacombes) © Francisco De Casa Gonzalez/123rf.com; (Cimetière du Père Lachaise) © Roger C. Lakhan; Page 27 (Verjus) Courtesy of Verjus; (L'Arpège) Courtesy of Restaurant L'Arpège, Paris; Page 31 (La Truffière) courtesy of La Truffière; (Fogón) © Vanina Herraiz/Fogón; Page 33 (Le Restaurant) © Amy Murrell/Restaurant and Hotel L'Hotel; (L'Arpège) Courtesy of Restaurant L'Arpège, Paris; Page 36 (Angelina) courtesy of Angelina Café; (Bread & Roses) Courtesy of Bread & Roses; Page 39 (Verjus) Courtesy of Verjus; (Drouant) courtesy of Drouant; Page 40 (A Priori Thé) © Julia Gilbert/A Priori Thé; (Willi's Wine Bar) Courtesy of Willi's Wine Bar; Page 43 (Café Pinson) Courtesy of Agence Source; (Jaja) courtesy of Jaja; Page 44 (Le Mary Celeste) © Valentine de Lagarde; (Le Baron Rouge) © Doume / © Roger C. Lakhan; Page 47 (Le Train Bleu) Courtesy of Le Train Bleu; (Milk) © Aurelia d'Andrea; Page 48 (Pink Flamingo Pizza) © Pink Flamingo; (Restaurant Pierre Sang Boyer) © NikiPhotograph; Page 50 (Epicure) © Romeo Blancourt; (Pétrelle) Courtesy of Jean-Luc André; Page 53 (top), Andy Wahloo, Courtesy of Andy Wahloo; (middle) Castel, Courtesy of Club Castel; Page 55 (Curio Parlor) Courtesy Monuments Nationaux; (Castel) Courtesy of Club Castel; Page 56 (Le Showcase) Courtesy of Le Showcase; (Le Bar du Plaza Athénée) Courtesy of L'Hôtel Plaza Athénée Paris/Eric Laignel; Page 59 (Club 18) Courtesy of Club 18; (1979) Courtesy of le 1979; Page 60 (Andy Wahloo) Courtesy of Andy Wahloo; (Wanderlust) © Docks-Cité de la Mode et du Design-Jakob+McFarlane-Les Barbus; Page 63 (Le Carmen) Courtesy of Le Carmen; (Chez Prune) Courtesy of Chez Prune; Page 65 (Point Èphémère) © Point Éphémère; (Bowling Mouffetard) Courtesy of Bowling Mouffetard; Page 67 (top) La Pâtisserie des Rêves, Courtesy of la Pâtisserie des Rêves; (middle) Marie Mercié, © Anne Roman; Page 69 (Shakespear and Co.) © Lauren Goldenburg for Shakespear and Co.; (Marie Mercié) © Anne Roman; Page 70 (La Grande Epicerie du Bon Marché) © Virgile Guinard/La Cave La Grande Epicerie de Paris; (La Pâtisserie des Rêves) Courtesy of la Pâtisserie des Rêves; Page 73 (Ladurée) © Aurelia d'Andrea; (Louis Vuitton) © Aurelia d'Andrea; Page 74 (Anne Fontaine) Courtesy of Anne Fontaine; (Fauchon) © Aurelia d'Andrea; Page 76 (W. H. Smith) © W. H. Smith; (Agnés B.) Courtesy of Agnés B.; Page 78 (Kiliwatch) © Aurelia d'Andrea; (Anna Rivka) Courtesy of Anna Rivka; Page 81 (The Broken Arm) Courtesy of The Broken Arm; (Merci) Courtesy of Merci; Page 83 (Muji) Courtesy of Muji; (BA&SH) © Aurelia d'Andrea; Page 84 (Rose Bunker) © Aurelia d'Andrea; (Antoine et Lili) © Paul Prescott; Page 87 (top) Musée Rodin, © Aurelia d'Andrea; (middle) Musée National d'Art Moderne, Courtesy of Musée National d'Art Moderne de La Ville de Paris/Christophe Walter; Page 89 (Conciergerie) © Fat Tire Bike and City Segway Tours; (Institut du Monde Arabe) © jophil / istockphoto.com; Page 90 (Musée Rodin) © Aurelia d'Andrea; (Palais de La Découverte) Chantal Rousselin for Palais de La Découverte; Page 93 (Jeu de Paume) Courtesy of Arno Gisinger/Jeu de Paume; (Musée des Arts Décoratifs) © Jean-Marie Del Moral/ Musée des Arts Décoratifs; Page 94 (Musée National d'Art Moderne) Courtesy of Musée National d'Art Moderne de La Ville de Paris/Christophe Walter (Espace Montmartre Dalí) Courtesy of Espace Dalí; Page 96 (Musée Marmottan) Courtesy of Musée Marmottan Monet, Paris; (Musée National d'Histoire Naturelle) © Patrick Lafaite/Museum Nationa lD'Historie Naturelle; Page 99 (Le Crazy Horse) © V. Krassilnikova; (Opéra Garnier) © tupungato /123rf.com; Page 100 (Bal du Moulin Rouge) © Paul Prescott; (La Cinémathèque Française) Courtesy of Stéphane Dabrowski for La Cinémathèque Française; Page 101 (Le Bataclan) © Aurelia d'Andrea; (Cabaret Sauvage) © Aurelia d'Andrea;

Page 105 (Citroën Tours of Paris) Courtesy of 4 Roues Sous 1 Parapluie; (Promenade Plantée) © Paul Prescott; Page 107 (Fat Tire Bike and City Segway Tours) © Fat Tire Bike and City Segway Tours; (Parc des Buttes Chaumont) © Paul Prescott; Page 108 (Parc des Princes) Courtesy of Parc des Princes; (Parc Montsouris) © Rrrainbow /istockphoto.com; Page 109 (Le Petit Bal Musette) © Christian Bassoul/Le Petit Bal Musette; (Tour Montparnasse) © SpaceManKris/istockphoto.com; Page 111 (top) Hôtel Mayet, Courtesy of Hôtel Mayet; (middle) Hôtel Bristol, © Roméo Balancourt / © Jean-Baptiste Leroux; Page 113 (Hôtel le Clos Medicis) Courtesy of Hôtel le Clos Medicis; (Artus) Courtesy of Hôtel Artus; Page 114 (Hôtel le Bellechasse) Courtesy of Hôtel le Bellechasse; (Hôtel Lenox) Courtesy of The Lenox; Page 117 (Hôtel Plaza Athénée) Courtesy of Hôtel Plaza Athénée Paris/Frédéric Ducout; (Hôtel le Meurice) © Guillaume de Laubier / Courtesy of Hôtel le Meurice; Page 118 (Hôtel Thérèse) Courtesy of l'Hôtel Thérèse; (Park Hyatt Paris-Vendôme) Courtesy of the Park Hyatt Paris-Vendôme; Page 120 (Hotel le Citizen du Canal Paris) Courtesy of Hotel le Citizen; (Hôtel Taylor) Courtesy of Hôtel Taylor; Page 121 (Hôtel 20 Prieure) Courtesy of Hôtel 20 Prieure; (Ai Sourire de Montmartre) Courtesy of Ai Sourire de Montmartre; Page 122 (Mama Shelter) Courtesy of Mama Shelter; (Saint James Paris) Courtesy of Saint James Paris

MOON MAPGUIDE PARIS
FIFTH EDITION

Avalon Travel
a member of the Perseus Books Group
1700 Fourth Street
Berkeley, CA 94710, USA
www.moon.com

ISBN-13: 978-1-61238-647-8
ISSN: 1539-1000

Editors: Elizabeth Hansen, Sabrina Young
Series Manager: Erin Raber
Interior Design: Jacob Goolkasian
Cover Design: Tabitha Lahr
Map Design: Mike Morgenfeld
Production Coordinator: Darren Alessi
Graphics Coordinator: Tabitha Lahr
Cartographers and Map Editor: Kat Bennett, Stephanie Poulain, Chris Henrick
Copy Editor and Proofreader: Deana Shields
Cover design: Faceout Studio

Printed in China through Asia Pacific Offset, San Francisco

Printing History
1st edition – 2002
5th edition – March 2014
5 4 3 2 1

Please send all feedback about this book to:

Moon MapGuide Paris
Avalon Travel
1700 Fourth Street
Berkeley, CA 94710, USA
email: feedback@moon.com
website: www.moon.com

MOON
TRAVEL GUIDES

MOON
HANDBOOKS
ISTANBUL
& THE TURKISH COAST

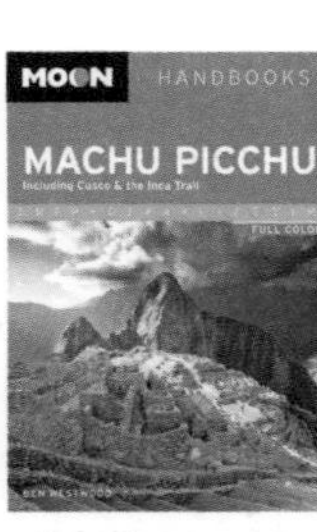
MOON
HANDBOOKS
MACHU PICCHU
Including Cusco & the Inca Trail
FULL COLOR

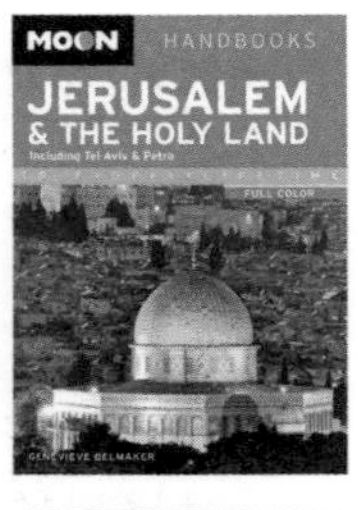
MOON
HANDBOOKS
JERUSALEM
& THE HOLY LAND
Including Tel Aviv & Petra
FULL COLOR

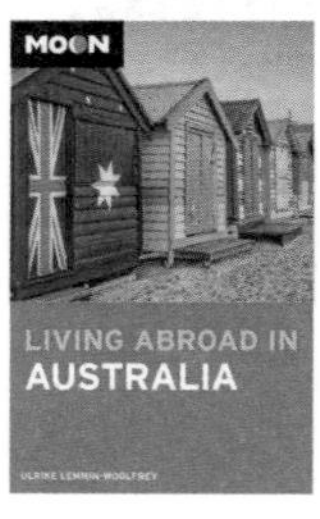
MOON
LIVING ABROAD IN
AUSTRALIA

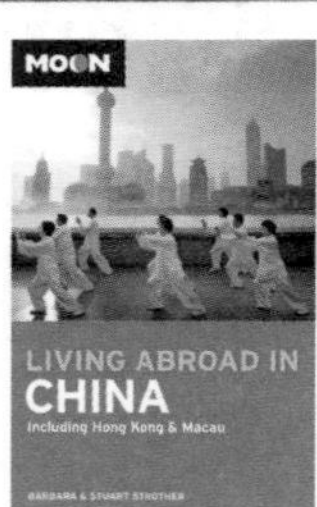
MOON
LIVING ABROAD IN
CHINA
Including Hong Kong & Macau

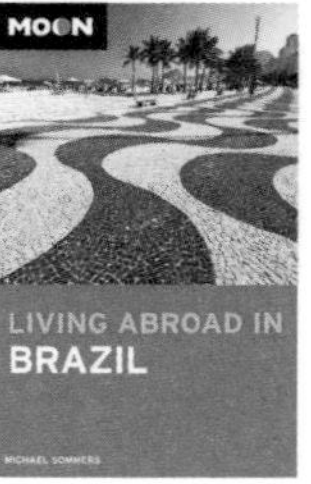
MOON
LIVING ABROAD IN
BRAZIL

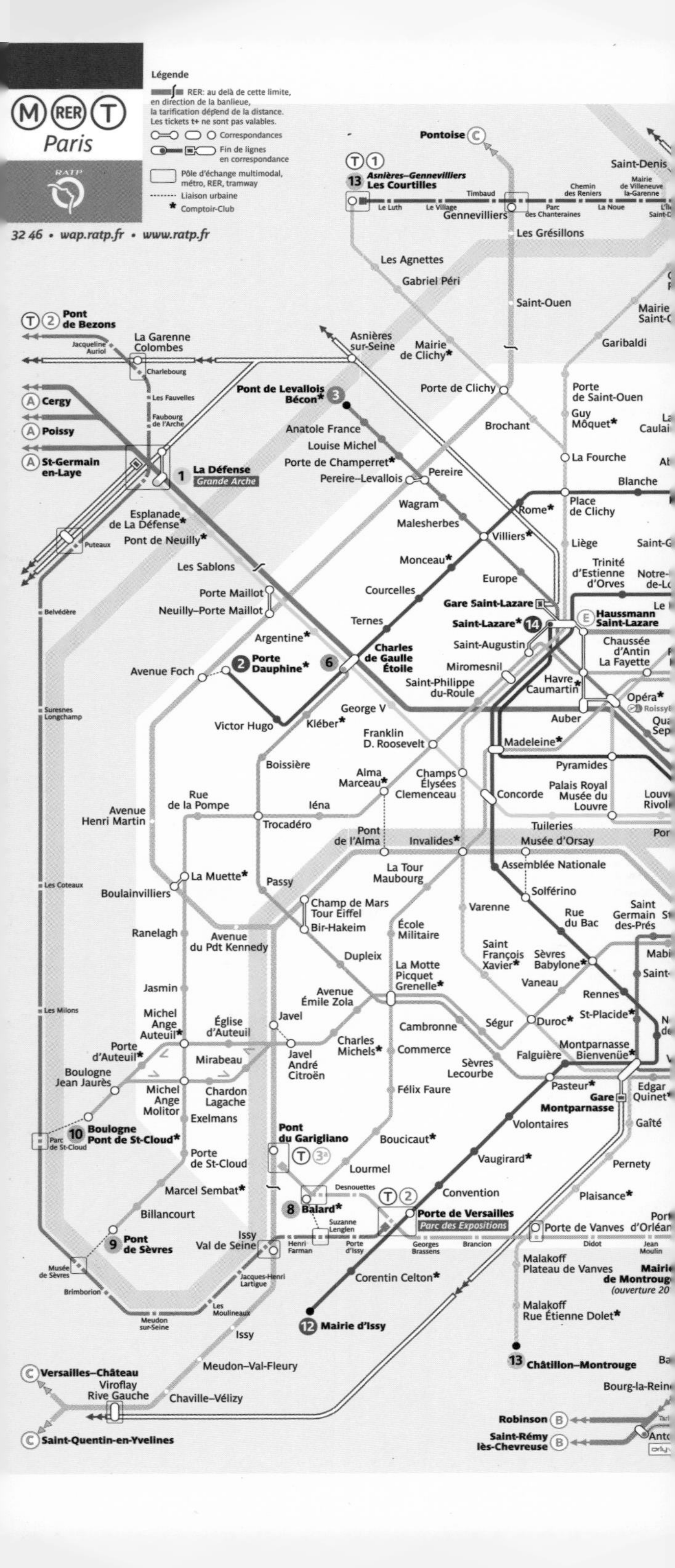

M RER T
Paris
RATP
Légende
RER: au delà de cette limite, en direction de la banlieue, la tarification dépend de la distance. Les tickets t+ ne sont pas valables.
Correspondances
Fin de lignes en correspondance
Pôle d'échange multimodal, métro, RER, tramway
Liaison urbaine
Comptoir-Club
32 46 • wap.ratp.fr • www.ratp.fr
Pontoise C
T 1
13 Asnières–Gennevilliers Les Courtilles
Timbaud
Chemin des Reniers
Mairie de Villeneuve la-Garenne
Saint-Denis
Le Luth
Le Village
Gennevilliers
Parc des Chanteraines
La Noue
Les Grésillons
Les Agnettes
Gabriel Péri
Saint-Ouen
Garibaldi
T 2 Pont de Bezons
Jacqueline Auriol
La Garenne Colombes
Charlebourg
Asnières sur-Seine
Mairie de Clichy*
Les Fauvelles
Faubourg de l'Arche
A Cergy
A Poissy
A St-Germain en-Laye
Pont de Levallois Bécon* 3
Porte de Clichy
Porte de Saint-Ouen
Guy Môquet*
Brochant
La Fourche
Blanche
1 La Défense Grande Arche
Anatole France
Louise Michel
Porte de Champerret*
Pereire–Levallois
Pereire
Wagram
Malesherbes
Rome*
Place de Clichy
Villiers*
Liège
Esplanade de La Défense*
Puteaux
Pont de Neuilly*
Les Sablons
Monceau*
Europe
Trinité d'Estienne d'Orves
Porte Maillot
Neuilly–Porte Maillot
Courcelles
Gare Saint-Lazare
Saint-Lazare* 14
E Haussmann Saint-Lazare
Belvédère
Ternes
Argentine*
2 Porte Dauphine*
6
Charles de Gaulle Étoile
Saint-Augustin
Chaussée d'Antin La Fayette
Avenue Foch
Miromesnil
Saint-Philippe du-Roule
Havre Caumartin*
Opéra*
Roissybus
Suresnes Longchamp
Victor Hugo
George V
Kléber*
Auber
Franklin D. Roosevelt
Madeleine*
Boissière
Alma Marceau*
Champs Élysées Clemenceau
Pyramides
Concorde
Palais Royal Musée du Louvre
Rue de la Pompe
Avenue Henri Martin
Iéna
Trocadéro
Tuileries
Pont de l'Alma
Invalides*
Musée d'Orsay
Assemblée Nationale
La Muette*
Boulainvilliers
Passy
La Tour Maubourg
Les Coteaux
Solférino
Champ de Mars Tour Eiffel
Bir-Hakeim
Varenne
Rue du Bac
Saint Germain des-Prés
Ranelagh
Avenue du Pdt Kennedy
École Militaire
Dupleix
Saint François Xavier*
Sèvres Babylone*
La Motte Picquet Grenelle*
Vaneau
Jasmin
Avenue Émile Zola
Rennes
Les Milons
Michel Ange Auteuil*
Église d'Auteuil
Javel
Cambronne
Ségur
Duroc*
St-Placide*
Porte d'Auteuil*
Mirabeau
Javel André Citroën
Charles Michels*
Commerce
Falguière
Montparnasse Bienvenüe*
Boulogne Jean Jaurès
Michel Ange Molitor
Chardon Lagache
Sèvres Lecourbe
Pasteur*
Gare Montparnasse
Edgar Quinet*
Félix Faure
Exelmans
Volontaires
Gaîté
Parc de St-Cloud
10 Boulogne Pont de St-Cloud*
Pont du Garigliano
T 3a
Boucicaut*
Porte de St-Cloud
Vaugirard*
Pernety
Lourmel
Marcel Sembat*
Desnouettes
T 2
Convention
Plaisance*
8 Balard*
Porte de Versailles Parc des Expositions
Billancourt
Suzanne Lenglen
Porte de Vanves
Porte d'Orléans
9 Pont de Sèvres
Issy Val de Seine
Henri Farman
Porte d'Issy
Georges Brassens
Brancion
Didot
Jean Moulin
Musée de Sèvres
Jacques-Henri Lartigue
Malakoff Plateau de Vanves
Mairie de Montrouge
Brimborion
Corentin Celton*
Les Moulineaux
Meudon sur-Seine
Malakoff Rue Étienne Dolet*
12 Mairie d'Issy
Issy
Meudon–Val-Fleury
13 Châtillon–Montrouge
C Versailles–Château
Viroflay Rive Gauche
Chaville–Vélizy
Bourg-la-Reine
C Saint-Quentin-en-Yvelines
Robinson B
Saint-Rémy lès-Chevreuse B